The Criminal Justice Student Writer's Manual

Sixth Edition

William A. Johnson, Jr.
University of Central Oklahoma

Richard P. Rettig
Eastern Oregon University

Gregory M. Scott
University of Central Oklahoma

Stephen M. Garrison
University of Central Oklahoma

PEARSON

Boston   Columbus   Indianapolis   New York   San Francisco   Upper Saddle River
Amsterdam   Cape Town   Dubai   London   Madrid   Milan   Munich   Paris   Montreal   Toronto
Delhi   Mexico City   Sao Paulo   Sydney   Hong Kong   Seoul   Singapore   Taipei   Tokyo

Editorial Director: Vernon R. Anthony
Acquisition Editor: Sara Eilert
Program Manager: Alicia Ritchey
Editorial Assistant: Lynda Cramer
Director of Marketing: David Gesell
Marketing Manager: Mary Salzman
Senior Marketing Coordinator: Alicia Wozniak
Marketing Assistant: Les Roberts
Team Lead for Project Management: JoEllen Gohr
Senior Project Manager: Steve Robb and Susan Hannahs
Senior Operations Specialist: Deidra M. Skahill

Creative Director: Andrea Nix
Art Director: Jayne Conte
Text and Cover Designer: Suzanne Behnke
Cover Image:
Media Project Manager: Leslie Brado
Media Project Coordinator: April Cleland
Full-Service Project Management: Integra Software Services, Ltd.
Composition: Integra Software Services, Ltd.
Printer/Binder: Edwards Brothers Malloy State Street
Cover Printer: Phoenix Color, Hagerstown
Text Font: Palatino 10/12

Credits and acknowledgments borrowed from other sources and reproduced, with permission, in this textbook appear on the appropriate page within text.

Library of Congress Cataloging-in-Publication Data

Johnson, William A.,
  The criminal justice student writer's manual/William A. Johnson, Jr., University of Central Oklahoma, Richard P. Rettig, Eastern Oregon University, Gregory M. Scott, University of Central Oklahoma, Stephen M. Garrison, University of Central Oklahoma. — 6th ed.
    pages cm
  ISBN-13: 978-0-13-351438-4 (alk. paper)
  ISBN-10: 0-13-351438-2 (alk. paper)
  1. Criminal justice, Administration of—Research—United States. 2. Legal composition—United States.
3. Report writing—United States. I. Title.
  HV9950.J643 2015
  808.06'6364—dc23

                                                                            2013035297

PEARSON

ISBN 10:   0-13-351438-2
ISBN 13: 978-0-13-351438-4

Contents

Preface

NEW TO THE SIXTH EDITION

- Updated material on "Citing Sources in ASA Style," Chapter 4
- Updated material on "Citing Sources in APA Style," Chapter 5
- Updated material on "Criminal Justice Online," Chapter 7
- New example for "Writing Probation and Parole Reports," Chapter 12
- Extensive renovation of Chapter 14, "Criminal Justice Policy Analysis Papers"
- Updates and revisions throughout the entire manual

The more complex criminal justice systems become, the greater the need for clear, direct communication. The sad reality is that many people have difficulty writing a simple declarative sentence. In all areas of criminal justice, no skill is recognized as more important than the ability to get messages on paper clearly in order to get business done. If you learn to write well, you will be more valuable in whatever line of work you pursue.

Administrators in criminal justice agencies are looking for people who can condense a mass of data to one sheet of clear comment. They are looking for men and women who can report the day-to-day activities of a complex system concisely and accurately. Administrators want more than undigested, descriptive data; they want to know what the experts in each area believe the data mean.

This book is designed to help you improve your writing. You will find principles and guidelines to help you write complex reports as well as summarize information into condensed presentations. Good writers know and use the terminology of their discipline. In writing reports and professional communication, criminal justice professionals often need to draw from the lexicon of several disciplines, for example law enforcement, forensics, psychology, sociology, law, and management. We have included a broad and extensive glossary to aid you in writing the assignments in this manual. As you continue to use this manual throughout your college and professional career, we hope your writing skills evolve and aid you in attaining your professional goals and objectives.

INSTRUCTOR SUPPLEMENTS

To access supplementary materials online, instructors need to request an instructor access code. Go to **www.pearsonhighered.com/irc**, where you can register for an instructor access code. Within 48 hours after registering, you will receive a confirming email, including an instructor access code. Once you have received your code, go to the site and log on.

ALTERNATE VERSIONS

eBooks This text is also available in multiple eBook formats including Adobe Reader and CourseSmart. *CourseSmart* is an exciting new choice for students looking to save money. As an alternative to purchasing the printed textbook, students can purchase an electronic version of the same content. With a *CourseSmart* eTextbook, students can search the text, make notes online, print out reading assignments that incorporate lecture notes, and bookmark important passages for later review. For more information, or to purchase access to the *CourseSmart* eTextbook, visit **www.coursesmart.com**.

ACKNOWLEDGMENTS

We thank Gary Bauer, Sara Eilert, Lynda Cramer, and all who assisted in the production of this book. A special thanks to Judge Sid Brown for his assistance in the new example for "Writing Probation and Parole Reports."

William Johnson
Richard Rettig
Gregory Scott
Stephen Garrison

PART 1

A HANDBOOK OF STYLE FOR CRIMINAL JUSTICE

Chapter **1**

Writing as Communication

WRITING TO LEARN

Writing is a way of ordering your experience. Think about it: No matter what you are writing—it may be a paper for your introductory criminal justice class, a short story, a limerick, a grocery list—you are putting pieces of your world together in new ways and making yourself freshly conscious of these pieces. This is one of the reasons writing is so hard. From the infinite welter of data that your mind continually processes and locks in your memory, you are selecting only certain items significant to the task at hand, relating them to other items, and phrasing them in a new coherence. You are mapping a part of your universe that has hitherto been unknown territory. You are gaining a little more control over the processes by which you interact with the world around you.

Writing is, therefore, one of the best ways to learn. This statement may sound odd at first. If you are an unpracticed writer, you may share a common notion that the only purpose writing can have is to express what you already know or think. Any learning that you as a writer might do has already been accomplished by the time your pen meets the paper. In this view, your task is to inform and even surprise the reader. But if you are a practiced writer, you know that at any moment as you write, you are capable of surprising yourself by discovering information you never knew that you knew. And it is surprise that you look for: the shock of seeing what happens in your own mind when you drop an old, established opinion into a batch of new facts or bump into a cherished belief from a different angle. Writing synthesizes new understanding for the writer. E. M. Forster's famous question—"How do I know what I think until I see what I say?"—is one that all of us could ask. We make meaning as we write, jolting ourselves by little discoveries into a larger and more interesting universe.

THE IRONY OF WRITING

Good writing helps the reader become aware of the ironies and paradoxes of human existence. One such paradox is that good writing expresses both that which is unique about the writer and, at the same time, that which is common, not to the writer alone, but to every human being. Many of America's most famous political statements share this double attribute of mirroring the singular and the ordinary. For example, read the following excerpts from President Franklin Roosevelt's first inaugural address, spoken on March 4, 1933, in the middle of the Great Depression; then answer this question: Is what Roosevelt said famous in history because its expression is extraordinary or because it appeals to something that is basic to every human being?

> This is pre-eminently the time to speak the truth, the whole truth, frankly and boldly. Nor need we shrink from honestly facing conditions in our country today. This great nation will endure as it has endured, will revive and will prosper. So first of all let me assert my firm belief that the only thing we have to fear is fear itself—nameless, unreasoning, unjustified terror which paralyzes needed efforts to convert retreat into advance. In every dark hour of our national life a leadership of frankness and vigor has met with that understanding and support of the people themselves which is essential to victory. I am convinced that you will again give that support to leadership in these critical days.
>
> In such a spirit on my part and on yours we face our common difficulties. They concern, thank God, only material things. Values have shrunken to fantastic levels; taxes have risen; our ability to pay has fallen, government of all kinds is faced by serious curtailment of income; the means of exchange are frozen in the currents of trade; the withered leaves of industrial enterprise lie on every side; farmers find no markets for their produce; the savings of many years in thousands of families are gone.
>
> More important, a host of unemployed citizens face the grim problem of existence, and an equally great number toil with little return. Only a foolish optimist can deny the dark realities of the moment.
>
> Yet our distress comes from no failure of substance. We are stricken by no plague of locusts. Compared with the perils which our forefathers conquered because they believed and were not afraid, we have still much to be thankful for. Nature still offers her bounty and human efforts have multiplied it. Plenty is at our doorstep, but a generous use of it languishes in the very sight of the supply....

The measure of the restoration lies in the extent to which we apply social values more noble than mere monetary profit.

Happiness lies not in the mere possession of money; it lies in the joy of achievement, in the thrill of creative effort.

The joy and moral stimulation of work no longer must be forgotten in the mad chase of evanescent profits. These dark days will be worth all they cost us if they teach us that our true destiny is not to be ministered unto but to minister to ourselves and to our fellow-men.

(Roosevelt 1933)

The help that writing gives us with learning and with controlling what we learn is one of the major reasons why your criminal justice instructors will require a great deal of writing from you. Learning the complex and diverse world of the criminal justice professional takes more than a passive ingestion of facts. You have to come to grips with social issues and with your own attitudes toward them. When you write in a class on criminal justice or juvenile delinquency, you are entering into the world of professional researchers in the same way they do—testing theory against fact and fact against belief.

Virtually everything that happens in the discipline of criminal justice happens on paper first. Documents are wrestled into shape before their contents can affect the public. Meaningful social programs are written before they are implemented. The written word has helped bring slaves to freedom, end wars, create new opportunities in the workplace, and shape the values of nations. Often, gaining recognition for ourselves and our ideas depends less upon what we say than upon how we say it. Accurate and persuasive writing is absolutely vital to the criminal justice professional.

Learning by Writing

A way of testing the notion that writing is a powerful learning tool is by rewriting your notes from a recent class lecture. The type of class does not matter; it can be history, chemistry, criminal justice, whatever. If possible, choose a difficult class, one in which you are feeling somewhat unsure of the material and one for which you have taken copious notes.

As you rewrite, provide the transitional elements (the connecting phrases like *in order to*, *because of*, and, *but*, *however*) that you were unable to supply in class because of the press of time. Furnish your own examples or illustrations of the ideas expressed in the lecture.

This experiment will force you to supply necessary coherence out of your own thought processes. See if the loss of time it takes you to rewrite the notes is not more than compensated for by a gain in your understanding of the lecture material.

CHALLENGE YOURSELF

There is no way around it: Writing is a struggle. Do you think you are the only one to feel this way? Take heart! Writing is hard for everybody, great writers included. Bringing order into the world is never easy. Isaac Bashevis Singer, winner of the 1978 Nobel Prize in literature, once wrote, "I believe in miracles in every area of life except writing. Experience has shown me that there are no miracles in writing. The only thing that produces good writing is hard work" (Lunsford and Connors 1992:2).

Hard work was evident in the words of John F. Kennedy's Inaugural Address. As you read the following excerpts from Kennedy's speech, what images come to mind? Historians tend to consider a president "great" when his words live longer than his deeds in the minds of the people. Do you think this will be—or has been—true of Kennedy?

> We observe today not a victory of party but a celebration of freedom—symbolizing an end as well as a beginning—signifying renewal as well as change. For I have sworn before you and Almighty God the same solemn oath our forebears prescribed nearly a century and three-quarters ago.
>
> The world is very different now. For man holds in his mortal hands the power to abolish all forms of human poverty and all forms of human life. And yet the same revolutionary beliefs for which our forebears fought are still at issue around the globe—the belief that the rights of man come not from the generosity of the state but from the hand of God.
>
> We dare not forget today that we are the heirs of that first revolution. Let the word go forth from this time and place, to friend and foe alike, that the torch has been passed to a new generation of Americans—born in this century, tempered by war, disciplined by a hard and bitter peace, proud of our ancient heritage—and unwilling to witness or permit the slow undoing of those human rights to which this nation has always been committed, and to which we are committed today at home and around the world....
>
> In the long history of the world, only a few generations have been granted the role of defending freedom in its hours of maximum danger. I do not shrink from this responsibility—I welcome it. I do not believe that any of us would exchange places with any other people or any other generation. The energy, the faith, the devotion which we bring to this endeavor will light our country and all who serve it—and the glow from that fire can truly light the world.
>
> And so, my fellow Americans: ask not what your country can do for you—ask what you can do for your country.
>
> My fellow citizens of the world: ask not what America will do for you, but what together we can do for the freedom of man.

(Kennedy 1961)

One reason writing is difficult is that it is not actually a single activity at all but a process consisting of several activities that can overlap each other, with two or more sometimes operating *simultaneously* as you labor to organize and phrase your thoughts. (We will discuss these activities later in this chapter.) The writing process tends to be sloppy for everyone; it is often a frustrating search for meaning and for the best way to articulate that meaning.

Frustrating though that search may sometimes be, it need not be futile. Remember this: The writing process makes use of skills that we all have. The ability to write, in other words, is not some magical competence bestowed on the rare, fortunate individual. While few of us may achieve the proficiency of Isaac Singer, we are all capable of phrasing thoughts clearly and in a well-organized fashion. But learning how to do so takes practice.

The one sure way to improve your writing is to write.   One of the toughest but most important jobs in writing is to maintain enthusiasm for your writing project. Commitment may sometimes be complicated, given the difficulties that are inherent in the writing process and that can be made worse when the project is unappealing at first glance. How, for example, can you be enthusiastic about having to write a paper analyzing prison reform when you know little about the American correctional system and see no real use in writing about it?

One of the worst mistakes that unpracticed student writers make is to fail to assume responsibility for keeping themselves interested in their writing. No matter how hard it may seem at first to drum up interest in your topic, *you have to do it*—that is, if you want to write a paper you can be proud of, one that contributes useful material and a fresh point of view to the topic. One thing is guaranteed: If you are bored with your writing, your reader will be, too. So what can you do to keep your interest and energy level high?

Challenge yourself.   Think of your paper not as an assignment but as a piece of writing that has a point to make. To get this point across persuasively is the real reason why you are writing, not the simple fact that a teacher has assigned you a project. If someone were to ask you why you are writing your paper and your immediate, unthinking response is, "Because I've been given a writing assignment," or "Because I want a good grade," or some other nonanswer along these lines, your paper may be in trouble.

If, on the other hand, your first impulse is to explain the challenge of your main point—"I'm writing to show how prison reform will benefit both inmates and the American taxpayer"—then you are thinking usefully about your topic.

Maintain Self-Confidence

Having confidence in your ability to write well about your topic is essential for good writing. This does not mean that you will always know what the end result of a particular writing activity will be. In fact, you have to cultivate your ability to tolerate a high degree of uncertainty while weighing evidence, testing hypotheses, and experimenting with organizational strategies and wording. Be ready for temporary confusion and for seeming dead ends, and remember that every writer faces these obstacles. It is from your struggle to combine fact with fact, to buttress conjecture with evidence, that order arises.

Do not be intimidated by the amount and quality of work that others have already done in your field of inquiry. The array of opinion and evidence that confronts you in the published literature can be confusing. But remember that no important topic is ever exhausted. *There are always gaps*—questions that have not yet been satisfactorily explored either in the published research on a subject or in the prevailing popular opinion. It is in these gaps that you establish your own authority, your own sense of control.

Remember that the various stages of the writing process reinforce each other. Establishing a solid motivation strengthens your sense of confidence about the project, which in turn influences how successfully you organize and write. If you start out well, using good work habits, and give yourself ample time for the various activities to coalesce, you should produce a paper that will reflect your best work, one that your audience will find both readable and useful.

THE WRITING PROCESS

LEARNING THE NATURE OF THE PROCESS

As you engage in the writing process, you are doing many different things at once. While planning, you are no doubt defining the audience for your paper at the same time that you are thinking about the paper's purpose. As you draft the paper, you may organize your next sentence while revising the one you have just written. Different parts of the writing process overlap, and much of the difficulty of writing is that so many things happen at once. Through practice—in other words, through *writing*—it is possible to learn how to control those parts of the process that can in fact be controlled and to encourage those mysterious, less controllable activities.

No two people go about writing in exactly the same way. It is important for you to recognize routines—modes of thought as well as individual exercises— that help you negotiate the process successfully. And it is also important to give yourself as much time as possible to complete the process. Procrastination is one of the writer's greatest enemies. It saps confidence, undermines energy, destroys concentration. Working regularly and following a well-planned schedule as closely as possible often make the difference between a successful paper and an embarrassment.

Although the various parts of the writing process are interwoven, there is naturally a general order to the work of writing. You have to start somewhere!

What follows is a description of the various stages of the writing process—*planning*, *drafting*, *revising*, *editing*, and *proofreading*—along with suggestions on how to approach each most successfully.

PLANNING

Planning includes all activities that lead up to the writing of the first draft. The particular activities in this stage differ from person to person. Some writers, for instance, prefer to compile a formal outline before writing that draft. Some writers perform brief writing exercises to jump-start their imaginations. Some draw diagrams; some doodle. Later we will look at a few starting strategies, and you can determine which may help you.

Now, however, let us discuss certain early choices that all writers must make during the planning stage. These choices concern *topic*, *purpose*, and *audience*, three elements that make up the writing context, or the terms under which we all write. Every time you write, even if you are writing a diary entry or a note to your banker, these elements are present. You may not give conscious consideration to all of them in each piece of writing that you do, but it is extremely important to think carefully about them when writing a criminal justice paper. Some or all of these defining elements may be dictated by your assignment, yet you will always have a degree of control over them.

Selecting a Topic

No matter how restrictive an assignment may seem, there is no reason to feel trapped by it. Within any assigned subject you can find a range of topics to explore. What you are looking for is a topic that engages your own interest. Let your curiosity be your guide. If, for example, you have been assigned the subject of prison reform, then guide yourself to find some issue concerning prison reform that interests you. (How does inmate education—for example, taking college courses by correspondence or television—affect recidivism? Should inmates incarcerated for violent offenses be allowed to "bulk up" by lifting weights?) Any good topic comes with a set of questions; you may well find that your interest picks up if you simply begin asking questions.

One strong recommendation: Ask your questions on paper. Like most other mental activities, the process of exploring your way through a topic is transformed when you write down your thoughts as they come instead of letting them fly through your mind unrecorded. Remember the old adage from Louis Agassiz: "A pen is often the best of eyes" (Pearce 1958:106).

While it is vital to be interested in your topic, you do not have to know much about it at the outset of your investigation. In fact, having too heartfelt a commitment to a topic can be an impediment to writing about it; emotions can get in the way of objectivity. Better often to choose a topic that has piqued your interest yet remained something of a mystery to you: a topic discussed in one of your classes, perhaps, or mentioned on television or in a conversation with friends.

Narrowing a Topic

The task of narrowing your topic offers you a tremendous opportunity to establish a measure of control over the writing project. It is up to you to hone your topic to just the right shape and size to suit both your own interests and the requirements of the assignment. Do a good job of it, and you will go a long way toward guaranteeing yourself sufficient motivation and confidence for the tasks ahead of you. If you do not narrow your topic well, somewhere along the way you may find yourself directionless and out of energy.

Generally, the first topics that come to your mind will be too large to handle in your research paper. For example, the topic of gun control has generated a tremendous number of published news articles and reports recently by experts in the field. Despite all the attention turned toward this topic, however, there is still plenty of room for you to investigate it on a level that has real meaning to you and that does not merely recapitulate the published research. What about an analysis of how enactment of the Brady bill has affected handgun crimes in your city? The problem with most topics is not that they are too narrow or too completely explored, but rather that they are so rich it is difficult to choose the most useful

---

Narrowing Topics

Without doing research, see how you can narrow the following general topics; for example:

General topic	Narrowed topics
Juvenile delinquency	Labeling serious habitual offenders: harassment or public safety?
	Substance abuse and delinquent behavior
	Kids that kill: juvenile delinquents or adult murderers?

Now try narrowing the following general topics:

Crime in America	Political corruption
International terrorism	Costs of incarceration
Education	Affirmative action hiring policies
Freedom of speech	Freedom to bear arms
Gun control	Training police officers

ways to address them. Take some time to narrow your topic. Think through the possibilities that occur to you, and as always, jot down your thoughts.

Students in an undergraduate course on criminology were told to write an essay of 2500 words on one of the following topics. Next to each general topic is an example of how students narrowed it to make a manageable paper topic.

General Topic	Paper Topic
Homicide	The effect of homicide on the black male population in the United States
Teenage Crimes	The role of drug involvement in teenage crimes in the United States
Prisons	Should U.S. prisons be run by the private sector?

Finding a Thesis

As you plan your writing, be on the lookout for an idea that can serve as your thesis. A thesis is not a fact, which can be immediately verified by data, but an assertion worth discussing, an argument with more than one possible conclusion. Your thesis sentence will reveal to your reader not only the argument you have chosen but also your orientation toward it and the conclusion that your paper will attempt to prove.

In looking for a thesis, you are doing many jobs at once:

1. You are limiting the amount and kind of material that you must cover, thus making it manageable.
2. You are increasing your own interest in the narrowing field of study.
3. You are working to establish your paper's purpose, the reason why you are writing about your topic. (If the only reason you can see for writing is to earn a good grade, then you probably won't!)
4. You are establishing your notion of who your audience is and what sort of approach to the subject might best catch their interest.

In short, you are gaining control over your writing context. For this reason, it is a good idea to come up with a thesis early on, a *working thesis*, which will very probably change as your thinking deepens but which will allow you to establish a measure of order in the planning stage.

The Thesis Sentence

The introduction of your paper will contain a sentence that expresses the task that you intend to accomplish. This thesis sentence communicates your main idea, the one you are going to support, defend, or illustrate. The thesis sets up an expectation in the reader's mind that is your job to satisfy. But in the planning stage a thesis sentence is more than just the statement that informs your reader of your goal. It is a valuable tool to help you narrow your focus and confirm in your own mind your paper's purpose.

Developing a Thesis

A Crime and Society class was assigned to write a 20-page paper studying a problem currently being faced by the municipal authorities in their own city. The choice of the problem was left up to the students. One class member, Mark Gonzales, decided to investigate the problem posed to the city by the large number of abandoned buildings in a downtown neighborhood that he drove through on his way to the university. His first working thesis read as follows:

Abandoned houses breed crime.

The problem with this thesis, as Mark found out, was that it was not an idea that could be argued but rather a fact that could be easily corroborated by the sources he began to consult. As Mark read reports from such sources as the Urban Land Institute and the City Planning Commission and talked with representatives from the Community Planning Department, he began to get interested in the dilemma his city faced in responding to the problem of abandoned buildings. Here is Mark's second working thesis:

Removal of abandoned buildings is a major problem facing the city.

This thesis narrowed the topic somewhat and gave Mark an opportunity to use material from his research, but there was still no real comment attached to it. It still stated a bare fact, easily proved. At this point, Mark became interested in the still narrower topic of how building removal should best be handled. He found that the major issue was funding the demolition and that different civic groups favored different funding methods. As Mark explored the arguments for and against funding plans, he began to feel that one of them might be best for the city. Mark's third working thesis:

Providing alternative shelter for homeless people reduces crime associated with abandoned buildings.

Note how this thesis narrows the focus of Mark's paper even further than the other two while also presenting an arguable hypothesis. It tells Mark what he has to do in his paper, just as it tells his reader what to expect.

At some time during your preliminary thinking on a topic, you should consult the library to see how much published work has already been done. This search is beneficial in at least two ways:

1. It acquaints you with a body of writing that will become very important in the research phase of the paper.

2. It gives you a sense of how your topic is generally addressed by the community of scholars you are joining. Is the topic as important as you think it is? Has there already been so much research on the topic as to make your inquiry, in its present formulation, irrelevant?

As you go about determining your topic, remember that one goal of criminal justice writing in college is to enhance your own understanding of the social and social-psychological process, to build an accurate model of the way social institutions work. Let this goal help you to aim your research into those areas that you know are important to your knowledge of the discipline.

Defining Your Purpose

There are many ways to classify the purposes of writing, but in general, most writing is undertaken either to inform or to persuade an audience. The goal of informative or expository writing is, simply, to impart information about a particular subject, while the aim of persuasive writing is to convince your reader of your point of view on an issue. The distinction between expository and persuasive writing is not hard and fast, and most criminal justice writing has elements of both types. Most effective writing, however, is clearly focused on either exposition or persuasion. When you begin writing, consciously select a primary approach of exposition or persuasion and then set out to achieve that goal.

Suppose you have been required to write a paper explaining how parents' attitudes affect their children's choice of colleges. If you are writing an expository paper, your task could be to describe in as coherent and impartial a way as possible the attitudes of the parents and the choices of their children. If, however, your paper attempts to convince your reader that parental attitudes often result in children making poor choices, you are now writing to persuade, and your strategy is radically different. You will now need to explain the negative effects of parental attitudes. Persuasive writing seeks to influence the opinions of its audience toward its subject.

Know what you want to say.   By the time of your final draft, you must have a very sound notion of the point you wish to argue. If, as you write that final draft, someone were to ask you to state your thesis, you should be able to give a satisfactory answer with a minimum of delay and no prompting. If, on the other hand, you have to hedge your answer because you cannot easily express your thesis, you may not yet be ready to write a final draft.

Watch out for bias!   There is no such thing as pure objectivity. You are not a machine. No matter how hard you may try to produce an objective paper, the fact is that every choice you make as you write is influenced to some extent by your personal beliefs and opinions. What you tell your readers is *truth*, in other words, is influenced, often without your knowing, by a multitude of factors: your environment, upbringing, and education; your attitude toward your audience; your political affiliation; your race and gender; your career goals; and your ambitions for the paper you are writing. The influence of such factors can be very subtle, and it is something you must work to identify in your own writing as well as in the writing

Knowing What You Want to Say

Two writers have been asked to state the theses of their papers. Which one of the writers better understands the writing task?

- *Writer 1:* "My paper is about police–community relations."
- *Writer 2:* "My paper argues that improving communication between the police and citizens in the community raises morale among police officers and helps people take greater responsibility for important issues within the community."

The second writer has a clear view of her task. The first knows what her topic is—police–community relations—but may not yet know what it is about these relations that fosters important changes within the community. It may be that you will have to write a rough draft or two or engage in various prewriting activities in order to arrive at a secure understanding of your task.

of others in order not to mislead or be misled. Remember that one of the reasons for writing is *self-discovery*. The writing you will do in criminal justice classes—as well as the writing you will do for the rest of your life—will give you a chance to discover and confront honestly your own views on your subjects. Responsible writers keep an eye on their own biases and are honest about them with their readers.

Defining Your Audience

In any class that requires you to write, it may sometimes be difficult to remember that the point of your writing is not simply to jump through the technical hoops imposed by the assignment. The point is *communication*, the transmission of your knowledge and your conclusions to the reader in a way that suits you. Your task is to pass to your reader the spark of your own enthusiasm for your topic. Readers who were indifferent to your topic should look at it in a new way after reading your paper. This is the great challenge of writing: to enter into your reader's mind and leave behind both new knowledge and new questions.

It is tempting to think that most writing problems would be solved if the writer could view the writing as if it had been produced by another person. The discrepancy between the understanding of the writer and that of the audience is the single greatest impediment to accurate communication. To overcome this barrier, you must consider your audience's needs. By the time you begin drafting, most if not all of your ideas will have begun to attain coherent shape in your mind, so that virtually any words in which you try to phrase those ideas will reflect your thought accurately—*to you*. Your readers, however, do not already hold the conclusions that you have so painstakingly achieved. If you omit from your writing the material that is necessary to complete your readers' understanding of your argument, they may well not be able to supply that information themselves.

The potential for misunderstanding is present for any audience, whether it is made up of general readers, experts in the field, or your professor, who is reading, in part, to see how well you have mastered the constraints that govern the relationship between writer and reader. Make your presentation as complete as possible, bearing in mind your audience's knowledge of your topic.

Using Invention Strategies

We have discussed various methods of selecting and narrowing the topic of a paper. As your focus on a specific topic sharpens, you will naturally begin to think about the kinds of information that will go into the paper. In the case of papers not requiring formal research, that material comes largely from your own recollections. Indeed, one of the reasons instructors assign such papers is to convince you of the incredible richness of your memory, the vastness and variety of the "database" you have accumulated and which, moment by moment, you continue to build.

So vast is your horde of information that it is sometimes difficult to find within it the material that would best suit your paper. In other words, finding out what you already know about a topic is not always easy. *Invention*, a term borrowed from classical rhetoric, refers to the task of discovering, or recovering from memory, such information. As we write, we go through some sort of invention procedure that helps us explore our topic. Some writers seem to have little problem coming up with material; others need more help. Over the centuries writers have devised different exercises that can help locate useful material housed in memory. We shall look at a few of these briefly.

Freewriting

Freewriting is an activity that forces you to get something down on paper. There is no waiting around for inspiration. Instead, you set yourself a time limit—perhaps three or five minutes—and write for that length of time without stopping, not even to lift the pen from the paper or your hands from the keyboard. Focus on the topic, and don't let the difficulty of finding relevant material stop you from writing. If necessary, you may begin by writing, over and over, some seemingly useless phrase, such as "I cannot think of anything to write about" or perhaps the name of your topic. Eventually, something else will occur to you. (It is surprising how long a three-minute freewriting session can seem to last!) At the end of the freewriting, look over what you have produced for anything of use. Much of the writing will be unusable, but there may be an insight or two that you did not know you possessed.

Besides helping to recover from your memory usable material for your paper, freewriting has other benefits. First, it takes little time to do, which means you may repeat the exercise as often as you like within a relatively short span of time. Second, it breaks down some of the resistance that stands between you and the act of writing. There is no initial struggle to find something to say; you just *write*.

Freewriting

The teacher in Shelby Johnson's second-year Family as a Social Institution class assigned Shelby a paper to write focusing on some aspect of American family life. Shelby, who felt her understanding of the family as an institution was slight, tried to get her mind started on the job of finding a topic that interested her with a two-minute freewriting. Thinking about the family and child development, Shelby wrote steadily for three minutes without lifting her pen from the paper. Here is the result of her freewriting:

Family family family family family family family what do I know? My family—father mother sister. Joely. Parents Mom and Dad. Carole and Don. Child development. My development. Okay okay okay okay okay. Both parents were present all my life. Both worked. Professionals. Dad at the school, Mom at the office. Sometimes we wished Mom was at home. The bedtimes she missed, Joely griping and that night she cried. That old empty feeling. Emptinesssssss. The way the air conditioner sounded when the house was quiet. That might be interesting: working parents, the effects on kids. A personal view. Two-paycheck families. Necessary nowadays—why not before? What's happened to make two jobs necessary. No. Back up. Go back to life in two-income family. I like it. Where to start. I could interview Mom. Get recent statistics on two-paycheck families. Where???? Ask in library tomorrow.

Brainstorming

Brainstorming is simply making a list of ideas about a topic. It can be done quickly and at first without any need to order items into a coherent pattern. The point is to write down everything that occurs to you quickly and as briefly as possible, using individual words or short phrases. Once you have a good-sized list of items, you can then group the items according to relationships that you see among them. Brainstorming thus allows you to uncover both ideas stored in your memory and useful associations among those ideas.

Brainstorming

A professor in a criminal justice class asked her students to write a 700-word paper, in the form of a letter to be translated and published in a Warsaw newspaper, giving Polish readers useful advice about living in a democracy. One student, Chelsea Blake, started thinking about the assignment by brainstorming. First, she simply wrote down anything that occurred to her:

Voting rights	Welfare	Freedom of press
Protest movements	Everybody equal	Minorities
Racial prejudice	The American Dream	Injustice

The individual	No job security	Lobbyists and PACs
Justice takes time	Psychological factors	Aristocracy of wealth
Size of bureaucracy	Market economy	Many choices

Thinking through her list, Chelsea decided to rearrange it into two lists, one devoted to positive aspects of life in a democracy, the other to negative aspects. At this point she decided to discard some items that were redundant or did not seem to have much potential. As you can see, Chelsea had some questions about where some of her items would fit.

Positive	**Negative**
Voting rights	Aristocracy of wealth
Freedom of the press	Justice takes time
Everybody equal	Racial prejudice
The American Dream	Welfare
Psychological factors	Lobbyists and PACs
Protest movements (positive?)	Size of bureaucracy

At this point, Chelsea decided that her topic would be the ways in which money and special interests affect a democratically elected government. Which items on her lists would be relevant to Chelsea's paper?

Asking Questions

It is always possible to ask most or all of the following questions about any topic: *Who? What? When? Where? Why? How?* These questions force you to approach the topic as a journalist does, setting it within different perspectives that can then be compared.

Asking Questions

For a class in criminal law, a professor asked her class to write a paper describing the impact of Supreme Court clerks on the decision-making process. One student developed the following questions as he began to think about a thesis:

- *Who* are the Supreme Court's clerks? (How old? Of what ethnicity and gender are they? What are their politics?)
- *What* are their qualifications for the job?

(continued)

- *What* exactly is their job?
- *When* during the Court term are they most influential?
- *Where* do they come from? (Is there any geographical pattern discernible in the way they are chosen? Any pattern regarding religion? Do certain law schools contribute a significantly greater number of clerks than any others?)
- *How* are they chosen? (appointed? elected?)
- *When* in their careers do they serve?
- *Why* are they chosen as they are?
- *Who* have been some influential Court clerks? (Have any gone on to sit on the bench themselves?)

Can you think of other questions that would make for useful inquiry?

Maintaining Flexibility

As you engage in invention strategies you are also doing other work. You are still narrowing your topic, for example, as well as making decisions that will affect your choice of tone or audience. You are moving forward on all fronts, with each decision you make affecting the others. This means you must be flexible to allow for slight adjustments in your understanding of the paper's development and of your goal. Never be so determined to prove a particular theory that you fail to notice when your own understanding of it changes. *Stay objective.*

Organizing Your Writing

A paper that has all the facts but gives them to the reader in an ineffective order will confuse rather than inform or persuade. While there are various methods of grouping ideas, none is potentially more effective than *outlining*. Unfortunately, no organizing process is more often misunderstood.

Outlining for Yourself

Outlining can do two jobs. First, it can force you, the writer, to gain a better understanding of your ideas by arranging them according to their interrelationships. There is one primary rule of outlining: Ideas of equal weight are placed on the same level within the outline. This rule requires you to determine the relative importance of your ideas. You have to decide which ideas are of the same type or order and into which subtopic each idea best fits.

If, in the planning stage, you carefully arrange your ideas in a coherent outline, your grasp of the topic will be greatly enhanced. You will have linked your ideas logically together and given a basic structure to the body of the paper. This sort of subordinating and coordinating activity is difficult, however, and as a result, inexperienced writers sometimes begin to write their first draft without an effective outline, hoping for the best. This hope is usually unfulfilled, especially in complex papers involving research.

Outlining for Your Reader

The second job an outline can perform is to serve as a reader's blueprint to the paper, summarizing its points and their interrelationships. A busy person can quickly get a sense of your paper's goal and the argument you have used to promote it by consulting your outline. The clarity and coherence of the outline help to determine how much attention your audience will give to your ideas.

While neither the American Sociological Association (ASA) nor the American Psychological Association (APA) in their style guides formally require the inclusion of an outline with a paper submitted for publication to a professional journal, both the fourth edition of the *ASA Style Guide* (2010:42) and the sixth edition of the *Publication Manual of the APA* (2010:62–63) advocate the use of organizational headings, based on formal outline patterning, within the paper's text. Indeed, a formal outline is such a useful tool that your criminal justice instructor may require you to submit one. A look at the model presented in other chapters of this manual will show you how strictly these formal outlines are structured. But while you must pay close attention to the requirements of the accompanying outline, do not forget how powerful a tool an outline can be in the early planning stages of your paper.

Organizing Thoughts

Juan, a student in a second-year criminal justice class, researched the impact of a worker-retraining program in his state and came up with the following facts and theories. Number them in logical order.

_____ A growing number of workers in the state do not possess the basic skills and education demanded by employers.

_____ The number of dislocated workers in the state increased from 21,000 in 1982 to 32,000 in 1992.

_____ A public policy to retrain uneducated workers would allow them to move into new and expanding sectors of the state economy.

_____ Investment in high technology would allow the state's employers to remain competitive in the production of goods and services in both domestic and foreign markets.

_____ The economy is becoming more global and more competitive.

Formal Outline Pattern

Following this pattern accurately during the planning stage of your paper helps to guarantee that your ideas are placed logically. A thesis sentence prefaces an organized outline.

Thesis sentence (prefaces the organized outline)

I. First main idea
   A. First subordinate idea
      1. Reason, example, or illustration
      2. Reason, example, or illustration
         a. Detail supporting reason #2
         b. Detail supporting reason #2
         c. Detail supporting reason #2
   B. Second subordinate idea

II. Second main idea

Notice that each level of the paper must have more than one entry; for every A there must be at least a B (and, if required, a C, D, etc.); for every 1 there must be a 2. This arrangement forces you to compare ideas, looking carefully at each one to determine its place among the others. The insistence on assigning relative values to your ideas is what makes your outline an effective organizing tool.

Knowing the Patterns of Criminal Justice Papers

The structure of any particular type of criminal justice paper is governed by a formal pattern. When rigid external controls are placed on their writing, some writers tend to feel stifled, their creativity impeded by this kind of "paint-by-numbers" approach to structure. It is vital to the success of your paper that you never allow yourself to be overwhelmed by the pattern rules for any type of paper. Remember that such controls exist not to limit your creativity but to make the paper immediately and easily useful to its intended audience. It is as necessary to write clearly and confidently in a case study or a policy analysis paper as in a term paper for English literature, a résumé, a short story, or a job application letter.

DRAFTING

The planning stage of the writing process is followed by the writing of the first draft. Using your thesis and outline as direction markers, you must now weave your amalgam of ideas, researched data, and persuasion strategies into logically ordered sentences and paragraphs. Though adequate prewriting may facilitate the drafting, it still will not be easy. Writers establish their own individual methods of encouraging themselves to forge ahead with the draft, but here are some tips to bear in mind.

1. Remember that this is a *rough draft*, not the final paper. At this stage, it is not necessary that every word be the best possible word. Do not put that sort of pressure on yourself. You must not allow anything to slow you down now. Writing is not like sculpting in stone, where every chip is permanent; you can always go back to your draft later and add, delete, reword, or rearrange. *No matter how much effort you have put into planning, you cannot be sure how much of this first draft you will eventually keep.* It may take several drafts to get one that you find satisfactory.

2. Give yourself sufficient time to write. Don't delay the first draft by telling yourself there is still more research to do. You cannot uncover all the material there is to know on a particular subject, so don't fool yourself into trying. Remember that writing is a process of discovery. You may have to begin writing before you can see exactly what sort of final research you need to do. Keep in mind that there are other tasks waiting for you after the first draft is finished, so allow for them as you determine your writing schedule. It is also very important to give yourself time to write because the more time that passes after you have written a draft, the better your ability to view it with greater objectivity. It is very difficult to evaluate your writing accurately soon after you complete it. You need to cool down, to recover from the effort of putting all those words together. The "colder" you get on your writing, the better able you are to read it as if it were written by someone else and thus acknowledge the changes you will need to make to strengthen the paper.

3. Stay sharp. Keep in mind the plan you created for yourself as you narrowed your topic, composed a thesis sentence, and outlined the material. But if you begin to feel a strong need to change the plan a bit, do not be afraid to do so. Be ready for surprises dealt to you by your own growing understanding of the topic. Your goal is to record your best thinking on the subject as accurately as possible.

Paragraph Development

There is no absolute requirement for the structure of any paragraph in your paper except that all its sentences must be clearly related to each other and each must carry the job of saying what you want to say about your thesis *one step farther*. In other words, any sentence that simply restates something said in another sentence anywhere else in the paper is a waste of your time and the reader's. It is not unusual for a paragraph to have, somewhere in it, a *topic* sentence that serves as the key to the paragraph's organization and announces the paragraph's connection to the paper's thesis. But not all paragraphs need topic sentences.

What all paragraphs in the paper *do* need is an organizational strategy. Here are four typical organizational models, any one of which—if you keep it in mind—can help you build a coherent paragraph:

- *Chronological organization.* The sentences of the paragraph describe a series of events or steps or observations as they occur over time. This happens, then that, and then that.
- *Spatial organization.* The sentences of the paragraph record details of its subject in some logical order: top to bottom, up to down, outside to inside.
- *General-to-specific organization.* The paragraph starts with a statement of its main idea and then goes into detail as it discusses that idea.
- *Specific-to-general organization.* The paragraph begins with smaller, nuts-and-bolts details, arranging them into a larger pattern that, by the end of the paragraph, leads to the conclusion that is the paragraph's main idea.

These are not the only organizational strategies available to you, and, of course, different paragraphs in a paper can use different strategies, though a paragraph that employs more than one organizational plan is risking incoherence. The essential thing to remember is that each sentence in the paragraph must bear a logical relationship to the one before it and the one after it. It is this notion of *interconnectedness* that can prevent you from getting off track and stuffing extraneous material in your paragraphs.

Let's look, for example, at a paragraph in a student paper whose thesis idea is that recent research is locating and charting factors that lead to marital dissatisfaction. The following paragraph occurs, roughly, in the middle of the paper:

> The large majority of professional literature agrees that the transition to parenthood affects marital satisfaction (Abbey, Andrews, and Halman 1994; Campbell 1989; Hunt 1995; Kephart and Jedlicka 1991; Levy-Skiff 1994; Lewis 1989; Stephenson 1988; Turner and Helms 1994). Although some researchers conclude otherwise, most believe children cause a decrease in marital happiness (Lewis 1989; Turner and Helms 1994). Usually this unhappiness is greater among women, probably due to the added responsibilities. This unhappiness increases if the husband does little to help out with the added responsibilities (Abbey, Andrews, and Halman 1994; Hunt 1995; Levy-Skiff 1994).

Does the paragraph's organization correspond to any of the four strategies listed earlier in the chapter? It clearly moves from a general topic—the fact that parenthood may affect a couple's marital happiness—to the more specific topic of *how* having children can cause such a change in marital satisfaction.

Do not expect paragraphs as precise as this one to come to you easily as you write your first draft. Like all other aspects of the writing process, paragraph development is a challenge. But remember, one of the helpful facts about paragraphs is that they are relatively small, especially compared to the overall scope of your paper. Each paragraph can basically do only one job—handle or help to handle a single idea, which is itself only a part of the overall development of the larger thesis idea. The fact that paragraphs are small and are aimed at a single task means that it is relatively easy to revise them. By focusing clearly on the single job a paragraph does and filtering out all the paper's other claims for your attention, you should gain enough clarity of vision during the revision process to understand what you need to do to make that paragraph work better.

Language Choices

To be convincing, your writing needs to be authoritative. That is, you have to sound as if you have confidence in your ability to convey your ideas in words. Sentences that sound stilted or that suffer from weak phrasing or the use of clichés are not going to win supporters for the positions that you express in your paper. So a major question becomes: How can I sound confident? Here are some points to consider as you work to convey to your reader that necessary sense of authority.

Level of Formality

Tone is one of the primary methods by which you signal to the readers who you are and what your attitude is toward them and toward your topic. Your major decision is which level of language formality is most appropriate to your audience. The informal tone you would use in a letter to a friend might well be out of place in a paper on police corruption written for your criminal justice professor. Remember that tone is only part of the overall decision that you make about how to present your information. Formality is, to some extent, a function of individual word choices and phrasing. Is it appropriate to use contractions like *isn't* or *they'll*? Would the strategic use of a sentence fragment for effect be out of place? The use of informal language, the personal *I*, and the second-person *you* is traditionally forbidden—for better or worse—in certain kinds of writing. Often part of the challenge of writing a formal paper is simply how to give your prose bite while staying within the conventions.

Jargon

One way to lose readers quickly is to overwhelm them with jargon—phrases that have a special, usually technical, meaning within your discipline but which are unfamiliar to the average reader. The occasional use of jargon may add an effective touch of atmosphere, but anything more than that will severely dampen a reader's enthusiasm for the paper. Often the writer uses jargon in an effort to impress the reader by sounding lofty or knowledgeable. Unfortunately, all jargon usually does is cause confusion. In fact, the use of jargon indicates a writer's lack of connection to the audience.

Criminal justice writing is a haven for jargon. Perhaps writers of professional journals and certain policy analysis papers believe their readers are all completely attuned to their terminology. It may be that these writers occasionally hope to obscure damaging information or potentially unpopular ideas in confusing language. In other cases, the problem could simply be unclear thinking by the writer.

Revising Jargon

What words in the following sentence, from a published article in a journal, are examples of jargon? Can you rewrite the sentence to clarify its meaning?

The implementation of statute-mandated regulated inputs exceeds the conceptualization of the administrative technicians.

Whatever the reason, the fact is that criminal justice papers too often sound like prose made by machines to be read by machines.

Students may feel that, in order to be accepted as criminal justice professionals, their papers should conform to the practices of their published peers. *This is a mistake.* Remember that it is never better to write a cluttered or confusing sentence than a clear one and that burying your ideas in jargon defeats the effort that you went through to form them.

Clichés

In the heat of composition, as you are looking for words to help form your ideas, it is sometimes easy to plug in a *cliché*—a phrase that has attained universal recognition by overuse. (Note: Clichés differ from jargon in that clichés are part of the general public's everyday language, while jargon is specific to the language of experts in a particular field.) Our vocabularies are brimming with clichés:

- It's *raining cats and dogs.*
- That issue is *dead as a doornail.*
- It's time for the governor to *face the music.*
- Angry voters *made a beeline* for the ballot box.

The problem with clichés is that they are virtually meaningless. Once colorful means of expression, they have lost their color through overuse, and they tend to bleed energy and color from the surrounding words. When revising, replace clichés with wording that more accurately conveys your point.

Descriptive Language

Language that appeals to the readers' senses will always engage their interest more fully than language that is abstract. This is especially important for writing in disciplines that tend to deal in abstracts, such as criminal justice. The typical criminal justice paper, with its discussions of abstract principles, demographics, or deterministic outcomes, is usually in danger of floating off into abstraction, with each paragraph drifting farther away from the felt life of the readers. Whenever appropriate, appeal to your readers' sense of sight, hearing, taste, touch, or smell.

Using Descriptive Language

Which of the following two sentences is more effective?

1. The housing project had deteriorated since the last inspection.
2. Since the last inspection, deterioration of the housing project had become evident in the stench rising from the plumbing, grime on the walls and floors, and the sound of rats scurrying in the hallways.

Gender-Neutral Writing

Language can be a very powerful method of either reinforcing or destroying cultural stereotypes. By treating the sexes in subtly different ways in your language, you may unknowingly be committing an act of discrimination. A common example is the use of the pronoun *he* to refer to a person whose gender has not been identified. But there are many other writing situations in which sexist and/or ethnic bias may appear. In order to avoid gender bias, the fourth edition of the *ASA Style Guide* (2010:4) recommends replacing words like *man*, *men*, or *mankind* with *person*, *people*, or *humankind*. When both sexes must be referred to in a sentence, use *he or she*, *her or him*, or *his or hers* instead of *he/she*, *him/her*, or *his/hers*.

Some writers, faced with this dilemma, alternate the use of male and female personal pronouns; others use the plural to avoid the need to use a pronoun of either gender:

Sexist:	A lawyer should always treat his client with respect.
Nonsexist:	A lawyer should always treat his or her client with respect.
Nonsexist:	Lawyers should always treat their clients with respect.
Sexist:	Man is a political animal.
Nonsexist:	People are political animals.

Remember that language is more than the mere vehicle of your thought. Your words shape perceptions for your readers. How *well* you say something will profoundly affect your readers' response to *what* you say. Sexist language denies to a large number of your readers the basic right to fair and equal treatment. Be aware of this common form of discrimination.

REVISING

Revising is one of the most important steps in assuring the success of your essay. While unpracticed writers often think of revision as little more than making sure all the *i*'s are dotted and *t*'s are crossed, it is much more than that. Revising is *reseeing* the essay, looking at it from other perspectives, trying always to align your view with the one that will be held by your audience. Research indicates that we are actually revising all the time, in every phase of the writing process as we reread phrases, rethink the placement of an item in an outline, or test a new topic sentence for a paragraph. Subjecting your entire hard-fought draft to cold, objective scrutiny is one of the toughest activities to master, but it is absolutely necessary. You must make sure that you have said everything that needs to be said clearly and in logical order. One confusing passage, and the reader's attention is deflected from where you want it to be. Suddenly the reader has to become a detective, trying to figure out why you wrote what you did and what you meant by it. You do not want to throw such obstacles in the path of understanding. Here are some tips to help you with revision.

1. *Give yourself adequate time for revision.* As just discussed, you need time to become "cold" on your paper in order to analyze it objectively. After you have written your draft, spend some time away from it. When you return, try to think of it as someone else's paper.

2. *Read the paper carefully.* This is tougher than it sounds. One good strategy is to read it aloud or to have a friend read it aloud while you listen. (Note, however, that friends are usually not the best critics. They are rarely trained in revision techniques and are often unwilling to risk disappointing you by giving your paper a really thorough examination.)

3. *Have a list of specific items to check.* It is important to revise in an orderly fashion, in stages, looking first at large concerns, such as the overall structure, and then rereading for problems with smaller elements such as paragraph organization or sentence structure.

4. *Check for unity.* Unity is the clear and logical relation of all parts of the essay to its thesis. Make sure that every paragraph relates well to the whole of the paper and is in the right place.

5. *Check for coherence.* Make sure there are no gaps between the different parts of the argument. Look to see that you have adequate *transition* everywhere it is needed. Transitional elements are markers indicating places where the paper's focus or attitude changes. Transitional elements can be one word long—*however, although, unfortunately, luckily*— or as long as a sentence or a paragraph: *In order to appreciate fully the importance of democracy as a shaping presence in post–cold war Polish politics, it is necessary to examine briefly the Poles' last historical attempt to implement democratic government.* Transitional elements rarely introduce new material. Instead, they are direction pointers, either indicating a shift to new subject matter or signaling how the writer wishes certain material to be interpreted by the reader. Because you, the writer, already know where and why your paper changes direction and how you want particular passages to be received, it can be very difficult for you to catch those places in your paper where transition is needed.

6. *Avoid unnecessary repetition.* Two types of repetition can annoy a reader: repetition of content and of wording.

Repetition of content occurs when you return to a subject that you have already discussed. Ideally, you should consider a topic *once*, memorably, and then move on to your next topic. Organizing a paper is a difficult task, however, that usually occurs through a process of enlightenment in terms of purposes and strategies, and repetition of content can happen even if you have used prewriting strategies. What is worse, it can be difficult for you to be aware of the repetition in your own writing. As you write and revise, remember that any unnecessary repetition of content in your final draft is potentially annoying to your readers, who are working to make sense of the argument they are reading and do not want to be distracted by a passage repeating material they have already encountered. You must train yourself, through practice, to look for material that you have repeated unnecessarily.

Repetition of wording occurs when you overuse certain phrases or words. This can make your prose sound choppy and uninspired, as the following examples demonstrate:

- The subcommittee's report on prison reform will surprise a number of people. A number of people will want copies of the report.
- The chairman said at a press conference that he is happy with the report. He will circulate it to the local news agencies in the morning. He will also make sure that the city council has copies.
- I became upset when I heard how the committee had voted. I called the chairman and expressed my reservations about the committee's decision. I told him I felt that he had let the teachers and students of the state down. I also issued a press statement.

The last passage illustrates a condition known by composition teachers as the *I-syndrome*. Can you hear how such duplicated phrasing can hurt a paper? Your language should sound fresh and energetic. Make sure, before you submit your final draft, to read through your paper carefully, looking for such repetition.

Not all repetition is bad. You may wish to repeat a phrase for rhetorical effect or special emphasis: *I came. I saw. I conquered.* Just make sure that any repetition in your paper is intentional, placed there to produce a specific effect.

EDITING

Editing is sometimes confused with the more involved process of revising. But editing happens later, after you have wrestled through your first draft—and maybe your second and third—and arrived at the final draft. Even though your draft now contains all the information you want to impart and has arranged the information to your satisfaction, there are still many factors to check, such as sentence structure, spelling, and punctuation. It is at this point that an unpracticed writer might be less than vigilant. After all, most of the work on the paper is finished; the big jobs of discovering material and organizing and drafting it have been completed. But watch out! Editing is as important as any other job in the writing process. Any error that you allow in the final draft will count against you in the mind of the reader. It may not seem fair, but a minor error—a misspelling or the confusing placement of a comma—will make a much greater impression on your reader than perhaps it should. Remember that everything about your paper is your responsibility, including getting even the supposedly little jobs right. Careless editing undermines the effectiveness of your paper. It would be a shame if all the hard work you put into prewriting, drafting, and revising were to be damaged because you carelessly allowed a comma splice!

Most of the tips given for revising hold for editing as well. It is best to edit in stages, looking for only one or two kinds of errors each time you reread the paper. Focus especially on errors that you remember committing in the past. If, for instance, you know you have a tendency to misplace commas, go through your paper looking at each comma carefully. If you have a weakness for writing unintentional sentence fragments, read each sentence aloud to make sure that it is indeed a complete sentence. Have you accidentally shifted verb tenses anywhere, moving from past to present tense for no reason? Do all the subjects in your sentences agree in number with their verbs? Now is the time to find out.

Watch out for *miscues*—problems with a sentence that the writer simply does not see. Remember that your search for errors is hampered in two ways:

1. As the writer, you hope not to find any errors with your writing. This desire not to find mistakes can cause you to miss sighting them when they occur.

2. Since you know your material so well, it is easy as you read to supply a missing word or piece of punctuation unconsciously, as if it is present.

How difficult is it to see that something is missing in the following sentence:

Unfortunately, legislators often have too little regard their constituents.

We can even guess that the missing word is probably *for*, which should be inserted after *regard*. It is quite possible, however, that the writer of the sentence would automatically supply the missing *for*, as if it were on the page. This is a miscue, which can be hard for writers to spot because they are so close to their material.

One tactic for catching mistakes in sentence structure is to read the sentences aloud, starting with the last one in the paper and then moving to the next-to-last, then the previous sentence, thus going backward through the paper (reading each sentence in the normal, left-to-right manner, of course) until you reach the first sentence of the introduction. This backward progression strips each sentence of its rhetorical context and helps you to focus on its internal structure.

Editing is the stage where you finally answer those minor questions that you put off earlier when you were wrestling with wording and organization. Any ambiguities regarding the use of abbreviations, italics, numerals, capital letters, titles (when do you capitalize *president*, for example?), hyphens, dashes (usually created on a typewriter or computer by striking the hyphen key twice), apostrophes, and quotation marks have to be cleared up now. You must also check to see that you have used the required formats for footnotes, endnotes, margins, and page numbers.

Guessing is not allowed. Sometimes unpracticed writers who realize that they don't quite understand a particular rule of grammar, punctuation, or format do nothing to fill that knowledge gap. Instead, they rely on guesswork and their own logic—which is not always up to the task of dealing with so contrary a language as English—to get them through problems that they could solve if only they referred to a writing manual. Remember that it does not matter to the reader why or how an error shows up in your writing. It only matters that you have dropped your guard. You must not allow a careless error to undo the good work that you have done.

PROOFREADING

Before you hand in your final version of the paper, it is vital that you check it over one more time to make sure there are no errors of any sort. This job is called *proofreading* or *proofing*. In essence, you are looking for many of the same things you checked for during editing, but now you are doing it on the last draft, which is about to be submitted to your audience. Proofreading is as important as editing; you may have missed an error that you still have time to find, or an error may have been introduced when the draft was last revised. Like every other stage of the writing process, proofreading is your responsibility.

At this point, you must check for typing mistakes: transposed or deleted letters, words, phrases, or punctuation. If you have had the paper professionally keyed, you still must check it carefully. Do not rely solely on the proofreader. If you are creating your paper on a computer or a word processor, it is possible for you unintentionally to insert a command that alters your document drastically by slicing out a word, line, or sentence at the touch of a key. Make sure such accidental deletions have not occurred.

Above all else, remember that your paper represents you. It is a product of your best thinking, your most energetic and imaginative response to a writing challenge. If you have maintained your enthusiasm for the project and worked through the different stages of the writing process honestly and carefully, you should produce a paper you can be proud of and one that will serve its readers well.

2

Writing Competently

GUIDELINES FOR THE COMPETENT WRITER

Good writing places your thoughts in your readers' minds in exactly the way you want them to be there. It tells your readers just what you want them to know without telling them anything you do not wish to say. That may sound odd, but the fact is that writers have to be careful not to let unwanted messages slip into their writing. Look, for example, at the following passage, taken from a paper analyzing the impact of a worker-retraining program in the writer's state. Hidden within the prose is a message that jeopardizes the paper's success. Can you detect the message?

> Recent articles written on the subject of dislocated workers have had little to say about the particular problems dealt with in this paper. Since few of these articles focus on the problem at the local level.

Chances are, when you reached the end of the second "sentence," you felt that something was missing and perceived a gap in logic or coherence, so you went back through both sentences to find the place where things had gone wrong. The second sentence is actually not a sentence at all. It does have certain features of a sentence—a subject (*few*) and a verb (*focus*)—but its first word (*Since*) subordinates the entire clause that follows, taking away its ability to stand on its own as a complete idea. The second "sentence," which is properly called a *subordinate clause*, merely fills in some information about the first sentence, telling us why recent articles about dislocated workers fail to deal with problems discussed in the present paper.

The sort of error represented by the second "sentence" is commonly called a *sentence fragment*, and it conveys to the reader a message that no writer wants to send: that the writer either is careless or—worse—has not mastered the language. Language errors such as fragments, misplaced commas, or shifts in verb tense send out warnings in the readers' minds. As a result the readers lose a little of their concentration on the issue being discussed. They become distracted and begin to wonder about the language competency of the writer. The writing loses effectiveness.

Note: Whatever goal you set for your paper, whether you want it to persuade, describe, analyze, or speculate, you must also set another goal: to *display language competence*. If your paper does not meet this goal, it will not completely achieve its other aims. Language errors spread doubt like a virus; they jeopardize all the hard work you have done on your paper.

Credibility in the job market depends upon language competence. Anyone who doubts this should remember the beating that Vice President Dan Quayle took in the press for misspelling the word *potato* at a spelling bee in 1992. His error caused a storm of humiliating publicity for the hapless Quayle, adding to an impression of his general incompetence.

Correctness is relative. Although they may seem minor, the sort of language errors we are discussing—often called *surface errors*—can be extremely damaging in certain kinds of writing. Surface errors come in a variety of types, including misspellings, punctuation problems, grammar errors, and the inconsistent use of abbreviations, capitalization, or numerals. These errors are an affront to your reader's notion of correctness, and therein lies one of their biggest problems. Different audiences tolerate different levels of correctness. You know that you can get away with surface errors in, say, a letter to a friend, who will not judge you harshly for them, while those same errors in a job application letter might eliminate you from consideration for the position. Correctness depends to an extent upon context.

Another problem is that the rules governing correctness shift over time. What would have been an error to your grandmother's generation—the splitting of an infinitive, for example, or the ending of a sentence with a preposition—is taken in stride today by most readers. So how do you write correctly when the rules shift from person to person and over time? Here are some tips.

CONSIDER YOUR AUDIENCE

One of the great risks of writing is that even the simplest choices regarding wording or punctuation can sometimes prejudice your audience against you in ways that may seem unfair. For example, look again at the old grammar rule forbidding the splitting of infinitives. After decades of counseling students to *never* split an infinitive (something this sentence has just done), composition experts now concede that a split infinitive is not a grammar crime. But suppose you have written a position paper trying to convince your city council of the need to hire security personnel for the library, and half of the council members—the people you wish to convince—remember their eighth-grade grammar teacher's now outdated warning about splitting infinitives. How will they respond when you tell them, in your introduction, that librarians are compelled *to always accompany* visitors to the rare book room because of the threat of vandalism? How much of their attention have you suddenly lost because of their automatic recollection of what is now a nonrule? It is possible, in other words, to write correctly and still offend your readers' notions of language competence.

Make sure that you tailor the surface features and the degree of formality of your writing to the level of competency that your readers require. When in doubt, take a conservative approach. Your audience might be just as distracted by contractions as by a split infinitive.

AIM FOR CONSISTENCY

When dealing with a language question for which there are different answers—such as whether or not to place a comma after the second item in a series of three ("The mayor's speech addressed taxes, housing for the poor, and the job situation")—always use the same strategy. If, for example, you avoid splitting one infinitive, avoid splitting all infinitives in your paper.

HAVE CONFIDENCE IN WHAT YOU ALREADY KNOW ABOUT WRITING!

It is easy for inexperienced writers to allow their occasional mistakes to shake their confidence in their writing ability. The fact is, however, most of what we know about writing is correct. We are all capable, for example, of writing grammatically sound phrases, even if we cannot list the rules by which we achieve coherence. Most writers who worry about their chronic errors have fewer than they think. Becoming distressed about errors makes writing more difficult.

Grammar

As various composition theorists have pointed out, the word *grammar* has several definitions. One meaning is "the formal patterns in which words must be arranged in order to convey meaning." We learn these patterns very early in life and use them spontaneously without thinking about them. Our understanding of grammatical patterns is extremely sophisticated, despite the fact that few of us can actually cite the rules by which the patterns work. Hartwell (1985:111) tested grammar learning by asking native English speakers of different ages and levels of education, including high school teachers, to arrange these words in natural order:

French   the   young   girls   four

Everyone could produce the natural order for this phrase: "the four young French girls." Yet none of Hartwell's respondents said they knew the rule that governs the order of the words.

ELIMINATE CHRONIC ERRORS

But if just thinking about our errors has a negative effect on our writing, how do we learn to write more correctly? Perhaps the best answer is simply to write as often as possible. Give yourself practice in putting your thoughts into written shape—and get lots of practice in revising and proofing your work. And as you write and revise, be honest with yourself—and patient. Chronic errors are like bad habits; getting rid of them takes time.

You probably know of one or two problem areas in your writing that you could have eliminated but have not done so. Instead, you have fudged your writing at the critical points, relying upon half-remembered formulas from past English classes or trying to come up with logical solutions to your writing problems. (*Warning*: The English language does not always work in a way that seems logical.) You may have simply decided that comma rules are unlearnable or that you will never understand the difference between the verbs *lay* and *lie*. And so you guess, and come up with the wrong answer a good part of the time. What a shame, when just a little extra work would give you mastery over those few gaps in your understanding and boost your confidence as well.

Instead of continuing with this sort of guesswork and living with the gaps in your knowledge, why not face the problem areas now and learn the rules that have heretofore escaped you? What follows is a discussion of those surface features of writing where errors most commonly occur. You will probably be familiar with most if not all of the rules discussed, but there may well be a few you have not yet mastered. Now is the time to do so.

PUNCTUATION, GRAMMAR, AND SPELLING

APOSTROPHES

An apostrophe is used to show possession; when you wish to say that something belongs to someone or to something, you add either an apostrophe and an *s* or an apostrophe alone to the word that represents the owner.

When the owner is *singular* (a single person or thing), the apostrophe precedes an added *s*:

- According to Mr. Pederson's secretary, the board meeting has been canceled.
- The school's management team reduced crime problems last year.
- Somebody's briefcase was left in the classroom.

The same rule applies if the word showing possession is a plural that does not end in *s*:

- The women's club provided screening services for at-risk youth and their families.
- Professor Logan has proven himself a tireless worker for children's rights.

When the word expressing ownership is a *plural* ending in *s*, the apostrophe follows the *s*:

- The new procedure was discussed at the youth workers' conference.

There are two ways to form the possessive for two or more nouns:

1. To show joint possession (both nouns owning the same thing or things), the last noun in the series is possessive: Billy and Richard's first draft was completed yesterday.
2. To indicate that each noun owns an item or items individually, each noun must show possession: Professor Wynn's and Professor Camacho's speeches took different approaches to the same problem.

The apostrophe is important—an obvious statement when you consider the difference in meaning between the following two sentences:

1. Be sure to pick up the psychiatrist's things on your way to the airport.
2. Be sure to pick up the psychiatrists' things on your way to the airport.

In the first of these sentences, you have only one psychiatrist to worry about, while in the second, you have at least two!

CAPITALIZATION

When to Capitalize

Here is a brief summary of some hard-to-remember capitalization rules.

1. You may, if you choose, capitalize the first letter of the first word in a sentence that follows a colon, but you do not have to do so. Make sure, however, that you use one pattern consistently throughout your paper:
   - Our instructions are explicit: Do not allow anyone into the conference without an identification badge.
   - Our instructions are explicit: do not allow anyone into the conference without an identification badge.
2. Capitalize *proper nouns* (nouns naming specific people, places, or things) and *proper adjectives* (adjectives made from proper nouns). A common noun following the proper adjective is usually not

capitalized, nor is a common article preceding the proper adjective (such as *a, an,* or *the*):

Proper Nouns	Proper Adjectives
England	English sociologists
Iraq	the Iraqi educator
Shakespeare	a Shakespearean tragedy

Proper nouns include:

- Names *of monuments and buildings.* The Washington Monument, the Empire State Building, the Library of Congress
- *Historical events, eras, and certain terms concerning calendar dates.* The Civil War, the Dark Ages, Monday, December, Columbus Day
- *Parts of the country.* North, Southwest, Eastern Seaboard, the West Coast, New England

Note: When words like *north, south, east, west, northwest* are used to designate direction rather than geographical region, they are not capitalized: We drove *east* to Boston and then made a tour of the *East Coast.*

- *Words referring to race, religion, or nationality.* Islam, Muslim, Caucasian, Asian, African American, Slavic, Arab, Jewish, Hebrew, Buddhism, Buddhists, Southern Baptists, the Bible, the Koran, American
- *Names of languages.* English, Chinese, Latin, Sanskrit
- *Titles of corporations, institutions, businesses, universities, and organizations.* Dow Chemical, General Motors, the National Endowment for the Humanities, University of Tennessee, Colby College, Kiwanis Club, American Association of Retired Persons, the Oklahoma State Senate

Note: Some words once considered proper nouns or adjectives have, over time, become common, such as french fries, pasteurized milk, arabic numerals, and italics.

3. Titles of individuals may be capitalized if they precede a proper name; otherwise, titles are usually not capitalized.

- The committee honored Dean Furmanski.
- The committee honored the deans from the other colleges.
- We phoned Doctor MacKay, who arrived shortly afterward.
- We phoned the doctor, who arrived shortly afterward.
- A story on Queen Elizabeth's health appeared in yesterday's paper.
- A story on the queen's health appeared in yesterday's paper.
- Pope John Paul's visit to Colorado was a public relations success.
- The pope's visit to Colorado was a public relations success.

When Not to Capitalize

In general, you do not capitalize nouns when your reference is nonspecific. For example, you would not capitalize the phrase *the senator*, but you would capitalize *Senator Smith*. The second reference is as much a title as it is a mere term of identification, while the first reference is a mere identifier. Likewise, there is a difference in degree of specificity between the phrase the *state treasury* and the *Texas State Treasury*.

Note: The meaning of a term may change somewhat depending on capitalization. What, for example, might be the difference between a *Democrat* and a *democrat*? When capitalized, the word refers to a member of a specific political party; when not capitalized, it refers to someone who believes in a democratic form of government.

Capitalization depends to some extent on the context of your writing. For example, if you are writing a policy analysis for a specific corporation, you may capitalize words and phrases referring to that corporation—such as *Board of Directors*, *Chairman of the Board*, and *the Institute*—that would not be capitalized in a paper written for a more general audience. Likewise, in some contexts it is not unusual to see titles of certain powerful officials capitalized even when not accompanying a proper noun: The President's visit to the New York City bombing site was considered a success.

COLONS

We all know certain uses for the colon. A colon can, for example, separate the parts of a statement of time (4:25 A.M.), separate chapter and verse in a biblical quotation (John 3:16), and close the salutation of a business letter (Dear Senator Keaton:). But the colon has other uses that can add an extra degree of flexibility to sentence structure.

The colon can introduce into a sentence certain kinds of material, such as a list, a quotation, or a restatement or description of material mentioned earlier:

- *List.* The committee's research proposal promised to do three things: (1) establish the extent of the problem, (2) examine several possible solutions, and (3) estimate the cost of each solution.
- *Quotation.* In his speech, the mayor challenged us with these words: "How will your council's work make a difference in the life of our city?"
- *Restatement or description.* Ahead of us, according to the senator's chief of staff, lay the biggest job of all: convincing our constituents of the plan's benefits.

COMMAS

The comma is perhaps the most troublesome of all marks of punctuation, no doubt because its use is governed by so many variables, such as sentence length, rhetorical emphasis, and changing notions of style. The most common problems are outlined here.

The Comma Splice

A comma splice is the joining of two complete sentences by only a comma:

- An impeachment is merely an indictment of a government official, actual removal usually requires a vote by a legislative body.
- An unemployed worker who has been effectively retrained is no longer an economic problem for the community, he has become an asset.
- It might be possible for the city to assess fees on the sale of real estate, however, such a move would be criticized by the community of real estate developers.

In each of these passages, two complete sentences (also called *independent clauses*) have been spliced together by a comma, which is an inadequate break between the two sentences.

One foolproof way to check your paper for comma splices is to read carefully the structures on both sides of each comma. If you find a complete sentence on each side and if the sentence following the comma does not begin with a coordinating conjunction (*and, but, for, nor, or, so, yet*), then you have found a comma splice.

Simply reading the draft through to try to "hear" the comma splices may not work, since the rhetorical features of your prose—its "movement"—may make it hard to detect this kind of sentence completeness error. There are five commonly used ways to correct comma splices.

1. Place a period between the two independent clauses:

   Incorrect: Physicians receive many benefits from their affiliation with clients, there are liabilities as well.

   Correct: Physicians receive many benefits from their affiliation with clients. There are liabilities as well.

2. Place a comma and a coordinating conjunction (*and, but, for, or, nor, so, yet*) between the sentences:

   Incorrect: The chairperson's speech described the major differences of opinion over the department situation, it also suggested a possible course of action.

Correct: The chairperson's speech described the major differences of opinion over the departmental situation, and it also suggested a possible course of action.

3. Place a semicolon between the independent clauses:

Incorrect: Some people believe that the federal government should play a large role in establishing a housing policy for the homeless, many others disagree.

Correct: Some people believe that the federal government should play a large role in establishing a housing policy for the homeless; many others disagree.

4. Rewrite the two clauses of the comma splice as one independent clause:

Incorrect: Television programs play a substantial part in the development of delinquent attitudes, however, they were not found to be the deciding factor in determining the behavior of juvenile delinquents.

Correct: Television programs were found to play a substantial but not a decisive role in determining the delinquent behavior of juveniles.

5. Change one of the two independent clauses into a dependent clause by beginning it with a subordinating word (*although, after, as, because, before, if, though, unless, when, which, where*), which prevents the clause from being able to stand on its own as a complete sentence.

Incorrect: The student meeting was held last Tuesday, there was a poor turnout.

Correct: When the student meeting was held last Tuesday, there was a poor turnout.

Commas in a Compound Sentence

A *compound sentence* is comprised of two or more independent clauses—two complete sentences. When these two clauses are joined by a coordinating conjunction, the conjunction should be preceded by a comma to signal the reader that another independent clause follows. (This is the second method for fixing a comma splice described earlier.) When the comma is missing, the reader is not expecting to find the second half of a compound sentence and may be distracted from the text.

As the following examples indicate, the missing comma is especially a problem in longer sentences or in sentences in which other coordinating conjunctions appear. Notice how the comma sorts out the two main parts of the compound sentence, eliminating confusion:

- *Without the comma.* The senator promised to visit the hospital and investigate the problem and then he called the press conference to a close.
- *With the comma.* The senator promised to visit the hospital and investigate the problem, and then he called the press conference to a close.
- *Without the comma.* The water board can neither make policy nor enforce it nor can its members serve on auxiliary water committees.
- *With the comma.* The water board can neither make policy nor enforce it, nor can its members serve on auxiliary water committees.

An exception to this rule arises in shorter sentences, where the comma may not be necessary to make the meaning clear:

- The mayor phoned and we thanked him for his support.

However, it is never wrong to place a comma before the conjunction between the independent clauses. If you are the least bit unsure of your audience's notions about what makes for proper grammar, it is a good idea to take the conservative approach and use the comma:

- The mayor phoned, and we thanked him for his support.

Commas with Restrictive and Nonrestrictive Elements

A *nonrestrictive element* is part of a sentence—a word, phrase, or clause—that adds information about another element in the sentence without restricting or limiting its meaning. While this information may be useful, the nonrestrictive element is not needed for the sentence to make sense. To signal its inessential nature, the nonrestrictive element is set off from the rest of the sentence with commas.

The failure to use commas to indicate the nonrestrictive nature of a sentence element can cause confusion. See, for example, how the presence or absence of commas affects our understanding of the following sentence:

1. The judge was talking with the policeman, who won the outstanding service award last year.
2. The judge was talking with the policeman who won the outstanding service award last year.

Can you see that the comma changes the meaning of the sentence? In the first version, the comma makes the information that follows it incidental: *The judge was talking with the policeman, who happens to have won the service award last year.* In the second version, the information following the word *policeman* is important to the sense of the sentence; it tells us specifically *which* policeman—presumably there is more than one—the judge was addressing. Here the lack of a comma has transformed the material following the word *policeman* into a *restrictive element*, which means that it is necessary to our understanding of the sentence.

Be sure that in your paper you make a clear distinction between nonrestrictive and restrictive elements by setting off the nonrestrictive elements with commas.

Commas in a Series

A series is any two or more items of a similar nature that appear consecutively in a sentence. The items may be individual words, phrases, or clauses. In a series of three or more items, the items are separated by commas:

- *The senator, the mayor, and the police chief* all attended the ceremony.
- Because of the new zoning regulations, *all trailer parks must be moved out of the neighborhood, all small businesses must apply for recertification and tax status*, and *the two local churches must repave their parking lots.*

The final comma in the series, the one before the *and*, is sometimes left out, especially in newspaper writing. This practice, however, can make for confusion, especially in longer complicated sentences, like the second example. Here is the way that sentence would read without the final, or *serial*, comma:

- Because of the new zoning regulations, all trailer parks must be moved out of the neighborhood, all small businesses must apply for recertification and tax status and the two local churches must repave their parking lots.

Notice that without a comma the division between the second and third items in the series is not clear. This is the sort of ambiguous structure that can cause a reader to backtrack and lose concentration. You can avoid such confusion by always using that final comma. Remember, however, that if you do decide to include it, do so *consistently*; make sure it appears in every series in your paper.

MISPLACED MODIFIERS

A *modifier* is a word or group of words used to describe, or modify, another word in a sentence. A *misplaced modifier*, sometimes called a dangling modifier, appears at either the beginning or end of a sentence and seems to be describing some word other than the one the writer obviously intended. The modifier therefore "dangles," disconnected from its correct meaning. It is often hard for the writer to spot a dangling modifier, but readers can—and will—find them, and the result can be disastrous for the sentence, as the following examples demonstrate:

Incorrect: Flying low over Washington, the White House was seen.

Correct: Flying low over Washington, we saw the White House.

Incorrect: Worried at the cost of the program, sections of the bill were trimmed in committee.

Correct: Worried at the cost of the program, the committee trimmed sections of the bill.

Incorrect: To lobby for prison reform, a lot of effort went into the TV ads.

Correct: The lobby group put a lot of effort into the TV ads advocating prison reform.

Incorrect: Stunned, the TV broadcast the defeated senator's concession speech.

Correct: The TV broadcast the stunned senator's concession speech.

Note that in the first two incorrect sentences, the confusion is largely due to the use of *passive-voice verbs*: "the prison *was seen*," "sections of the proposal *were trimmed*." Often, though not always, a dangling modifier results from the fact that the actor in the sentence—*we* in the first sentence, *the committee* in the second—is either distanced from the modifier or obliterated by the passive-voice verb. It is a good idea to avoid passive voice unless you have a specific reason for using it.

One way to check for dangling modifiers is to examine all modifiers at the beginnings or endings of your sentences. Look especially for *to be* phrases (to lobby) or for words ending in *-ing* or *-ed* at the start of the modifier. Then check to see if the word being modified is always in plain sight and close enough to the phrase to be properly connected.

PARALLELISM

Series of two or more words, phrases, or clauses within a sentence should have the same grammatical structure, which is called *parallelism*. Parallel structures can add power and balance to your writing by creating a strong rhetorical rhythm. Here is a famous example of parallelism from the Preamble to the U.S. Constitution. (The capitalization follows that of the original eighteenth-century document; parallel structures have been italicized.)

> We the People of the United States, in Order *to form a more perfect Union, Establish Justice, insure Domestic Tranquility, provide for the common defense, promote the general Welfare, and secure the Blessings of Liberty to ourselves and our Posterity, do ordain and establish* this Constitution for the United States of America.

There are actually two series in this sentence, the first composed of six phrases that each complete the infinitive phrase beginning with the word *to* (*to form, [to] Establish, [to] insure, [to] provide, [to] promote, [to] secure*), the second consisting of two verbs (*do ordain and [do] establish*). These parallel series appeal to our love of balance and pattern, and they give an authoritative tone to the sentence. The writer, we feel, has thought long and carefully about the matter at hand and has taken firm control of it.

Because we find a special satisfaction in balanced structures, we are more likely to remember ideas phrased in parallelisms than in less highly ordered language. For this reason, as well as for the sense of authority and control that they suggest, parallel structures are common in well-written speeches:

> We hold these truths to be self-evident, that all men are created equal, that they are endowed by their Creator with certain unalienable Rights, that among these are Life, Liberty, and the pursuit of Happiness.
>
> Declaration of Independence, 1776

> But, in a larger sense, we can not dedicate—we can not consecrate—we can not hallow—this ground. The brave men, living and dead, who struggled here, have consecrated it, far above our poor power to add or detract. The world will little note, nor long remember what we say here, but it can never forget what they did here.
>
> Abraham Lincoln, Gettysburg Address, 1863

> Let us never negotiate out of fear. But never let us fear to negotiate....Ask not what your country can do for you; ask what you can do for your country.
>
> John F. Kennedy, Inaugural Address, 1961

Faulty Parallelism

If the parallelism of a passage is not carefully maintained, the writing can seem sloppy and out of balance. Scan your writing to make sure that all series and lists have parallel structure. The following examples show how to correct faulty parallelism:

Incorrect: The mayor promises not only to reform the police department but also *the giving of raises* to all city employees. [Connective structures such as *not only ... but also* and *both ... and* introduce elements that should be parallel.]

Correct: The mayor promises not only *to reform* the police department but also *to give raises* to all city employees.

Incorrect: The cost *of doing nothing* is greater than the cost *to renovate* the apartment block.

Correct: The cost *of doing* nothing is greater than the cost *of renovating* the apartment block.

| Incorrect: | Here are the items on the committee's agenda: (1) *to discuss* the new property tax, (2) *to revise* the wording of the city charter, (3) *a vote* on the city manager's request for an assistant. |
| Correct: | Here are the items on the committee's agenda: (1) *to discuss* the new property tax, (2) *to revise* the wording of the city charter, (3) *to vote* on the city manager's request for an assistant. |

FUSED (RUN-ON) SENTENCES

A *fused sentence* is one in which two or more independent clauses (passages that can stand as complete sentences) have been joined together without the aid of any suitable connecting word, phrase, or punctuation. The sentences have been run together. As you can see, there are several ways to correct a fused sentence:

Incorrect:	The council members were exhausted they had debated for two hours.
Correct:	The council members were exhausted. They had debated for two hours. [The linked independent clauses have been separated into two sentences.]
Correct:	The council members were exhausted; they had debated for two hours. [A semicolon marks the break between the two clauses.]
Correct:	The council members were exhausted, having debated for two hours. [The second independent clause has been rephrased as a dependent clause.]
Incorrect:	Our policy analysis impressed the committee it also convinced them to reconsider their action.
Correct:	Our policy analysis impressed the committee and also convinced them to reconsider their action. [The second clause has been rephrased as part of the first clause.]
Correct:	Our policy analysis impressed the committee, and it also convinced them to reconsider their action. [The two clauses have been separated by a comma and a coordinating word.]

Although a fused sentence is easily noticeable to the reader, it can be maddeningly difficult for the writer to catch in proofreading. Unpracticed writers tend to read through the fused spots, sometimes supplying the break that is usually heard when sentences are spoken. To check for fused sentences, read the independent clauses in your paper carefully, making sure that there are adequate breaks among all of them.

PRONOUN ERRORS

Its versus It's

Do not make the mistake of trying to form the possessive of *it* in the same way that you form the possessive of most nouns. The pronoun *it* shows possession by simply adding an *s*:

- The prosecuting attorney argued the case on *its* merits.

The word *it's* is a contraction, meaning *it is*:

- It's the most expensive program ever launched by the prison.

What makes the *its*/*it's* rule so confusing is that most nouns form the singular possessive by adding an apostrophe and an *s*:

- The *jury's* verdict startled the crowd.

When proofreading, any time you come to the word *it's*, substitute the phrase *it is* while you read. If the phrase makes sense, you have used the correct form. Consider the following uses of *it's*:

- The newspaper article was misleading in *it's* analysis of the election.

Now read it as *it is*:

- The newspaper article was misleading in *it is* analysis of the election.

If the phrase makes no sense, substitute *its* for *it's*:

- The newspaper article was misleading in *its* analysis of the election.

Vague Pronoun Reference

Pronouns are words that stand in place of nouns or other pronouns that have already been mentioned in your writing. The most common pronouns include *he, she, it, they, them, those, which,* and *who*. You must make sure that there is no confusion about the word to which each pronoun refers:

- The mayor said that *he* would support our bill if the city council would also back *it*.
- The piece of legislation *which* drew the most criticism was the bill concerning housing for the poor.

The word that is replaced by the pronoun is called its *antecedent*. To check the accuracy of your pronoun references, ask yourself this question: To what does the pronoun refer? Then answer the question carefully, making sure that there is not more than one possible antecedent. Consider the following example:

- Several special interest groups decided to defeat the new health care bill. *This* became the turning point of the government's reform campaign.

To what does the word *This* refer? The immediate answer seems to be the word *bill* at the end of the previous sentence. It is more likely the writer was referring to the attempt of the special interest groups to defeat the bill, but there is no word in the first sentence that refers specifically to this action. The reference is unclear. One way to clarify the reference is to change the beginning of the second sentence:

- Several special interest groups decided to defeat the new health-care bill. *Their attack on the bill* became the turning point of the government's reform campaign.

Here is another example:

- When John F. Kennedy appointed his brother Robert to the position of U.S. Attorney General, *he* had little idea how widespread the corruption in the Teamsters Union was.

To whom does the word *he* refer? It is unclear whether the writer is referring to John or to Robert Kennedy. One way to clarify the reference is simply to repeat the antecedent instead of using a pronoun:

- When President John F. Kennedy appointed his brother Robert to the position of U.S. Attorney General, *Robert* had little idea how widespread the corruption in the Teamsters Union was.

Pronoun Agreement

Remember that a pronoun must agree with its antecedent in both gender and number, as the following examples demonstrate:

- Mayor Smith said that *he* appreciated our club's support in the election.
- One reporter asked the senator what *she* would do if the President offered *her* a cabinet post.
- Having listened to our case, the judge decided to rule on *it* within the week.
- Engineers working on the housing project said *they* were pleased with the renovation so far.

The following words, however, can become troublesome antecedents. They may look like plural pronouns but are actually singular:

Anyone	Each	Either	Everybody	Everyone
Nobody	No one	Somebody	Someone	

A pronoun referring to one of these words in a sentence must be singular, too.

Incorrect: *Each* of the women in the support group brought *their* children.

Correct: *Each* of the women in the support group brought *her* children.

Incorrect: Has *everybody* received *their* ballot?

Correct: Has *everybody* received *his or her* ballot? [The two gender-specific pronouns are used to avoid sexist language.]

Correct: Have *all* the delegates received *their* ballots? [The singular antecedent has been changed to a plural one.]

Shifts in Person

It is important to avoid shifting among first person (*I, we*), second person (*you*), and third person (*she, he, it, one, they*) unnecessarily. Such shifts can cause confusion:

Incorrect: *Most people* [third person] who seek a job find that if *you* [second person] tell the truth during *your* interviews, *you* will gain the voters' respect.

Correct: *Most people* who seek a job find that if *they* tell the truth during *their* interviews, *they* will win the voters' respect.

Incorrect: *One* [third person singular] cannot tell whether *they* [third person plural] are cut out for public office until they decide to run.

Correct: *One* cannot tell whether *one* is cut out for public office until *one* decides to run.

QUOTATION MARKS

It can be difficult to remember when to use quotation marks and where they go in relation to other marks of punctuation. When faced with these questions, inexperienced writers often try to rely on logic rather than on a rulebook, but the rules do not always seem to rely on logic. The only way to make sure of your use of quotation marks is to *memorize* the rules. Luckily, there are not many.

Quotation Marks and Direct Quotations

Use quotation marks to enclose direct quotations that are not longer than four typed lines:

> It remains for history to pass judgment on what one scholar calls "the strangest verdict ever given in such a case" (Rollins 2001:45).

Longer quotes, called block quotes, are handled in different ways according to the particular style guide you are using. For example, the fourth edition of the *ASA Style Guide* (2010:25), which is often used by criminal justice professionals, requires that quotes of 50 or more words in length appear in an indented block, without quotation marks:

> Sowell's position, which changed the position of the entire East Coast League, is summarized by Scott (1997):
>> The constrained vision sees people as fundamentally limited in terms of their abilities to live peaceful, cooperative, public-spirited lives. People are morally limited, and therefore, although they may do a good deed, they are not to be trusted to act as they ought to toward one another. If we hear of a disaster in another part of the world, we may take a moment to feel sorry for the victims, but then we proceed with our lives as if nothing had happened. (p. 46)

In this example, the author's name and the date of publication appear within the paper's text, while the page number of the quote is given, in parentheses, following the quote. (Note that the *p* representing *page number* is capitalized when it is the first item in the parentheses.) You may, if you wish, include author's name and date within the parentheses instead of in your text.

The block quote format recommended in the sixth edition of the *Publication Manual of the APA* (2010:92), another style guide often used by criminal justice professionals, requires quotations of 40 words or longer to be indented and presented without quotation marks, and does not capitalize the *p* representing page number if it appears at the beginning of the parenthetical reference following the quote: (p. 46).

Note: Bibliographical formatting styles for both the *ASA Style Guide* and the *Publication Manual of the APA* are given in Chapter 4. Whichever bibliographical format you use, *be consistent.*

Use single quotation marks to set off quotations within quotations:

- "One of the defendants objected," Officer Smith explained, "saying that he refused 'to acknowledge any wrongdoing in the case whatsoever.' "

When the interior quote occurs at the end of the sentence, both single and double quotation marks are placed outside the period.

Use quotation marks to set off titles of the following:

- a short poem (one not printed as a separate volume)
- a short story

- an article or essay
- a song title
- an episode of a television or radio show

Use quotation marks to set off words or phrases used in special ways:

- *To convey irony.* The "liberal" administration has done nothing but cater to big business.
- *To set off a technical term.* To have "charisma," Weber would argue, is to possess special powers. Many believe that John F. Kennedy had great charisma.

Note: Once the term is defined, it is not placed in quotation marks again.

Quotation Marks in Relation to Other Punctuation

Always place commas and periods *inside* closing quotation marks:

- "My fellow Americans," said the President, "there are tough times ahead of us."

Place colons and semicolons *outside* closing quotation marks:

- In his speech on voting, the sociologist warned against "an encroaching indolence"; he was referring to the attitude of the middle class.
- There are several victims of the government's campaign to "Turn Back the Clock": the homeless, the elderly, and the mentally impaired.

Use the context to determine whether to place question marks, exclamation points, and dashes inside or outside closing quotation marks. If the punctuation is part of the quotation, place it *inside* the quotation mark:

- "When will the tenure committee make up its mind?" asked the dean.
- The demonstrators shouted, "Free the hostages!" and "No more slavery!"

If the punctuation is not part of the quotation, place it *outside* the quotation mark:

- Which president said, "We have nothing to fear but fear itself"? [Although the quote is a complete sentence, you do not place a period after it. There can only be one piece of "terminal" punctuation that ends a sentence.]

SEMICOLONS

The semicolon is another little-used punctuation mark you should learn to incorporate into your writing strategy because of its many potential applications. For example, a semicolon can be used to correct a comma splice:

Incorrect: The union representatives left the meeting in good spirits, their demands were met.

Correct: The union representatives left the meeting in good spirits; their demands were met.

Incorrect: Several guests at the fund-raiser had lost their invitations, however, we were able to seat them anyway.

Correct: Several guests at the fund-raiser had lost their invitations; however, we were able to seat them anyway. [Conjunctive adverbs like *however, therefore,* and *thus* are not coordinating words (such as *and, but, or, for, so, yet*) and cannot be used with a comma to link independent clauses. If the second independent clause begins with *however*, it must be preceded by either a period or a semicolon.]

As you can see from the second example, connecting the two independent clauses with a semicolon instead of a period strengthens the relationship between the clauses.

Semicolons can also separate items in a series when the series itself contain commas:

- The newspaper account of the rally stressed the march, which drew the biggest crowd; the mayor's speech, which drew tremendous applause; and the party afterwards in the park.

Avoid misusing semicolons. For example, use a comma, not a semicolon, to separate an independent clause from a dependent clause:

Incorrect: Students from the college volunteered to answer phones during the pledge drive; which was set up to generate money for the new arts center.

Correct: Students from the college volunteered to answer phones during the pledge drive, which was set up to generate money for the new arts center.

Do not overuse semicolons. Although they are useful, too many semicolons in your writing can distract your readers' attention. Avoid monotony by using semicolons sparingly.

SENTENCE FRAGMENTS

A *fragment* is a part of a sentence that is punctuated and capitalized as if it were an entire sentence. It is an especially disruptive kind of error because it obscures the connections that the words of a sentence must make in order to complete the reader's understanding.

Students sometimes write fragments because they are concerned that a particular sentence is growing too long and needs to be shortened. Remember that cutting the length of a sentence merely by adding a period somewhere along its length often creates a fragment. When checking your writing for fragments, it is essential that you read each sentence carefully to determine whether it has (1) a complete subject and a verb, and (2) a subordinating word before the subject and verb, which makes the construction a subordinate clause rather than a complete sentence.

Types of Sentence Fragments

Some fragments lack a verb:

Incorrect: The chairperson of our committee, having received a letter from the mayor. [Note that the word *having*, which can be used as a verb, is here being used as a gerund introducing a participial phrase. *Watch out* for words that look like verbs but are being used in another way.]

Correct: The chairperson of our committee received a letter from the mayor.

Some fragments lack a subject:

Incorrect: Our study shows that there is broad support for improvement in the health-care system. And in the unemployment system.

Correct: Our study shows that there is broad support for improvement in the health care system and in the unemployment system.

Some fragments are subordinate clauses:

Incorrect: After the latest edition of the newspaper came out. [This clause has the two major components of a complete sentence: a subject (*edition*) and a verb (*came*). Indeed, if the first word (*After*) were deleted, the clause would be a complete sentence. But that first word is a *subordinating word*, which acts to prevent the following clause from standing on its own as a complete sentence. *Watch out* for this kind of construction. It is called a *subordinate clause*, and it is not a sentence.]

Correct: After the latest edition of the newspaper came out, the mayor's press secretary was overwhelmed with phone calls. [A common method of correcting a subordinate clause that has been punctuated as a complete sentence is to connect it to the complete sentence to which it is closest in meaning.]

Incorrect: Several congressmen asked for copies of the Vice President's position paper. Which called for reform of the Environmental Protection Agency.

Correct: Several congressmen asked for copies of the Vice President's position paper, which called for reform of the Environmental Protection Agency.

SPELLING

All of us have problems spelling certain words that we have not yet committed to memory. But most writers are not as bad at spelling as they believe themselves to be. Usually it is a handful of words that the individual finds troubling. It is important to be as sensitive as possible to your own particular spelling problems—and to keep a dictionary handy. There is no excuse for failing to check spelling.

Do not rely on your computer's spell checker. There are certain kinds of spelling errors that computers cannot catch, as the following two sentences demonstrate:

- Wilbur wood rather dye than admit that he had been their.
- When he cited the bare behind the would pile, he thought, "Isle just lye hear until he goes buy."

Here are a list of commonly confused words and a list of commonly misspelled words. Read through the lists, looking for those words that tend to give you trouble. If you have any questions, *consult your dictionary.*

Commonly Confused Words

accept/except	council/counsel	its/it's
advice/advise	dairy/diary	know/no
affect/effect	descent/dissent	later/latter
aisle/isle	desert/dessert	lay/lie
allusion/illusion	device/devise	lead/led
an/and	die/dye	lessen/lesson
angel/angle	dominant/dominate	loose/lose
ascent/assent	elicit/illicit	may be/maybe
bare/bear	eminent/immanent/	miner/minor
brake/break	imminent	moral/morale
breath/breathe	envelop/envelope	of/off
buy/by	every day/everyday	passed/past
capital/capitol	fair/fare	patience/patients
choose/chose	formally/formerly	peace/piece
cite/sight/site	forth/fourth	personal/personnel
complement/compliment	hear/here	plain/plane
conscience/conscious	hole/whole	precede/proceed
corps/corpse	human/humane	presence/presents

principal/principle	scene/seen	track/tract
quiet/quite	sense/since	waist/waste
rain/reign/rein	stationary/stationery	waive/wave
raise/raze	straight/strait	weak/week
reality/realty	taught/taut	weather/whether
respectfully/respectively	than/then	were/where
reverend/reverent	their/there/they're	which/witch
right/rite/write	threw/through	whose/who's
road/rode	too/to/two	your/you're

Commonly Misspelled Words

a lot	courteous	harass
acceptable	definitely	hero
accessible	dependent	heroes
accommodate	desperate	humorous
accompany	develop	hurried
accustomed	different	hurriedly
acquire	disappear	hypocrite
against	disappoint	ideally
annihilate	easily	immediately
apparent	efficient	immense
arguing	environment	incredible
argument	equipped	innocuous
authentic	exceed	intercede
before	exercise	interrupt
begin	existence	irrelevant
beginning	experience	irresistible
believe	fascinate	irritate
benefited	finally	knowledge
bulletin	foresee	license
business	forty	likelihood
cannot	fulfill	maintenance
category	gauge	manageable
committee	guaranteed	meanness
condemn	guard	mischievous

missile	pursue	sincerely
necessary	pursuing	skiing
nevertheless	questionnaire	stubbornness
no one	realize	studying
noticeable	receipt	succeed
noticing	received	success
nuisance	recession	successfully
occasion	recommend	susceptible
occasionally	referring	suspicious
occurred	religious	technical
occurrences	remembrance	temporary
omission	reminisce	tendency
omit	repetition	therefore
opinion	representative	tragedy
opponent	rhythm	truly
parallel	ridiculous	tyranny
parole	roommate	unanimous
peaceable	satellite	unconscious
performance	scarcity	undoubtedly
pertain	scenery	until
practical	science	vacuum
preparation	secede	valuable
probably	secession	various
process	secretary	vegetable
professor	senseless	visible
prominent	separate	without
pronunciation	sergeant	women
psychology	shining	writing
publicly	significant	

PART 2

PAPER FORMATS AND CITATIONS

3

Student Paper Formats

PRELIMINARY CONSIDERATIONS

Your format makes your paper's first impression. Justly or not, accurately or not, it announces your professional competence—or lack of competence. A well-executed format implies that your paper is worth reading. More importantly, however, a proper format brings information to your readers in a familiar form that has the effect of setting their minds at ease. Your paper's format should therefore impress your readers with your academic competence by following accepted professional standards for criminal justice writing. Like the style and clarity of your writing, your format communicates messages that are often more readily and profoundly received than the content of the document itself.

This chapter contains instructions for the following format elements:

- Margins
- Pagination
- Title page
- Abstract
- Executive summary
- Outline summary
- Table of contents

- List of tables and figures
- Text
- Headings and subheadings
- Tables
- Illustrations and figures
- Reference listing
- Appendixes

There are many format styles available to the criminal justice professional and no consensus as to which one is most appropriate. On its Web site, the *Justice Quarterly*, the official journal of the Academy of Criminal Justice Sciences, requires its contributors to use the format established by the American Psychological Association (APA), the most recent revision of which is published in the sixth edition of the *Publication Manual of the APA* (2010). The format described in this chapter is based on elements from the APA manual and from the fourth edition of the *ASA Style Guide* (2010), but it is styled more for the student writer than for the professional.

When preparing a paper for submission to an accredited journal in criminal justice, you should always carefully follow that journal's guidelines for submitting manuscripts; but for now, unless you receive instructions to the contrary from your course instructor, follow the format directions in this manual exactly. Guidelines for citing and referencing sources—using both ASA and APA standards—are explained in Chapters 4 and 5.

Criminal justice assignments should be printed on 8½-by-11-inch premium white bond, 20-lb. or heavier. Do not use any other color or size except to comply with special instructions from your instructor, and do not use an off-white or poor quality (draft) paper. *Always submit to your instructor an original computer (preferably laser) printed manuscript. Do not submit a photocopy!* Always make a second copy to keep for your own files and to keep in case the original is lost. As you would most likely be working on a computer, it's a good idea to keep a copy of your paper on the hard drive or a flash drive, another on a disc you can store in a safe place, and a hard copy of the paper, or e-mail the file to yourself in case the computer crashes and the disc is lost.

When you have completed your paper and you are ready to turn it in, do not bind it or enclose it within a plastic cover sheet unless instructed to do so. Place one staple in the upper left corner, or use a paper clip at the top of the paper. Note that a paper to be submitted to a journal for publication should not be clipped, stapled, or bound in any form.

MARGINS

Except for theses and dissertations, margins should be 1 inch from all sides of the paper. (*Note*: The fourth edition of the *ASA Style Guide* [2010:88] requires margins to be no less than 1¼ inches on all sides for papers submitted for publication to a journal sponsored by the ASA.) Unless otherwise instructed, all submissions should be *double-spaced* in a 12-point word-processing font. Select a font that is plain and easy to read, such as Helvetica, Courier, Garamond, or Times Roman. According to the fourth edition of the *ASA Style Guide* (2010:88), papers submitted for publication to an ASA journal should use 12-point Times New Roman. Do not use script, decorative, or elaborate fonts.

PAGINATION

Page numbers should appear in the upper right-hand corner of each page, starting with the second page of the text and continuing consecutively through the paper. No page number should appear on the title page or on the first page of the text. Page numbers should appear 1 inch from the right side and ½ inch from the top of the page. You should use lowercase roman numerals (*i, ii, iii,* etc.) for the front matter, such as the title page, table of contents, and table of figures that precede the first page of text. These roman numerals should begin with *ii* for the page that immediately follows the title page and be centered ½ inch from the bottom of the page.

In special cases, as when your instructor wants no pages preceding the first page of text, the title of the paper should appear 1 inch from the top of the first page, centered, followed by your name and course information. Most formats omit placing the page number on this first page of text, but some instructors may require it to be placed at the bottom center. All other page numbering should follow the guidelines just mentioned.

TITLE PAGE

The following information should be centered on the title page:

- Title of the paper
- Name of writer
- Course name and section number
- Name of instructor
- Name of college or university
- Date

As the sample title page shows, the title should clearly describe the problem addressed in the paper. If the paper discusses juvenile recidivism in Muskogee County jails, for example, the title "Recidivism in the Muskogee County Juvenile Justice System" is professional, clear, and helpful to the reader. "Muskogee County," "Juvenile Justice," or "County Jails" are all too vague to be effective. Also, the title should not be "cute." A cute title may attract attention for a play on Broadway, but it will detract from the credibility of a paper in criminal justice. "Inadequate Solid Waste Disposal Facilities in Muskogee" is professional; "Down in the Dumps" is not.

An Explanation of the Association between Crime and Unemployment

by

George Rockenbach

For
Criminology 4473, Section 3
Professor Sid Orange

Centerbury College
October 28, 2009

ABSTRACT

An abstract is a brief summary of a paper written primarily to allow potential readers to see if the paper contains information of sufficient interest for them to read. People conducting research want specific kinds of information, and they often read dozens of abstracts looking for papers that contain relevant data. The heading "Abstract" is centered near the top of the page. Next is the title, also centered, followed by a summary of the paper's topic, research design, results, and conclusions. The abstract should be written in one to three paragraphs, total-ing approximately 100–150 words. Remember, an abstract is not an introduction; instead, it is a brief summary, as demonstrated in the accompanying sample.

ABSTRACT

College Students' Attitudes on Capital Punishment

A survey of college students' beliefs about capital punishment was undertaken in October of 2007 at Ohio State University. The sample was comprised of 92 students in two lower-level criminal justice classes. The purpose of the study was to determine the extent to which students believe it is acceptable for the state to take the life of individuals who commit certain crimes.

Variables tested for association with capital punishment attitudes were age, sex, and ethnicity. Results indicated that the majority of students favor the use of capital punishment with certain crimes, and that young white males are the most pro–capital punishment. The students in this sample expressed a concern about what might happen to the rate of serious crimes if the death penalty were abolished. However, they were more concerned with those who committed certain heinous crimes being punished appropriately.

EXECUTIVE SUMMARY

An executive summary, like an abstract, summarizes the content of a paper but does so in more detail, as seen in the sample shown. Whereas abstracts are read by people who are doing research, executive summaries are more likely to be read by people who need some or all of the information in the paper in order to make a decision. Many people, however, will read the executive summary to fix clearly in their mind the organization and results of a paper before reading the paper itself.

The length of the executive summary is dictated to some extent by the length of the document being summarized. For example, a 150–200-page grant report might be summarized in an 8–10-page executive summary, while a 25-page research paper might need only a page or two of summary. The lengthier executive summary might also contain headings and subheadings similar to those used in the actual report. By following the outline of the actual paper, the executive summary serves as a sort of summary of each of the sections in the much lengthier report.

The executive summary that follows summarizes a fictitious report on the second year of a *Drug Assessment Study with Juvenile Offenders in a Secure Detention Setting*. This example gives you an idea of the details that should be included in your summary.

EXECUTIVE SUMMARY

This Drug Assessment Study is written for practitioners who deal with drug-involved juvenile offenders repeatedly cycling through detention centers. The assessment process was initiated sometime after they were placed in detention. Two psychologists interviewed 198 youth over a six-month period and recorded the information they obtained on a specially designed "assessment" instrument. They also administered an instrument designed to measure the level of alcohol and other drug use, coupled with an unobtrusive measurement of denial and other underlying manifestations of substance abuse. The results of this study are summarized below.

One important finding had to do with interpersonal relationships. Those who used and abused alcohol and/or other drugs were generally friends of users and abusers. Those who did not use and abuse these substances almost always reported much less association with those who use and abuse drugs. Young people on probation and parole for substance abuse–related offenses probably should be restrained by the court from association with those who have a serious alcohol and/or drug history.

The findings from this study support the hypothesis that where youth are distanced from the family, in terms of communication, feelings, and disorganized relationships, their chances of alcohol and/or other drug involvement increase, at times dramatically. Significant progress in helping delinquents change and adjust might be attained by a serious commitment to family therapy and family development, especially with the cooperation and insistence of the court. There is good reason to believe that significant differences exist between white and minority families with respect to child-rearing philosophy and practice. If this is true, it may well affect alcohol and/or other drug use, attitudes toward families, school, and other areas of juvenile misbehavior. It would follow that detention treatment plans, court-ordered probation, and aftercare alternatives should be differentiated, where feasible and legal, to respond to minority families at the point of their needs.

Findings from this study imply that for those youth who come in contact with the juvenile justice system: (1) blacks are much less addicted than either whites or other minorities, at least in very early adolescence; (2) black parents are significantly more concerned with their children's use of alcohol and/or other drugs when compared with white parents; (3) blacks report much more emotional support from their family members; and (4) there appears to be, at least on the surface, more dysfunctional family interaction among white families than black. Perhaps the juvenile justice system should develop neighborhood programs to provide positive support within the strong kinship networks already in place in the black culture; early intervention could reach black children before they fully enter the rebellious youth culture.

The body of literature cited in this report is fairly unified in asserting that common etiological roots cannot be shown between substance abuse and delinquency. Even the relationship between violent crime and substance abuse remains clouded (Johnson 2009). A relationship between substance use and more serious delinquency appears to be developmental rather than causal (Scott 2011). More than ever, this suggests that attention should be given to the National Council of Juvenile and Family Court Judges' report, which argues from a systemic and holistic perspective (Garrison 2112). Drug use and abuse, child neglect, abandonment, sexual, physical and emotional abuse, family violence, family dysfunction, and juvenile delinquency are interactive variables that cannot be clearly identified, diagnosed, or treated without addressing them together.

Our study supports a vast body of literature that suggests meaningful intervention in the lives of juveniles at risk should include, whenever possible, a holistic approach. Not only must each youth be requested to take responsibility for his or her behavior and work toward resolution of his problems, but also family members should be called to account for their responsibility and compelled, when necessary, to participate in treatment.

OUTLINE SUMMARY

An outline page is a specific style of executive summary. It clearly shows the sections into which the paper is divided and the content of the information in each section. An outline summary is an asset to busy decision makers because it allows them to understand the entire content of a paper without reading it, or to refer quickly to a specific part of the paper for more information.

OUTLINE SUMMARY

   I. The problem is that picnic and restroom facilities at Hafer Community Park have deteriorated.
   A. Only one major renovation has occurred since 1967, when the park was opened.
   B. The Park Department estimates that repairs would cost about $33,700.
  II. Three possible solutions have been given extensive consideration:
   A. One option is to do nothing. Area residents will use the park less as deterioration continues.
   B. The first alternative solution is to make all repairs immediately, which will require a total of $33,700.
   C. A second alternative is to make repairs according to a priority list over a five-year period.
 III. The recommendation of this report is that alternative C be adopted by the city council. The benefit/cost analysis demonstrates that residents will be satisfied if basic improvements are made immediately.

TABLE OF CONTENTS

A table of contents does not provide as much information as an outline but does include the headings of the major sections and subsections of a paper. Tables of contents are not normally required in student papers or papers presented at professional meetings, but they may be included. (The fourth edition of the *ASA Style Guide* [2010] does not require a table of contents for manuscripts submitted for publication consideration.) Tables of contents are normally required, however, in books, theses, and dissertations. The table of contents should consist of the chapter or main section titles and the first level of headings within sections, along with their page numbers, as the accompanying example demonstrates.

TABLE OF CONTENTS

LISTS OF TABLES AND FIGURES

A list of tables or figures contains the titles of the tables or figures included in the paper in the order in which they appear, along with their page numbers. You may list tables, illustrations, and figures together under the title "Figures" (and call them all figures in the text), or if you have a list with more than a half-page of entries, you may have separate lists of tables, figures, and illustrations (and title them accordingly in the text). The format for all such lists should follow the accompanying example.

LIST OF FIGURES

TEXT

Ask your instructor for the number of pages required for the paper you are writing. The text should follow the directions explained in Chapters 1 and 2. Headings and subheadings within the text vary with the assignment. Procedures for applying headings and subheadings to your text are described next.

HEADINGS AND SUBHEADINGS

Generally, three heading levels should meet your organizational needs when writing criminal justice papers:

1. *Primary headings* should be centered and printed in all capital letters.
2. *Secondary headings* should be centered and italicized, with only the first letter in each word capitalized, excluding articles, prepositions, and conjunctions.
3. *Tertiary headings* should be indented and lead into the paragraph with only the first letter of the first word capitalized. They should be italicized and followed by a period. The text should follow.

The accompanying example has three heading levels that follow these guidelines.

Sample: Three Levels of Headings

> # RESULTS
>
> ## *Alcohol and Other Drugs*
>
> *Risk factors.* Characteristics of risk can be found in families from all social and economic strata, especially where adolescents...

TABLES

Tables are used in the text to show relationships among data to help the reader come to a conclusion or understand a certain point. Tables that show simple results or "raw" data should be placed in an appendix. Tables should not reiterate the content of the text. They should say something new, and they should stand on their own. That is, the reader should be able to understand the table without reading the text. Clearly label the columns and rows in each table. Each word in the title (except articles, prepositions, and conjunctions) should be capitalized. The source of the information should be shown immediately below the table, not in a footnote or endnote. A hypothetical table on population change is shown as an example.

TABLE 3.1 *Population Change in Ten U.S. Cities, 1980–1986*

City	1986 Rank	1980 Population	1986 Population	Percentage Change, 1980–1986
New York	1	7,071,639	7,262,700	2.7
Los Angeles	2	2,968,528	3,259,300	9.8
Chicago	3	33,005,072	3,009,530	0.2
Houston	4	41,611,382	1,728,910	7.3
Philadelphia	5	1,688,210	1,642,900	–22.3
Detroit	6	1,203,369	1,086,220	–29.7
San Diego	7	875,538	1,015,190	16.0
Dallas	8	904,599	1,003,520	10.9
San Antonio	9	810,353	914,350	12.8
Phoenix	10	790,183	894,070	13.1

Source: U.S. Bureau of the Census (1988).

ILLUSTRATIONS AND FIGURES

Illustrations are not normally inserted in the text of a paper; they are only included in the appendix if they are necessary to explain the material in the text. If illustrations are necessary, do not paste or tape photocopies of photographs or similar materials to the text or the appendix. Instead, photocopy each one on a separate sheet of paper and center it, along with its typed title, within the normal margins of the paper. The format of the illustration titles should be the same as that for tables and figures.

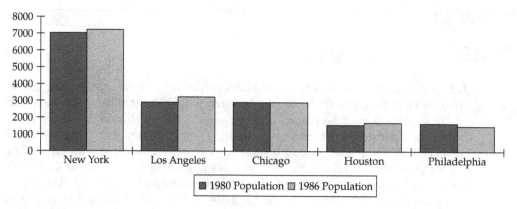

FIGURE 3.1   *Population Growth in Five U.S. Cities, 1980–1986*
Source: U.S. Bureau of the Census. 1988. *County and City Data Book.*

Figures in the form of charts and graphs may be very helpful in presenting certain types of information. The example above demonstrates how data in the preceding table can be presented in a bar chart.

REFERENCE LISTING

Chapters 4 and 5 discuss and give models of two standard citation systems for the references in your paper, the ASA style and the APA style. Some instructors prefer papers to be structured in *article format,* with everything presented as tightly compressed and succinct as possible. If your instructor favors this system, your reference section should immediately follow (double-spaced) the last line of your discussion section. Other instructors prefer the references to be listed on a separate page. Ask your instructor which system you should follow.

APPENDIXES

Appendixes are reference materials set for the convenience of the reader at the back of the paper, after the text. Providing information that supplements the important facts contained in the text, they may include maps, charts, tables, and selected documents. Do not place materials that are merely interesting or decorative in your appendix. Include only items that will answer questions raised by the text or that are necessary to explain the text.

Follow the format guidelines for illustrations, tables, and figures when adding material in an appendix. At the top center of the page, label your first appendix "Appendix A," your second appendix "Appendix B," and so on. If you are only appending one item, it should be labeled "Appendix," with no letter indicating sequence. Do not append an entire government report, journal article, or other publication, but only the portions of such documents that are necessary to support your paper. The source of the information should always be evident on the appended pages.

4

Citing Sources in ASA Style

INTRODUCTION TO ASA STYLE

One of your most important jobs as a research writer is to document your use of source material carefully and clearly. Failure to do so will cause your reader confusion, damage the effectiveness of your paper, and perhaps make you vulnerable to a charge of plagiarism. Proper documentation is more than just good form. It is a powerful indicator of your own commitment to scholarship and the sense of authority that you bring to your writing. Good documentation demonstrates your expertise as a researcher and increases your reader's trust in you and your work.

Unfortunately, as anybody who has ever written a research paper knows, getting the documentation right can be a frustrating, confusing job, especially for the novice writer. Positioning each element of a single reference citation accurately can require what seems an inordinate amount of time spent thumbing through the style manual. Even before you begin to work on specific citations, there are important questions of style and format to answer.

WHAT TO DOCUMENT

Direct quotes must always be credited, as must certain kinds of paraphrased material. Information that is basic—important dates, facts, or opinions universally acknowledged—need not be cited. Information that is not widely known, whether fact or opinion, should be documented.

What if you are unsure whether or not a certain fact is widely known? You are, after all, very probably a newcomer to the field in which you are conducting your research. If in doubt, supply the documentation. It is better to overdocument than to fail to do justice to a source.

Read through the following pages before trying to use them to structure your notes. Unpracticed student researchers tend to ignore the documentation section of their style manual until the moment the first note has to be worked out, and then they skim through the examples looking for the one that perfectly corresponds to the immediate case in hand. But most style manuals do not include every possible documentation model, so the writer must piece together a coherent reference out of elements from several models. Reading through all the models before using them gives you a feel for where to find different aspects of models as well as for how the referencing system works in general.

ASA STYLE IN PAPERS

The American Sociological Association (ASA) has its own citation system, widely used by sociology students and professionals, and published in the *ASA Style Guide*, currently in its fourth edition (2010). The formats used in the *ASA Style Guide* are a modification of the author–date style elaborated in the *Chicago Manual of Style* (*CMS*), perhaps the most universally approved of all documentation authorities. Note that, while the *CMS* is currently in its sixteenth edition (2010), the fourth edition of the *ASA Style Guide* is based on the fifteenth edition (2003) of the *CMS*.

One of the advantages of using the ASA style is that it is designed to guide the professional sociologist in preparing a manuscript for submission to a journal. The ASA style is required for all papers submitted to the *American Sociological Review*, the official journal of the ASA and the most influential sociology journal in publication. It is also required for all the leading journals in sociology and some in criminal justice. Throughout this section, where answers to questions of style are not clearly defined and explained in the fourth edition of the *ASA Style Guide* (2010), we have referred to the *CMS* for recommendations.

The ASA style uses an author–date system of referencing, also known as a parenthetical-reference system, which requires two components for each significant reference to a source: (1) a note placed within the text, in parentheses, closely following the location where the source material occurs, and (2) a full bibliographical reference for the source, placed in a list of references following the entire text of the paper. In order not to distract the reader from the argument, the parenthetical note within the text is as brief as possible, containing just enough information to refer the reader to the full reference listing that appears in the bibliography or reference section following the text. Usually the minimum information necessary is the author's last name—meaning the name by which the source is alphabetized in the references at the end of the paper—and the year of the publication of the source. As indicated by the following models, this information can be given in a number of ways. The next section of this chapter gives models of bibliographical entries corresponding to these parenthetical notes.

TEXT CITATIONS IN ASA STYLE

Citations within the text should include the author's last name and the year of publication. Page numbers should be included only when quoting directly from a source or referring to specific passages. Subsequent citations of the same source should be identified the same way as the first.

SAMPLES OF ASA CITATION STYLE

The following examples identify the *ASA Style Guide*'s (2010) citation system for a variety of possible sources.

Author's Name in Text

When the author's name is in the text, it should be followed by the publication year in parentheses:

Freedman (2013) postulates that when individuals...

Author's Name Not in Text

When the author's name is not in the text, the last name and publication should be enclosed in parentheses:

...encourage more aggressive play (Perrez 1999).

Citation Including Page Numbers

Page numbers are included only when quoting directly from a source or referring to specific passages. However, some instructors prefer page numbers for all citations in order to check for plagiarism. Ask your instructor what system you should follow. When the page number is included, it should follow the publication year and be preceded by a colon with no space between the colon and the page number:

Thomas (2011:741) builds on this scenario...

In both the in-text citations and the references, the *ASA Style Guide* (2010) follows the format recommended by the *CMS* (2003) for recording a range of page numbers.

For any range of numbers in which the first number is below 100, use all digits:

D'Ambrosio (2009:14–19) denies this possibility.

...endorses the project enthusiastically (Jenkins 2007:78–79).

For any range in which the first number is 100 or a multiple of 100, use all digits:

> ...according to Squires (2012:400–409).

> In which case the vote will fail (Piplin 2001:1200–1201).

For any range in which the first number is 101 through 109, 201 through 209, 301 through 309, etc., use the changed part only for the second number:

> ...counters any lateral move, according to Givan (1998:103–4).

> ...a cogent argument for the opposite opinion (Fells 2004:1108–9).

For any range in which the first number is 110 through 199, 210 through 299, 310 through 399, etc., use two or more digits as needed:

> Alexandro (2007:221–23) supports the proposition...

> ...in which case, according to Stevenson (1999), the Congress will act (1299–302).

In a range of page numbers in which the second number contains four digits, three of which are changed, use all four digits:

> ... refused to acknowledge the request (Austin 2008:1298–1305).

> Rankin (2013:3489–3510) claims attorney-client privilege...

Source with Two Authors

When the publication has two authors, cite both last names:

> ...establish a sense of self (Holmes and Watson 1872:114–16).

Source with Three Authors

When a publication has three authors, all three last names should be cited in the first citation, with "et al." used for subsequent citations in the text. Thus, a first citation would read:

> ...found the requirements very restrictive (Mollar, Querley, and McLarry 2008).

Thereafter, the following form is sufficient:

> ...proved to be quite difficult (Mollar et al. 2008).

Source with More Than Three Authors

For more than three authors, use "et al." in all citations.

> Kinneson et al. (2009) made the...

Two Authors with Same Last name

When citing two authors with the same last name, use a first initial to differentiate between them.

>...the new budget cuts (K. Grady 2004).

>...stimulate economic growth (B. Grady 2003).

Two Works by Same Author

When citing two works by the same author, in the same note, place a comma between the publication dates of the works.

>George (2002, 2006) argues for...

If the two works were published in the same year, differentiate between them by adding lowercase letters to the publication dates. Be sure to add the letters to the references in the bibliography too.

>...the city government (Estrada 2012a, 2012b).

Work with No Author Given

If the author's name is not provided within the work but you know the author's identity, then Section 17.34 of the *CMS* (2003) suggests you may give the name in brackets:

>...cannot be held accountable ([Logan] 1994).

According to Section 17.32 of the *CMS* (2003), if the name of the author of an anonymous work cannot be ascertained, the reference begins with the title of the work. The first of the following models refers to a magazine article, the second to a book. Note that in the case of the book title, the initial article "The" is moved to the end of the title.

>("The Case for Prosecuting Deadbeat Dads" 1996:36–38)

>(*Worst Way to Learn: The Government's War on Education, The* 2003)

Direct Quotes

Direct quotes of fewer than 50 words should be placed in the text, with quotation marks at the beginning and end. The citation should include the page number in one of the following formats:

>The majority of these ads promote the notion that "If you are slim, you will also be beautiful and sexually desirable" (Rockett and McMinn 1990:278).

Smith and Hill (1997) found that "women are far more likely to obsess about weight" (p. 127).

Direct quotes of 50 words or more should be indented as a block, with no tab set for the first line. Such longer quotes should not be contained within quotation marks:

> Especially pernicious is the fact that, according to what research has been done, the situation is universal and does not correct itself with age, education, or any type of socialization therapy. According to Brown (2005):
>
> > There are few girls and women of any age or culture raised in white America, who do not have some manifestation of the concerns discussed here, i.e., distortion of body image, a sense of "out-of-control" in relationship to food, addiction to dieting, binging, or self-starvation. (P. 161)

It should be noted that in the block quote the author, date, and page number follow the period at the end, and that the "P" for "page" is capitalized when the page number appears alone without the author and date, as in this example.

Source Cited in a Secondary Source

Sometimes information is obtained from a source that is cited in a secondary source. While it is always best to locate and cite the original source, sometimes this is not possible. When citing a source that is itself cited in a secondary source, refer in your parenthetical citation to the original source, and not the later source in which the original is cited. For example, if you wish to cite information from a 2005 article by John Smith that you found cited in a 2007 article by Allen Jones, your citation will look like this:

> … the promise of a subsequent generation (Smith 2005).

See "Article Cited in a Secondary Source" in the reference section later in this chapter for information on how to list this citation in your references.

Chapters, Tables, Appendixes, and So Forth

Cite chapters, tables, appendixes, and the like as follows:

> … (Johnson 2006, chap. 6).

> … (Blake 2001, table 4:34).

> … (Shelby 2013, appendix C:177).

Reprints

When citing a work reprinted from an earlier publication, give the earliest date of publication in brackets, followed immediately by the date of version you have used:

> … Baldwin ([1897] 1992) interpreted the results of the survey positively.

More Than One Source in a Reference

When citing more than one source, separate citations by a semicolon and order them in a manner of your choice. You may arrange them in alphabetical order, date order, or order of importance to your argument, but whatever order you choose, use it consistently throughout your paper.

> ...are related (Harmatz 1987:48; Marble et al. 1986:909; Powers and Erickson 1986:48; Rackley et al. 1988:10; Thompson and Thompson 1986:1067).

Work with No Date of Publication Given

If no date of publication for a source can be determined, perhaps because of the age of the document or the fact that it has not yet been published, use the abbreviation "n.d." for "no date," unless the document is to be published, in which case use the word "forthcoming."

> ...gave the Roundheads no secure license (Hallows n.d.).

> Bartholi (forthcoming) places the blame squarely on Congress.

Archival Sources

According to Section 17.233 of the *CMS* (2003), manuscript collections are rarely cited in author–date citation style. When they are, the *CMS* recommends placing the date of the document under discussion in the body of the text rather than within the parentheses, since most collections include materials from different dates:

> Johnson wrote to Scott on March 12 (Nora Manuscripts) to explain the publishing disaster.

According to Section 17.324 of the *CMS* (2003), cite any of the unpublished documents of the United States Government housed in the National Archives (NA)—including films, photographs, and sound recordings as well as written materials—by the record group (RG) number.

> ...(NA, RG 43, Box 106, June 23, 1934).

Machine-Readable Data Files

When citing machine-readable data files, include authorship and date:

> ...(American Institute of Public Opinion 1989).

Classic Texts

When citing classic texts, such as the Bible, standard translations of ancient Greek texts, or numbers of the *Federalist Papers*, you may use the systems by which they are subdivided. Since any edition of a classic text employs the standard subdivisions, this reference method has the advantage of allowing your reader to find the source passage in any published edition of the text. It is not necessary to include a citation for a classic text in the reference section.

You may cite a biblical passage by referring to the particular book, chapter, and verse, all in roman type, with the translation given after the verse number:

"But the path of the just is as the shining light, that shineth more and more unto the perfect day" (Proverbs 4:18 King James Version).

The *Federalist Papers* are numbered:

Madison addresses the problem of factions in a republic (*Federalist* 10).

Newspapers

According to Section 17.191 of the *CMS* (2003), it is possible to cite newspapers in notes or in parenthetical references instead of in a reference list or bibliography:

In an August 10, 1993, editorial, the *New York Times* painted the new regime in glowing colors.

An article entitled "Abuse in the Inner City," written by Harry Black and published in the *Daily News* on December 24, 1996, took exception to the mayor's remarks.

If you wish to include newspaper references in the list of works cited or the bibliography, however, there is a model entry provided in the next section of this chapter.

Public Documents

When citing a public (government) document or one with institutional authorship, include in your text citation only a minimum of information from the beginning of the reference list citation, followed, if applicable, by the page number. While the information in the text citation is minimal, it must be sufficient to make the connection clearly with the full citation in the reference list.

…only in areas of large population growth (U.S. Bureau of the Census 1993:223).

Documents for which author's names are provided are cited just as nonpublic documents:

…making a positive impact on local economies (McSweeney and Marshall 2009:5).

The following models are based largely on information from the fourth edition of the *ASA Style Guide* (2010) and from the fifteenth edition of the *CMS* (2003). Corresponding reference list entries appear in the next section.

Congressional Journals

Parenthetical text references to both the *Senate Journal* and the *House Journal* start with the journal title, the session year, and, if applicable, the page:

(*U.S. Senate Journal* 1997:24)

Congressional Debates

Congressional debates are printed in the daily issues of the Congressional Record, which are bound biweekly and then collected and bound at the end of the session. Whenever possible, you should consult the bound yearly collection instead of the biweekly compilations. The "H" preceding the page number stands for House of Representatives.

(U.S. Congress. House 1930:H10403)

Congressional Reports and Documents

References to congressional reports and documents, which are numbered sequentially in one- or two-year periods, include the name of the body generating the material, the year, and the page.

(U.S. Congress. House 2004:12)

Note: Any reference that begins with "U.S. Congress," "U.S. Senate," or "U.S. House" may omit the "U.S." if it is clear from the context that you are referring to the United States. Whichever form you use, be sure to use it consistently, in both the notes and the bibliography.

State and Local Government Documents

References for state and local government publications are modeled on those for corresponding national government documents:

(Oklahoma Legislature 2008)

(Marder 1977:37)

Laws

You must structure a citation to a law according to the place where you found the law published. Initially published separately in pamphlets, as slip laws, statutes are eventually collected and incorporated, first into a set of volumes called *U.S. Statutes at Large* and later into the *U.S. Code*, a multivolume set that is revised every six years. You should use the latest edition.

Statutes at Large:

(*Statutes at Large* 2006:2083)

U.S. Code:

(*Declaratory Judgment Act, U.S. Code* 28, sec. 1562)

State law:

(*Ohio Revised Code Annotated*)

U.S. Constitution

References to the United States Constitution include the number of the article or amendment, the section number, and the clause, if necessary:

(U.S. Constitution, art. 3, sec. 3)

Executive Department Documents

A reference to a report, bulletin, circular, or any other type of material issued by the Executive Department starts with the name of the agency issuing the document, although you may use the name of the author, if known:

(Department of Labor 1984:334)

Legal References

Court decisions at any level of government are rarely given their own citations in the author–date system but are instead identified in the running text. If you wish to use a formal reference, however, this manual recommends that, for the text citation, you place within the parentheses only the title of the case, in italics, followed by the year.

(*AT&T Corporation v. Iowa Utilities Board* 1999)

The next section of this manual provides models of citations for court decisions suitable to the list of references.

Publications of Government Commissions

According to Section 17.320 of the *CMS* (2003), references to bulletins, circulars, reports, and study papers that are issued by various government commissions should include the name of the commission, the date of the document, and the page:

(Securities and Exchange Commission 1984:57)

Corporate Authors

Because government documents are often credited to a corporate author with a lengthy name, you may devise an acronym or a shortened form of the name and indicate in your first reference to the source that this name will be used in later citations:

(*Bulletin of Labor Statistics* 1997:154; *hereafter BLS*)

Interviews

According to the *CMS* (Sections 17.205, 17.208), citations to interviews should be handled by references within the text or in notes.

In a March 1997 interview with O. J. Simpson, Barbara Walters asked questions that seemed to upset and disorient the former superstar.

For published or broadcast interviews, no parenthetical reference is necessary, but there should be a complete citation under the interviewer's name in the bibliography.

An unpublished interview conducted by the writer of the paper should also be cited in the syntax of the sentence:

In an interview with the author on April 23, 2003, Dr. Kennedy expressed her disappointment with the new court ruling.

If you are citing material from an interview that you conducted, identify yourself as "the author" and give the date of the interview. Cite the interview by placing the date in parentheses following the name of the person interviewed:

Marsha Cummings (2009), Director of the Children's Hospital in Oklahoma City, was interviewed by the author on November 14, 2009.

REFERENCES IN ASA STYLE

In the author–date referencing system, parenthetical citations in the text point the reader to the fuller source descriptions at the end of the paper, known as the references or bibliography. This reference list, which always directly follows the text under the heading "References," is arranged alphabetically according to the first element in each citation. As stated in Chapter 3, some instructors prefer papers to be structured in article format, with everything presented as tightly compressed and succinct as possible. If your instructor favors this system, your reference section should immediately follow (after a double space) the last line of your discussion section. Other instructors prefer the references to be listed on a separate page. Ask your instructor which system you should follow.

As with most alphabetically arranged bibliographies, there is a kind of reverse-indentation system, or "hanging indent": After the first line of a citation, all subsequent lines are indented five spaces. The entire references section is double-spaced.

The ASA uses standard, or "headline style," capitalization for titles in the reference list. In this style, all first and last words in a title, and all other words except articles (*a, an, the*), coordinating words (*and, but, or, for, nor*), and prepositions (*among, by, for, of, to, toward*, etc.), are capitalized.

Remember that every source cited in the text, with those exceptions noted in the following examples, must have a corresponding entry in the references section. Do not include references to any work not cited in the text of your paper.

SAMPLES OF ASA REFERENCE STYLE

Many of the following formats are based on those given in the fourth edition of the *ASA Style Guide* (2010). Formats for bibliographical situations not covered by the ASA guide are taken from the fifteenth edition of the *CMS* (2003).

Books

One Author

First comes the author's name, inverted, then the date of publication, followed by the title of the book, the place of publication, and the name of the publisher. Use first names for all authors or use initials if no first name is provided. Add a space after each initial, as in the following example. For place of publication, identify the state, with its postal abbreviation, only if the city of publication is not clear otherwise. There is no need, in other words, to identify the state for cities such as New York, Los Angeles, Boston, or Dallas, or Chicago. If the city is located in a country other than the United States, however, cite the name of the country.

Periods are used to divide most of the elements in the citation, although a colon is used between the place of publication and publisher. Custom dictates that the main title and subtitle be separated by a colon, even though a colon may not appear in the title as printed on the title page of the book.

> Northrup, A. K. 2008. *Living High off the Hog: Recent Pork Barrel Legislation in the Senate*. Cleveland: Johnstown.

If no date of publication can be determined, perhaps because of the age of the document or the fact that it has not yet been published, use the abbreviation "N.d." for "no date." If the document is to be published, end the reference with the word "forthcoming."

> Hallows, Gerard. N.d. *On the Latest Indignities Suffered by the Crown*. London: Southwall.

> Bartholi, Kenneth. N.d. *Ineptitudes of Scale: Courtroom Practices in the New Century*. London, England: Balfour. Forthcoming.

Two Authors

Only the name of the first author is reversed, since it is the one by which the citation is alphabetized. Note that there is no comma between the first name of the first author and the *and* following:

> Spence, Michelle and Kristen Ruell. 1996. *Hiring and the Law*. Boston, MA: Tildale.

Three or More Authors

The use of *et al.* is not acceptable in the references section; list the names of all authors of a source. Place commas between all names. Note also that the ASA does not advocate abbreviating the word "University" in the name of a press, as indicated in the following model:

> Moore, J. B., Allen Rice, and Natasha Traylor. 2009. *Criminals and Class*. Norman, OK: University of Oklahoma Press.

No Author Given

Section 17.34 of the *CMS* (2003) states that if you can ascertain the name of the author when that name is not given in the work itself, place the author's name in brackets:

> [Morey, Cynthia]. 2013. *How We Mate: American Dating Customs, 1950–2000*. New York: Putney.

Do not use the term *anonymous* to designate an author whose name you cannot determine; instead, according to Section 17.32 of the *CMS* (2003), begin your reference entry with the title of the book, followed by the date. You may, if you wish, move initial articles (*a, an, the*) to the end of the title:

> Worst Way to Learn: The Government's War on Education, The. 1997. San Luis Obispo, CA: Blakeside.

Editor, Compiler, or Translator as Author

When no author is listed on the title page, begin the citation with the name of the editor, compiler, or translator:

> Trakas, Dylan, comp. 2012. *Making the Road-Ways Safe: Essays on Highway Crime Prevention*. El Paso, TX: Del Norte Press.

Editor, Compiler, or Translator with Author

> Pound, Ezra. 1953. *Literary Essays*, edited by T. S. Eliot. New York: New Directions.

> Stomper, Jean. 2005. *Grapes and Wrath*, translated by John Picard. New York: Baldock.

Untranslated Book

If your source is in a foreign language, it is not necessary, according to Section 17.64 of the *CMS* (2003), to translate the title into English. Use the capitalization format of the original language.

> Picon-Salas, Mariano. 1950. *De la Conquesta a la Independencia*. Mexico, DF: Fondo de Cultura Económica.

If you wish to provide a translation of the title, do so in brackets or parentheses following the title. Set the translation in roman type and capitalize only the first word of the title and subtitle, proper nouns, and proper adjectives:

> Wharton, Edith. 1916. *Voyages au front* (Visits to the Front). Paris, France: Plon.

Two or More Works by Same Author

If you wish you may replace the author's name in all citations after the first by a three-em dash (six strokes of the hyphen). List the works in the order of the year of publication, starting with the earliest year:

> Russell, Henry. 1978. *Famous Last Words: Notable Supreme Court Cases of the Last Five Years*. New Orleans, LA: Liberty Publications.

> ———. 1988. *Great Court Battles*. Denver, CO: Axel and Myers.

Chapter in Multiauthor Collection

> Gray, Alexa North. 2008. "Foreign Policy and Crime." Pp. 188–204 in *Current Issues in Criminal Justice*, edited by Barbara Bonnard and Luke F. Guinness. New York: Boulanger.

The parenthetical text reference may include the page reference:

(Gray 1998:195–97)

You must repeat the name if the author and the editor are the same person:

> Farmer, Susan P. 1995. "Literary Crimes of the Last Century." Pp. 58–73 in *A Brief History of Fraud*, edited by Susan A. Farmer. Nashville, TN: Burkette and Hyde.

Author of Foreword or Introduction

According to Section 17.46 of the *CMS* (2003), there is no need to cite the author of a foreword or introduction in your bibliography, unless you have used material from that author's contribution to the volume. In that case, list the bibliography entry under the name of the author of the foreword or introduction. Place the name of the author of the work itself after the title of the work:

> Farris, Carla. 2010. Foreword to *Sex Crimes among the Professoriat: A Case Study*, by Basil Givan. New York: Galapagos.

> The parenthetical text reference cites the name of the author of the foreword or introduction, not the author of the book:

(Farris 2010)

Articles in Encyclopedias and Other Reference Books

According to Section 17.238 of the *CMS* (2003), well-known reference books such as the *Encyclopedia Britannica* or the *American Heritage Dictionary* are not given a citation in the reference list. They should be credited within the running text of the paper:

> …as explained in Rondal Gould's article on welfare in the twelfth edition of *Collier's Encyclopedia*.

Subsequent Editions

If you are using an edition of a book other than the first, you must cite the number of the edition or the status, such as Rev. ed., in roman type, for revised edition, if there is no edition number:

> Hales, Sarah. 2010. *The Coming Water Wars*. 3d ed. Pittsburgh, PA: Blue Skies.

Multivolume Work

If you are citing a multivolume work in its entirety, use the following format:

> Graybosch, Charles. 1988–89. *The Rise of the Unions*. 3 vols. New York: Starkfield.

If you are citing only one of the volumes in a multivolume work, use the following format:

> Graybosch, Charles. 1988. *The Beginnings*. Vol. 1, *The Rise of the Unions*. New York: Starkfield.

Reprints

Adams, Sterling R. [1964] 2007. *How to Fix an Election: Criminal Campaign Strategies*. New York: Starkfield.

Classic Texts

According to the fifteenth edition of the *CMS* (2003: Sections 15.250 and 17.247), references to classic texts such as sacred books and Greek verse and drama are usually confined to the text and not given citations in the bibliography.

Periodicals

Journal Article

Journals are periodicals, usually published either monthly or quarterly, that specialize in serious scholarly articles in a particular field.

Hunzecker, Joan. 2010. "Rehabilitating Juvenile Offenders in Texas." *Southwest Recidivism Review* 4(2):250–62.

Johnson, J. D., N. E. Noel and J. Sutter-Hernandez. 2000. "Alcohol and Male Acceptance of Sexual Aggression: The Role of Perceptual Ambiguity." *Journal of Applied Social Psychology* 30(6):1186–1200.

Note that the name of the journal, italicized, is followed without punctuation by the volume number. Include the issue number, in parentheses, followed by a colon and the inclusive page numbers, all without spaces in between. Do not use *p.* or *pp.* to introduce the page numbers.

Article Published in More than One Journal Issue

Crossitch, Vernelle. 1997. "Evaluating Evidence: Calibrating Ephemeral Phenomena," parts 1–4. *Epiphanic Review* 15(4):22–29; 16(1):46–58; 17(1):48–60.

Article Published in Foreign-Language Journal

Sczaflarski, Richard. 2001. "The Trumpeter in the Tower: Solidarity and Legend" (in Polish). *World Political Review* 32(3):79–95.

Article Cited in Secondary Source

When referencing a source that has itself been cited in a secondary source, first list the complete citation of the source you cited, followed by the phrase *cited in*, in roman type, and a listing of the source from which you obtained your citation.

Johnson, William A. and Richard P. Rettig. 2006. "Drug Assessment of Juveniles in Detention." *Social Forces* 28(3):56–69, cited in John Duncan and Mary Ann Hopkins. 2009. "Youth and Drug Involvement: Families at Risk." *British Journal of Addiction* 95:45.

Gonzalez, Tim, Lucy Hammond, Fred Luntz, and Virginia Land. 1999. "Free Love and Nickel Beer: On Throwaway Relationships."*Journal of Alcoholism and Religion* 12(2):14–29, cited in Emanuel Hiddocke, Cheryl Manson, and Ruth Mendez. 2001. *The Death of the American Family*. Upper Saddle River, NJ: Prentice Hall, p. 107.

Magazines and Newspapers

Magazines, which are usually published weekly, bimonthly, or monthly, appeal to the popular audience and generally have a wider circulation than journals. *Newsweek* and *Scientific American* are examples of magazines.

Monthly Magazine

Stapleton, Bonnie and Ellis Peters. 2010. "How It Was: On the Trail with Og Mandino." *Lifetime Magazine*, April, pp. 23–24, 57–59.

Weekly or Bimonthly Magazine

Bruck, Connie. 1997. "The World of White Collar Crime: A Mogul's Farewell." *Rebarbative Review*, October 18, pp. 12–15.

Newspaper Articles

Everett, Susan. 1996. "Beyond the Alamo: How Texans View Historic Violence." *Carrollton Tribune*, February 16, D1, D4.

Sources Stored in Archives

According to item five in the Appendix to the fourth edition of the *ASA Style Guide* (2010), if you refer to a number of archival sources, you should group them in a separate part of the references section and name it "Archival Sources."

Clayton Fox Correspondence, Box 12. July–December 1903. File: Literary Figures 2. Letter to Edith Wharton, dated September 11.

Section 17.324 of the *CMS* (2003) recommends that materials housed in the National Archives or in one of its branches be cited according to their RG number. The citation may also include title, subsection, and file number:

National Archives. RG 438. Records of the National Committee on Poverty and Aging. File 78A-M22.

Public Documents

Section 4.4.1 of the fourth edition of the *ASA Style Guide* (2010) notes that nonlegal works generally identify legal documents—for example, constitutions, executive orders, or amicus briefs—in the running text and not in the list of references. The ASA guide goes on, however, to say that it is possible to include public documents among the references and gives several examples. The following reference models are based on those found in the fourth edition of the *ASA Style Guide* (2010) and in the fifteenth edition of the *CMS* (2003).

Congressional Journals

References to either the Senate Journal or the House Journal begin with the journal's title and include the years of the session, the number of the Congress and session, and the month and day of the entry:

> *U.S. Senate Journal.* 1997. 105th Cong., 2d sess., 10 December.

While Section 2.5 of the fourth edition of the *ASA Style Guide* (2010) recommends that ordinal numbers *second* and *third* usually be expressed as "nd" (52nd) and "rd" (103rd), respectively, it makes an exception for legal citations, in which either ordinal may be expressed as "d" (52d, 103d).

Congressional Debates

Congressional debates are printed in the daily issues of the Congressional Record, which are bound biweekly and then collected and bound at the end of the session. Whenever possible, you should consult the bound yearly collection instead of the biweekly compilations. The "H" preceding the page number stands for House of Representatives.

> U.S. Congress. House of Representatives. 2001. *District of Columbia Police Coordination Amendment Act of 2001.* H.R. 2199, 107th Congress, 1st Session, 2001. *Congressional Record* 147 (December 19, 2001): H10403.

Congressional Reports and Documents

> U.S. Congress. Senate. Select Committee on Intelligence. 2004. *Report on the U.S. Intelligence Community's Prewar Intelligence Assessments on Iraq.* Committee Report. 108th Congress, 2nd Session.

Note: Any reference that begins with "U.S. Congress," "U.S. Senate," or "U.S. House" may omit the "U.S." if it is clear from the context that you are referring to the United States. Whichever form you use, be sure to use it consistently, in both the notes and the bibliography.

State and Local Government Documents

References for state and local government publications are modeled on those for corresponding national government documents:

> Oklahoma Legislature. Joint Committee on Public Recreation. 2008. *Final Report to the Legislature, Regular Session, on Youth Activities*. Oklahoma City.

> Sidney M. Marder. 1977. *Review and Synopsis of Public Participation regarding Sulfur Dioxide and Particulate Emissions*. Illinois Institute for Environmental Quality. IIEQ Document no. 77/21. Chicago.

Remember to start the reference with the author's name, when available, as in the second model.

Laws

According to Section 17.310 of the *CMS* (2003), laws may be cited to the *Statutes at Large* or the *U.S. Code* or both.

Statutes at Large:

> *National Defense Authorization Act for Fiscal Year 2007*. Public Law 109–364, 120 U.S. *Statutes at Large* 2083 (2006).

The number "120" designates the volume and "2083" the page number.

U.S. Code:

> *Declaratory Judgment Act*, 28 U.S.C., Section 2201 (1952).

The number "28" designates the volume number.

State Law:

> *Ohio Revised Code Annotated*, Section 3566 (West 2000).

U.S. Constitution

> U.S. Constitution, Article 2, Section 2.

Executive Department Documents

> U.S. Department of Labor. Employment Standards Administration. 2010. *Resource Book: Training for Federal Employee Compensations Specialists*. Washington, D.C.: U.S. Government Printing Office.

Legal References

Supreme Court

Since 1875 all Supreme Court decisions have been published in the *United States Supreme Court Reports*, which is designated by the abbreviation "U.S." The number preceding the abbreviation is the volume number, and the number following is the opening page of the decision:

> *AT&T Corporation v. Iowa Utilities Board*, 525 U.S. 366 (1999).

Before 1875, Supreme Court decisions were published under the names of official court reporters. The reference below is to William Cranch, *Reports of Cases Argued and Adjudged in the Supreme Court of the United States, 1801–1815*, 9 vols. (Washington, D.C., 1804–17). The number preceding the clerk's name is the volume number; the last number is the page:

> *Marbury v. Madison*. 1803. 1 Cranch 137.

Lower Federal Courts

Decisions of the lower federal courts are usually cited to the *Federal Reporter*, abbreviated as "F.," or the *Federal Supplement* (F. Supp.). The material in parenthesis in the model reference provided here is the name of the court, abbreviated, and the year of the decision:

> *Eaton v. IBM Corp.*, 925 F. Supp. 487 (S. D. Tex. 1996).

State Courts

In the model reference provided here, "Cal." is the abbreviated name of the official court reporter, "27" is the volume number, "2d" identifies the series number, and "746" is the opening page of the decision.

> *Williams v. Davis*, 27 Cal. 2d 746 (1946).

Note that the titles of court cases, including the "v," are italicized.

Government Commissions

U.S. Securities and Exchange Commission. 1984. *Annual Report of the Securities and Exchange Commission for the Fiscal Year*. Washington, D.C.: U.S. Government Printing Office.

Note: See the section on formatting citations for electronic sources, later in this chapter, for information on citing public documents found in Internet sources.

Interviews

According to Section 17.205 of the *CMS* (2003), interviews are best handled in the body of the text or in notes, but if you or your instructor wants to list such entries, here are possible formats.

Published Interview

Untitled Interview in a Book:

> Jorgenson, Mary. 2011. Interview by Alan McAskill. Pp. 62–86 in *Paroled Pioneers*, edited by Alan McAskill. Richmond, VA: Dynasty Press.

Titled Interview in a Periodical:

> Simon, Jan. 2013. "Picking the Right Argument: An Interview with John Simon," by Selena Fox. *Media Week*, March 14, pp. 40–54.

Television Interview

> Snopes, Edward. 2013. Interview by Clint Gordon. *Oklahoma Politicians*. WKY Television, June 4.

Unpublished Interview

> Kennedy, Melissa. 2006. Interview by author. Tape recording. Portland, ME, April 23.

Unpublished Sources

Personal Communications

According to Section 17.208 of the *CMS* (2003), references to personal communications may be handled completely in the text of the paper:

> In a letter to the author, dated July 16, 1997, Mr. Bentley admitted the organizational plan was flawed.

If, however, you wish to include a reference to an unpublished communication in the list of references, you may do so using one of the following models:

> Bentley, Jacob. 1997. Letter to author, July 16.

> Duberstein, Cindy. 2008. Telephone conversation with the author, June 5.

> Timrod, Helen. 2003. E-mail to author, April 25.

Thesis and Dissertation

Longley, Slim. 2006. "Populism and the Urge toward Larceny." Ph.D. dissertation, Department of Criminal Justice, Lamont University, Cleveland, OH.

Paper Presented at a Meeting

Zelazny, Kim and Ed Gilmore. 2010. "Crime for Crime's Sake: Dealing with the Habitual Offender." Presented at the annual meeting of the California State Conference on Crime and Jurisprudence, June 15, San Francisco, CA.

Unpublished Manuscript

Borges, Rita V. 1993. "Mexican-American Border Conflicts, 1915–1970." Department of History, University of Texas at El Paso, El Paso, TX. Unpublished manuscript.

Working and Discussion Papers

Blaine, Emory and Ralph Cohn. 1995. "Analysis of Social Structure in Closed Urban Environments." Discussion Paper No. 312, Institute for Sociological Research, Deadwood College, Deadwood, SD.

ELECTRONIC SOURCES

The need for a reliable online citation system continues to grow, but attempts to establish one are hampered by a number of factors. For one thing, there is no foolproof method of clearly reporting even such basic information as the site's author(s), title, or date of establishment. Occasionally, authors identify themselves clearly; sometimes they place a link to their home page at the bottom of the site. But it is not always easy to determine exactly who authored a particular site. Likewise, it can be difficult to determine whether a site has its own title or exists as a subsection of a larger document with its own title. Perhaps the biggest problem facing online researchers is the instability of Internet sites. While some sites may remain in place for weeks or months, many either move to another site—not always leaving a clear path for you to find it—or disappear.

As in other issues concerning the formatting of research material, the fourth edition of the *ASA Style Guide* (2010) has adopted methods established in the fifteenth edition of the *CMS* (2003) as a direction for its own system for handling electronic sources.

TEXT CITATIONS FOR ELECTRONIC SOURCES

Format parenthetical text citations for most types of electronic sources just as you do for text citations for printed materials. See exceptions later in this chapter for Web sites, blog entries, and e-mail documents.

REFERENCES FOR ELECTRONIC SOURCES

Books, Sections of Books, and Reports

To cite a book, a chapter or section of a book, or a separately published report that you have accessed online, begin the reference citation with the same format that you use for a print edition, including, if available, the place of publication, the name of the publisher, and the date of publication. Follow this information with the date on which you last retrieved the material and, in parentheses, the URL (uniform resource locator) (the address for the document on the World Wide Web). Model references in Section 5 of the third edition of the *ASA Style Guide* (2007) suggest that, when necessary, it is acceptable to break a lengthy URL address at the end of a line only after a period. Do not place a hyphen after the period. Remember, the one thing that is absolutely required in order to find a site on the Internet is the site address; so make sure you copy it accurately.

> Squires, Nora and Avery Cook. 2009. *Negotiating Stress in the Home: A Primer*. New York: Cally Press. Retrieved March 13, 2009 (http://www. jc.familiesagainstgloom.org/htmlbook09/s&c).

You may, if you wish, list other formats in which the book appears:

> Snyder, Howard N. and Melissa Sickmund. 2009. *Juvenile Offenders and Victims: 2009 National Report*. Pittsburgh, PA: National Center for Juvenile Justice. (Also available at http://ojjdp.ncjrs.gov/ojstatbb/ nr2006/downloads/NR2006.pdf)

Online Periodicals

Journal Article Available in Print and Online

Begin with the information required for a reference to the print edition and end with the date accessed and the online location, in parentheses.

> Bucknell, Vespasia. 2008. "Servitude as a Way of Life: Religious Denominations in Middle America." *Skeptic's Journal* 4(2):22–37. Retrieved September 25, 2009 (http://www.religio.org/protest/ skepjrnl/my03.html).

Journal Article Available Online Only

Include as much as possible of the information required for a citation for an article available in print, followed by the date you last retrieved the article and, in parentheses, the URL.

> Linklater, Philip and Lucy Beall. 2007. "My Papa's Waltz: Alcoholism and Culture." *High Art Quarterly* 12(2). Retrieved April 1, 2009 (http://www. linkbeall/lennox.org/litcult.html).

For journal articles you have accessed through an online database such as JSTOR or SocINDEX, list the database just before the retrieval date.

> Asbridge, Mark and Swarna Weerasinghe. 2009. "Homicide in Chicago from 1890 to 1930: Prohibition and Its Impact on Alcohol- and Non-Alcohol-Related Homicides." *Addiction* 104(3):355–64. (Retrieved from ScoINDEX on March 13, 2009.)

Online Newspaper Article

> Spires, Amanda. 2000. "Hard Times for Social Workers, Says Mayor." *El Paso Sun Times*, July 14, pp. A2, A8. Retrieved November 12, 2008 (http:// www.elpasosun.com/2000-12/12.html).

Newsletter

> Lampert, James. 2008. "Slouching toward Armageddon." *Desert Technologies*, July. Retrieved January 22, 2009 (http://www.phoenixites.org/destech/ Jul09/dt3.html).

Web Sites

Any Web site from which you have used material that is important to the work you are doing in your manuscript should receive a text citation and a full citation in the reference list.

Document Retrieved from an Institution with a Known Location

Text citation:

> (SPM 2008)

Reference:

> Society for the Prevention of Malnutrition. 2008. "Score Card for the Decade." Juneau, AL: Society for the Prevention of Malnutrition. Retrieved June 6, 2009 (http://www.spmal.org/rs/westhem/stat).

Document Retrieved from a Corporate Web Site with an Unknown Location

Text citation:

> (Okdata 2009)

Reference:

> Okydata Corp. 2009. "Sports that Stigmatize: The Impact of Noodling on the State's Cultural Profile." Retrieved September 12, 2009 (http://www.okydata.com/sportrec/channelcat.html).

Public Documents

A great number of public texts, including congressional debates, bills, and laws; federal, state, and local reports and documents; and court cases can now be found on the Internet. Over the last few years there has been a flowering of government-centered Web sites, such as THOMAS, a Web site established by the Library of Congress, under the direction of Congress, to make all manner of federal legislative information available to the general public.

Citations for public documents found on the Internet use the citation format for a print document as far as is practicable, ending with the date of retrieval and URL. For documents found on databases and Web sites such as LexisNexis and THOMAS, list the name of the database or Web site before the retrieval date.

> U.S. Congress. House of Representatives. 2009. *Omnibus Appropriations Act of 2009*. H.R. 1105, 111th Congress, 1st Session, 2009. (Retrieved from THOMAS on March 13, 2009.)

Blog Entries

Give full citations for any significant Web log references included in your manuscript.

Text citation:

> (Hochenauer 2009)

Reference:

> Hochenauer, Kurt. "No New Tax Cuts." *Okie Funk: Notes From The Outback,* March 13, 2009. Retrieved March 14, 2009 (http://www.okiefunk.com/).

E-mail Documents

A reference to an e-mail message should be handled within the text of the manuscript and referenced in a footnote or endnote. Do not cite the e-mail address, and be sure to obtain permission from the owner of the e-mail before using it.

Text citation:

> Bennett assured the author in an e-mail message that the negotiations would continue.

Footnote:

> [4]Albert Bennett, e-mail message to author, March 22, 2009.

CD-ROM

References to materials housed on CD-ROM are cited in much the same way as printed sources. You may omit the place of publication and date, unless relevant.

> *Complete National Geographic: 110 Years of National Geographic Magazine.* 2000. CD-ROM. Mindscape.

DVD-ROM and Videocassettes

Citations for video recordings resemble those for printed material. Section 17.273 of the *CMS* (2003) notes that scenes from a video work, which are accessible individually on DVDs, should be treated as book chapters and cited by title or number. Material incidental to the primary work on the DVD or videocassette—for example, critical commentaries—should be cited by author and title.

> "Crop Duster Attack." 1959; 2000. *North by Northwest*. DVD. Directed by Alfred Hitchcock. Burbank, CA: Warner Home Video.

The first date listed above is the date the film was first shown; the second is the date the DVD was published.

> Cleese, John, Terry Gilliam, Eric Idle, Terry Jones, and Michael Palin. 2001. "Commentaries." Disc 2. *Monty Python and the Holy Grail*, special ed. DVD. Directed by Terry Gilliam and Terry Jones. Culver City, CA: Columbia Tristar Home Entertainment.

The date in the above citation refers to the commentaries being cited, material original to the 2001 DVD edition of the movie. The original date of the film is omitted as irrelevant.

A sample reference page follows.

REFERENCES

Asbridge, Mark and Swarna Weerasinghe. 2009. "Homicide in Chicago from 1890 to 1930: Prohibition and Its Impact on Alcohol- and Non-Alcohol-Related Homicides." *Addiction* 104(3):355–64. (Retrieved from ScoINDEX on March 13, 2009.)

Johnson, J. D., N. E. Noel, and J. Sutter-Hernandez. 2000. "Alcohol and Male Acceptance of Sexual Aggression: The Role of Perceptual Ambiguity." *Journal of Applied Social Psychology* 30(6):1186–1200.

Johnson, William A. and Richard P. Rettig. 2006. "Drug Assessment of Juveniles in Detention." Social Forces 28(3):56–69, cited in John Duncan and Mary Ann Hopkins. 2009. "Youth and Drug Involvement: Families at Risk." *British Journal of Addiction* 95:45.

Moore, J. B., Allen Rice, and Natasha Traylor. 2009. *Criminals and Class.* Norman, OK: University of Oklahoma Press.

Sczaflarski, Richard. 2001 "The Trumpeter in the Tower: Solidarity and Legend" (in Polish). *World Political Review* 32(3):79–95.

Spires, Amanda. 2000. "Hard Times for Social Workers, Says Mayor." *El Paso Sun Times*, July 14, p. 2. Retrieved November 12, 2008 (http://www.elpasosun.com/2000–12/12.html).

Stapleton, Bonnie and Ellis Peters. 1981. "How It Was: On the Trail with Og Mandino." *Lifetime Magazine*, April, pp. 23–24, 57–59.

Stomper, Jean. 2005. *Grapes and Wrath.* Translated by John Picard. New York: Baldock.

5

Citing Sources
in APA Style

INTRODUCTION TO APA STYLE

Some criminal justice courses permit or encourage students to use APA (American Psychological Association) documentation style, and this chapter is for students in these courses.

As we mentioned in Chapter 4, one of your most important jobs as a research writer is to document your use of source material carefully and clearly. Failure to do so will cause your reader confusion, damage the effectiveness of your paper, and perhaps make you vulnerable to a charge of plagiarism. Proper documentation is more than just good form. It is a powerful indicator of your own commitment to scholarship and the sense of authority that you bring to your writing. Good documentation demonstrates your expertise as a researcher and increases your reader's trust in you and your work.

Unfortunately, as anybody who has ever written a research paper knows, getting the documentation right can be a frustrating, confusing job, especially for the novice writer. Positioning each element of a single reference citation accurately can require what seems an inordinate amount of time spent thumbing through the style manual. Even before you begin to work on specific citations, there are important questions of style and format to answer.

WHAT TO DOCUMENT

Direct quotes must always be credited, as must certain kinds of paraphrased material. Information that is basic—important dates, facts, or opinions universally acknowledged—need not be cited. Information that is not widely known, whether fact or opinion, should receive documentation.

What if you are unsure whether or not a certain fact is widely known? You are, after all, very probably a newcomer to the field in which you are conducting your research. If in doubt, supply the documentation. It is better to overdocument than to fail to do justice to a source.

The following formats are taken from the sixth edition of the *Publication Manual of the APA* (2010). Like the ASA style described in Chapter 4, the APA style uses an author–date system of referencing, also known as a parenthetical-reference system, which requires two components for each significant reference to a source: (1) a note placed within the text, in parentheses, near where the source material occurs, and (2) a full bibliographical reference for the source, placed in a list of references following the text and keyed to the parenthetical reference within the text. Models for both text citations and full references are given in the following section.

TEXT CITATIONS IN APA STYLE

SAMPLES OF APA CITATION STYLE

One Work by One Author

To cite both the author's name and the year of publication in the text, use this format:

> …was challenged by Lewissohn in 1999.

Here is an author's name in the text with the year of publication in parentheses:

> Freedman (2006) postulates that when individuals…

If you want both the author's name and the year of publication in parentheses, use this model:

> …encourage more aggressive play (Perrez, 1979) and contribute…

When the citation appears at the end of a sentence, the parenthetical reference is placed inside the period.

> …and avoid the problem (Keaster, 2003).

In all cases, use only the author's surname, and do not include suffixes such as *Jr*.

One Work by Two, Three, Four, or Five Authors

Every time a reference to a work with two authors occurs in your text, include the surnames of both authors in your citation. For works with three, four, or five authors, cite surnames for all authors in your first text citation, and in all subsequent citations include only the surname of the first author, followed by the phrase *et al.*, in roman type and followed by a period. End with the year if it is the first citation of the reference within the paragraph.

> ...however, according to Holmes and Bacon (2009), the victim never establishes a sense of self.

> ...establishes a sense of self (Holmes & Bacon, 1872).

> ...found the requirements very restrictive (Mollar, Querley, & McLarry, 1926).

> ...proved to be quite difficult (Mollar et al., 1926).

> ...according to Mollar et al. (1926)...

Note: For all sources with more than one author, separate the last two names with the word *and* if they are given within the text and by an ampersand if they appear within parentheses.

One Work by Six or More Authors

In all references to sources with six or more authors, cite only the surname of the first author, followed by a comma and the phrase *et al.*, in roman type, followed by a period and the date:

> Kineson, et al. (1933) made the following suggestion...

When references to two multiple-author sources with the same year shorten to the same abbreviated format, cite as many of the authors as needed to differentiate the sources. Consider these examples:

> Keeler, Allen, Pike, Johnson, and Keaton (1994)

> Keeler, Allen, Schmidt, Wendelson, Crawford, and Blaine (1994)

Using the standard method for abbreviating citations, these two sources would both shorten to the same format:

> Keeler, et al. (1994)

However, to avoid confusion, shorten the citations to these works as follows:

> Keeler, Allen, Pike, et al. (1994)

> Keeler, Allen, Schmidt, et al. (1994)

Group as Author

Use the complete name of a group author in the first citation:

> ...to raise the standard of living (National Association of Food Retailers, 1994).

If the name of the group is lengthy, and if its abbreviation is easily identified by the general public, you may abbreviate the group name in citations after the first one.

First citation:

> …usually kept in cages (Society for the Prevention of Cruelty to Animals, 1993).

Subsequent citations:

> …which, according to the SPCA (1990),…

Remember that you must be sure to give enough information in the text citation to point the reader clearly to the full entry in the reference list.

Authors with Same Surname

Use initials to differentiate authors with the same last name, even if the dates of publication are different.

> …the new sentencing laws (K. Grady, 1999).

> …to reduce recidivism (B. Grady, 2001).

Two Works by Same Author

If the two citations appear in the same note, place a comma between the publication dates:

> George (1992, 1994) argues for…

If the two works were published in the same year, differentiate them by adding lowercase letters as suffixes to the publication dates. Be sure also to add the suffixes to the entries in the list of references, where you will assign suffixes to the different works alphabetically by title of work.

> …the city government (Estrada, 1994a, 1994b).

Work with No Author Given

Begin the parenthetical reference of a work by an unnamed author with the first few words of the entry from the reference list—usually the title—either italicizing them if they are part of the title of a book or placing them in quotation marks if they are part of the title of an essay, newspaper article, or chapter:

> …economic recovery is unlikely (*Around the Bend*, 2000).

> …will run again in the next election ("Problems for Smithson," 1996).

Reference to Specific Parts of a Source

Page numbers should only be included when quoting directly from a source or referring to specific passages. Use *p.* or *pp.*, in roman type, to denote page numbers.

> Thomas (2005, p. 741) builds on this scenario...

> ...in the years to come (Dixon, 1997, pp. 34–35).

If your focus is limited to only a chapter, you can cite the chapter. Note that you do not abbreviate the word *chapter* in text citations.

> ...despite the fact that he never discovered the right mix of therapy and pharmaceuticals (Jessup, 2003, chapter 4).

For an electronic source that does not use page numbers but does number the article's paragraphs, denote the paragraph using the abbreviation *para.*, in roman type:

> Cordell (2008) insists that the court bear in mind the relatives' wishes (para. 12).

If the electronic source includes neither page nor paragraph numbers but does feature headings, you may cite the heading and the number of the paragraph, following it, from which you are taking material:

> ...shall be liable for damages in such a case (Johnson and Rettig, 2009, FAQs section, para. 4).

Direct Quotations

Direct quotes of fewer than 40 words should be placed in the text, with quotation marks at the beginning and end. The citation should include the author, year of publication, and page number.

> Traffic fines over the time period reflect "the local magistrate's bias against minorities as well as anyone living in Osage County" (Rockett & McMinn, 1990, p. 278).

If there is no page number but the paragraph is numbered, as is sometimes the case in online sources, include that number. The following example places the author name and date within the running text:

> The majority of these convictions, according to Peterson et al. (2009), were obtained "through the most fraudulent of courtroom practices" (para. 2), and should have been thrown out.

Direct quotes of 40 words or more should start on a new line as a block quotation and be double-spaced and indented approximately half an inch (about five spaces) from the left margin, just as the first line of a paragraph is indented. Indent the first line of any additional paragraphs within the quotation an additional half inch. The parenthetical reference following the block quote is placed after the final period:

> During this time Sartain (1889) and his men made a discovery that, briefly summarized in the published account, has caused consternation and confusion among American penologists for over one hundred years:
>
> > We came to a huge structure made of stone but covered in sheathing that looked to be composed of metal, and there we were accosted in an indecipherable tongue by a set of guards most fearsomely armed and exhibiting signs of extreme agitation. One, in fact, threw his spear toward us, but owing to the distance between him and us, it did no harm.
> >
> > It required the discharging of but a single rifle to scatter the defenders and leave us in possession of the pile, to which, alas, we could find no door nor opening of any kind, but from within which rose, faintly, the most piteous moans any of us had ever heard men make. (p. 204)

Chapters, Tables, Appendixes, and So Forth

...(see Table 4 of Blake, 1985, for complete information).

...(see Appendix B of Shelby, 2003).

Reprints

Cite by the original date of publication and the date of the edition you are using:

...complaints from Daniels (1922/1976), who takes a different view...

More Than One Source in Reference

Separate citations by a semicolon and place them in alphabetical order by author:

...are related (Harmatz, 1987, p. 48; Marble et al., 1986, p. 909; Powers & Erickson, 1986, p. 48; Rackley et al., 1988, p. 10; Thompson & Thompson, 1986, p. 62).

Unpublished Materials

If the source is scheduled for publication at a later time, use the designation in press, within parentheses, in roman type:

A study by Barle and Ford (in press) lends support...

Personal Communications

Materials such as letters to the author, memos, e-mails, messages from electronic discussion groups, and telephone conversations should be cited within the text but not listed among the references. Include in the text note the initials and last name of the person with whom you communicated and give as exact a date as possible:

> ...explained to the author and to the corporation that the work was flawed (P. L. Bingam, personal communication, February 20, 2000).

> ...agrees, for the most part, with the findings and opinions of W. E. Knight (personal communication, October 12, 1998).

Undated Materials

For undated materials, use "n.d." ("no date") in place of the date:

> ...except that Fox (n.d.) disagrees.

> ...cannot be ascertained (Fox, n.d.).

Classical and Historical Texts

Refer to classical and historical texts, such as the Bible, standard translations of ancient Greek writings, and the *Federalist Papers*, by using the systems by which they are subdivided, rather than the publication information of the edition you are using. Since all editions of such texts employ the standard subdivisions, this reference method has the advantage of allowing your readers to find the cited passage in any published version. You may cite a biblical passage by referring to the particular book, chapter, and verse, all in roman type, with the translation given after the verse number:

> "But the path of the just is as the shining light, that shineth more and more unto the perfect day" (Prov. 4:18, King James Version).

The *Federalist Papers* may be cited by their standard numbers:

> Madison addresses the problem of factions in a republic (*Federalist* 10).

If you are citing a work whose date is not known or is inapplicable, cite the year of the translation, preceded by the abbreviation *trans.*, in roman type, or the year of the version, followed by the word *version*, in roman type:

> Plato (trans. 1908) records that...

> ...disagrees with the formulation in Aristotle (1892 version).

Public Documents

Appendix 7.1: References to Legal Materials (pp. 216–24) in the sixth edition of the *Publication Manual of the APA* (2010) gives models for citations of such public documents as court decisions, statutes, and other legislative and executive materials, but the appendix also points authors to the eighteenth edition of *The Bluebook: A Uniform System of Citation* (2005) for more detail on how to cite such documents. Here are models for some sources frequently used by criminal justice professionals.

Legislative Hearings

Information concerning a hearing before a legislative subcommittee is published in an official pamphlet. A text citation for such a pamphlet begins with a shortened form of the pamphlet's title and includes the year in which the hearing was held:

> ...citing many of the dangers of underfunded school programs (*Funding for Inner City Schools*, 1990).

Bills and Resolutions

Both enacted and unenacted bills and resolutions are cited by their number and house of origin—Senate (S.) or House of Representatives (H.R.), in roman type—and year. For example, the parenthetical reference to Unenacted Bill Number 7658, originating in the Senate in 1996, would be handled in one of the following ways:

> ...cannot reject visa requests out of hand (S. 7658, 1996).

> ...cannot reject visa requests out of hand (Senate Bill 7658, 1996).

> ...according to Senate Bill 7658 (1996).

A parenthetical reference to enacted resolution 94, which originated in the House of Representatives in 1993, reads as follows:

> ...only to U.S. citizens (H.R. Res. 94, 1993).

> House Resolution 94 (1993) explains that...

Statutes in Federal Code

In the text, cite the popular or official name of the act and the year:

> ...in order to obtain a license (Fish and Game Act of 1990).

> ...as provided by the Fish and Game Act of 1990,...

Federal Reports

The text and parenthetical references, respectively, to a report from the Senate or House of Representatives are handled as follows:

> ...as was finally explained in Senate Report No. 85 (1989), the...

> ...was finally clarified (H.R. Rep. No. 114, 2009).

Court Decisions

...which she failed to meet (*State of Nevada v. Goldie Warren*, 1969).

...as was ruled in State of Nevada v. Goldie Warren (1969).

Executive Orders

Executive Order No. 13,521 (1993) states that...

It was clearly decided (Executive Order No. 13,521, 1993) that...

REFERENCES IN APA STYLE

Parenthetical citations in the text point the reader to the fuller source descriptions at the end of the paper, known as the reference list or bibliography. According to the sixth edition of the *Publication Manual of the APA* (2010:180, n. 1), there is a difference between a reference list and a bibliography of sources consulted for a paper. A reference list gives only those sources used directly in the paper for support, whereas a bibliography may also include materials used indirectly, perhaps for background or further reading—materials, in other words, that do not appear directly in the paper, either in actual quotations or in paraphrase. Ask your instructor which type of source list you should provide for your class paper.

Like all other parts of the paper, the reference list should be double-spaced. Entries are alphabetized by the first element in each citation. (See the sample reference page at the end of this chapter.) The APA reference system uses "sentence-style" capitalization for titles of books and articles, meaning that only the first word of the title and subtitle (if present) and all proper names are capitalized. Titles of periodicals, including journals and newspapers, are given standard, or "headline style," capitalization. In this style all words in a title, except articles (*a, an, the*), coordinating words (*and, but, or, for, nor*), and prepositions (*among, by, for, of, to, toward*), are capitalized. Although the titles of journals and books are italicized, titles of chapters or articles are neither italicized or underlined nor enclosed in quotation marks.

These capitalization and italicizing rules mean that your reproduction of the titles of works you cite in your reference list will very probably not look like they do in the original document. For example, while a book title may appear in all capital letters on the book's title page—STRESS IN THE AMERICAN WORKPLACE—in an APA-style reference page it will conform to APA format rules: *Stress in the American workplace.*

As with most alphabetically arranged bibliographies, there is a kind of reverse-indentation system, commonly called a *hanging indent*: After the first line of a citation, which is set flush left, all subsequent lines are indented five spaces. Certain word processing programs, such as Microsoft Word, offer a command that will apply hanging indent format to blocks of material.

Note: If there is only one reference in your list, title the section *Reference*, in roman type, instead of *References*. Capitalize only the first letter of the word.

SAMPLES OF APA REFERENCE STYLE

Books

One Author

For a single-author source, the author's last name comes first, then the initials of the first and, if available, middle names. Add a space after each initial. The date of publication follows in parentheses, followed by a period and then the title of the book in italics. The city of publication is cited next, then the state or territory, using U.S. Postal abbreviations. If the location is outside the United States, spell out the names of the city and country. The name of the publisher is given last and in as brief a form as possible while still clear. In other words, avoid such unnecessary terms as *Publishers, and Sons, Limited, Co.,* and *Inc.*

> Northrup, A. K. (2013). *Creative tensions in family units: Studies in behavior.* Cleveland, OH: Johnstown.

Periods divide most of the elements in the citation, although a colon is used between the place of publication and publisher. Custom dictates that the main title of a book and its subtitle are separated by a colon, even though a colon may not appear in the title as printed on the title page of the book. Capitalize the first word of the subtitle.

Two Authors

Reverse both names, placing a comma after the initials of the first name. Separate the names by an ampersand:

> Spence, M. L., & Ruel, K. M. (2007). *Therapy and the law.* London, England: Tildale.

Three or More Authors

List the names and initials, in reverse order, of all authors of a source if there are six or fewer authors. If there are more than six authors, place the phrase *et al.,* in roman type and with a period after *al,* following the name of the sixth author, and do not list the remaining names of authors.

> Moore, J. B., Macrory, K. L., Rice, A. D., Traylor, N. P., Wallo, B., Denison, W. L., et al. (2006). *Violence against women in the workplace: An overview.* Norman: University of Oklahoma Press.

As this model indicates, if the publisher is a university with the name of the state or province in its title, do not repeat that name in the location preceding the colon.

Multiple-author entries with the same first author should be alphabetized in the list of references by the surname of the second author. If the second author is the same also, then alphabetize by the surname of the third author, and so on.

Group as Author

Alphabetize such entries according to the first significant word in the group's name, and spell out the name completely:

> National Association of Physical Therapists. (2008). *Standardization of physical therapy techniques.* Trenton, NJ: Arkway.

Work with No Author Given

Begin the citation with the title of the work, alphabetizing according to the first significant word:

> *Around the bend: Physical and emotional distress among civic administrators.* (2010). Dallas, TX: Turbo.

Editor or Compiler as Author

> Jastow, X. R. (Comp.). (1990). *Saying good-bye: Pathologies in Soviet literature.* New York, NY: Broadus.

> Yarrow, P. T., & Edgarton, S. P. (Eds.). (1987). The *Waco protocol and the prevention of violence.* New York, NY: Halley.

Book with Author and Editor

When a book has both an author and an editor, there is no comma between the title and the parentheses enclosing the editor's name, and the editor's last name and initials are not reversed:

> Scarborough, D. L. (2010). *Written on the wind: Prison maxims* (E. K. Lightstraw, Ed.). Beaufort, SC: Juvenal.

Translated Book

Do not reverse the last name and initials of the translator:

> Zapata, E. M. (2008). *Beneath the wheel: Mental health of the prison population in Northern Mexico* (A. M. Muro, Trans.). El Paso, TX: Del Norte.

Untranslated Book

Provide a translation of the title, in brackets, following the title:

Wharton, E. N. (1916). *Voyages au front* [Visits to the front]. Paris, France: Plon.

Two Works by Same Author

Do not use a rule in place of the author's name in the second and subsequent entries; always state the author's name in full and give the earlier reference first:

George, J. B. (1981). *Who shot John: Psychological profiles of gunshot victims in the Midwest, 1950–1955.* Okarche, OK: Flench & Stratton.

George, J. B. (1989). *They often said so: Repetition and obfuscation in nineteenth-century psychotherapy.* Stroud, OK: Casten.

If both works by the same author were published in the same year, order the entries in your reference list alphabetically by title, excluding *A* or *The*.

Author of Foreword or Introduction

List the entry under the name of the author of the foreword or introduction, not the author of the book:

Farris, C. J. (2010). Foreword. In B. Givan, *Sex crimes among the professoriat: A case study* (pp. 1–24). New York, NY: Galapagos.

Selection in Multiauthor Collection

Gray, A. N. (1998). Foreign policy and the foreign press. In B. Bonnard & L. F. Guinness (Eds.), *Current psychotherapy issues* (pp. 188–204). New York, NY: Boulanger.

You must provide a complete citation for every selection from a multiauthor collection that appears in the references; do not abbreviate the name of the collection, even if it is included as a separate entry in the reference list.

Signed Article in a Reference Book

Jenks, S. P. (1983). Fuller, Buckminster. In L. B. Sherman & B. H. Sherman (Eds.), *International dictionary of psychology* (pp. 204–205). Boston, MA: R. R. Hemphill.

Unsigned Article in an Encyclopedia

Pathologies. (1968). In *Encyclopedia of criminals and criminology* (4th ed.). Boston, MA: Blankenship.

Subsequent Editions

If you are using an edition of a book other than the first, you must cite the number of the edition or the status (such as *Rev. ed.* for revised edition) if there is no edition number:

> Hales, S. A. (2010). *The water wars* (3d ed.). Pittsburgh, PA: Blue Skies.

> Peters, D. K. (1972). *Social conditioning in early childhood* (Rev. ed.). Riverside, CA: Ingot.

Republished Book

> Hollander, W. A. (2003). Causes of aggressive behavior in minority populations. In Y. Dearinger & J. Bowie (Eds.). *The published works of Walter Hollander* (Vol. 2, pp. 12–298). Tulsa, OK: Leesh. (Original work published 1952.)

Multivolume Work

If you are citing a multivolume work in its entirety, use the following format:

> Graybosch, C. S. (1988). *The rise of the unions* (Vols. 1–3). New York, NY: Starkfield.

If you are citing only one volume in a multivolume work, and that volume has its own title, use the following format:

> Graybosch, C. S. (1988). *The rise of the union: Vol. 1. Bloody beginnings.* New York, NY: Starkfield.

If the volume you use within the multivolume work does not have its own title, place the volume number in parentheses:

> Bradford, C. (2006). Foucault and punishment. In P. Bishop & L. Gortch (Eds.), *French theories of rehabilitation* (Vol. 2, pp. 231–270). Austin, TX: Wolverine.

Classical Texts

According to Section 6.18 of the sixth edition of the *Publication Manual of the APA* (2010), references to classical texts such as sacred books and ancient Greek verse and drama are usually confined to the text and not given citations in the list of references.

Periodicals

Journal Article

While the name of the article appears in sentence-style capitalization, the name of the journal is capitalized in standard, or headline, style and italicized. The volume number is also italicized, separated from the name of the journal by a comma and, in journals with continuous pagination (see the following text), followed by a comma. Do not use *p.* or *pp.* (in roman type) to introduce the page numbers, which are not italicized.

Journal with Continuous Pagination

Most print journals are paginated so that each issue of a volume continues the page numbering of the previous issue. The reason for such pagination is that most print journals are bound in libraries as complete volumes of several issues, and continuous pagination makes it easier to consult these large compilations. References for journals with continuous pagination do not need to include the issue number after the volume number:

> Hunzecker, J., & Roethke, T. (2012). Reaching the revived: Rehab programs in rural communities. *Review of Recidivism, 4,* 250–262.

Journal in Which Each Issue Is Paginated Separately

The issue number appears in parentheses immediately following the volume number. There is no space between the volume number and the parentheses. Unlike the volume number, which is in italics, the issue number and parentheses are in roman type. In the citation that follows, the quotation marks are necessary only because the title includes a quoted slogan:

> Skylock, B. L. (1991). "Fifty-four forty or fight!": Aggression sloganized in early America. *American History Digest, 28*(3), 25–34.

Non-English Journal Article

When using the original version of an article written in a language other than English, cite the original article, inserting a translation of the title, in brackets, after the original title:

> Kern, W. (1938). Waar verzamelde Pigafetta sijn Maleise woorden? [Where did Pigafetta collect his Malaysian words?]. *Tijdschrift voor Indische taal-, land- en volkenkunde, 78,* 191–200.

English Translation of a Journal Article

If the English translation of a non-English article is cited, give the English title without brackets:

> Sczaflarski, R. (2001). The trumpeter in the tower: Solidarity and legend. *World Psychological Review, 32,* 79–95.

Magazines and Newspapers

Magazines, which are usually published weekly, bimonthly, or monthly, appeal to the popular audience and generally have a wider circulation than journals. *Newsweek* and *Scientific American* are examples of magazines.

Article in Monthly Magazine

> Stapleton, B., & Peters, E. L. (1981, April). How it was: On the trail with Og Mandino. *Lifetime Magazine, 131*(2), 24–23, 57–59.

Article in Weekly or Bimonthly Magazine

> Bruck, C. (1997, October 18). Sentencing guidelines: A change in sight? *Behavior Weekly, 73,* 12–15.

Newspaper Article

Notice that, unlike in journal or magazine citations, page numbers for references to newspapers are preceded by *p.* or *pp.* (in roman type).

> *Newspaper Article with No Author Named:*

> Little left to do before hearing, says criminologist. (1996, January 16). *The Vernon Times*, p. A7.

> *Newspaper Article with Discontinuous Pages:*

> Give all the page numbers, separating them with commas:

> Everett, S. (1996, February 16). An entire state of illegal aliens: How Oklahomans view their "Sooner" past. *The Carrollton Tribune*, pp. D1, D4, D7–8.

Personal Communications

According to Section 6.20 of the sixth edition of the *Publication Manual of the APA* (2010), personal communications such as letters, memos, and telephone and e-mail messages are cited within the text but do not appear in the reference list since the data they provide are not recoverable.

Public Documents

Appendix 7.02: Text Citations of Legal Materials in the sixth edition of the *Publication Manual of the APA* (2010) gives models for citations of such public documents as court decisions, statutes, and other legislative and executive materials, but the appendix also points authors to the eighteenth edition of

The Bluebook: A Uniform System of Citation (2005) for more detailed instructions on how to cite such documents. Here are models for some sources frequently used by criminal justice professionals.

Legislative Hearings

Information concerning a hearing before a legislative subcommittee is published in an official pamphlet, which is cited as follows:

> *Funding for intelligence testing: Hearing before the Subcommittee on Education Reform of the Education Committee, House of Representatives*, 103d Cong., 2d Sess. 1 (1993).

This citation refers to the official pamphlet reporting on the hearing named, which was held in the U.S. House of Representatives during the second session of the 103d Congress. The report of the hearing begins on page 1 of the pamphlet.

Bills and Resolutions

Bills and resolutions are cited by their number, house of origin—Senate (*S.*) or House of Representatives (*H.R.*), in roman type—and year.

Unenacted Federal Bills and Resolutions

The following citation refers to Unenacted Bill Number 2010 from the U.S. Senate:

> Better Pharmaceuticals for Children Act, S. 2010, 103d Cong. (1993).

Enacted Federal Bills and Resolutions

The following citation refers to House Resolution number 192, reported on page 4281 of volume 152 of the *Congressional Record*:

> H.R. Res. 192, 104th Cong., 2d Sess. 152 Cong. Rec. 4281 (1994).

Statutes in Federal Codes

The following entry refers to an act located at section (§) 1043 of title 51 of the *United States Code Annotated*, the unofficial version of the *United States Code*:

> Fish and Game Act of 1990, 51 U.S.C.A. § 1043 *et seq.* (West, 1993).

The material in parentheses indicates that the volume of the *United States Code Annotated* in which the statute is found was published in 1993 by West Publishing. The phrase *et seq.*, Latin for "and following," indicates that the act is also mentioned in later sections of the volume.

Federal Reports

The following citation refers to a report from the House of Representatives. The report number is hyphenated, the first half referring to the year of Congress (101) and the second half to the number of the report.

> H. Rep. No. 101-409 (1990).

> Citation for a document from the Senate would start with *S.* instead of *H. Rep.*

Court Decisions

While the name of the case is italicized in the text citation, it appears in roman type in the full reference.

Unpublished Cases

The following citation refers to a case filed in the U.S. Supreme Court on October 3, 1992, under docket number 46-2097:

> Metrano v. Vandelay Industries, No. 46-2097 (U.S. Oct. 3, 1992).

Published Cases

The following citation refers to a case published in volume 102 of the *Federal Supplement*, beginning on page 482:

> Jacob v. Warren, 102 F. Supp. 482 (W. D. Nev. 1969).

> The decision in the case was rendered by the federal district court for the Western District of Nevada in 1969.

Executive Orders

Executive orders are reported in volume 3 of the *Code of Federal Regulations*. This order appears on page 305:

> Exec. Order No. 13,521, 3 C.F.R. 305 (1993).

Electronic Sources

Section 6.31 of the sixth edition of the *Publication Manual of the APA* (2010) recommends that, in general, a reference for an online source should begin with information that would be present in a reference for a fixed-media (print) source, followed by the additional information needed to allow readers to retrieve the electronic version that you have cited. Usually the additional information will include the URL of the electronic source. The URL (uniform resource locator) is in effect the address of the source on the Internet, and it must be rendered with absolute accuracy. This means that, since the URL is generally the final element in the reference, you should not place a final period at the end of a reference that includes a URL, because the period may be misinterpreted as part of the URL path. You may break a URL that wraps from one line to the next immediately before most punctuation (an exception to this rule is http://   ). Do not add a hyphen at the break.

The DOI System

Because of the ephemeral nature of all content on the Internet—the ease with which material is often moved, altered, or deleted—a group of international publishers is working to establish a reliable, persistent identification system for managing online content. The DOI (digital object identifier) system provides a stable method for finding Internet content by tagging such content with a unique alphanumeric string that will serve as a persistent link to the content's Internet location. The alphanumeric string, called a DOI, is assigned by a registration agency that provides linking services for publishers. The agency called CrossRef, for example, serves as a linking service for materials published by the scientific community. A reader searching for an article whose entry in a reference list includes a DOI can enter that DOI into the *DOI resolver* search field provided by CrossRef.org and be directed to the article, or else to a link for purchasing it.

A DOI can be attached to print as well as electronic material; when a book or an article has been assigned a DOI, that string can be made part of a reference entry, and no further retrieval information is necessary to identify and locate the material. This means that, if you include the DOI in your reference, you need not also include the source's URL. The referencing system presented in the sixth edition of the *Publication Manual of the APA* (2010) provides models for references using the DOI system. Examples of such models follow.

A DOI string usually begins with a *10*, in roman type, followed by a prefix of four or more digits that identifies the organization that has established the DOI for the content. A slash separates the prefix from a suffix, a list of alphanumeric digits, often quite long, determined by the publisher. A DOI typically looks like this:

10.1008/ambi.2119.0568

The four-digit string following the first period—"1008"—is the prefix; the material following the slash is the suffix.

If a DOI has been assigned to an electronic text—an electronic journal article, for example—the string can usually be found on the text's first page near the copyright notice, as well as on the database landing page for the article. It is important to reproduce the DOI in your reference exactly. Do not place a period after the DOI in the reference, since the period may be misinterpreted as part of the DOI.

Here are models for several of the kinds of references commonly required in criminal justice research work.

Books

Electronic Version of Print Book

It is unnecessary to include the name and place of the publisher, even if there is a print version of the book.

> Moore, J. B., Macrory, K. L., Rice, A. D., Traylor, N. P., Wallo, B., Denison, W. L., et al. (2006). *Violence against women in the workplace: An overview.* Retrieved from http://www.crjus.org/lectronic/fb99/indata.html

With editor as author:

> Barton, P. L. (Ed.). (2009). *Sex offenders and residency laws.* Retrieved from https://www.aacjdir.org/reports/survey-205/publications/jinx.htm

Electronic-Only Book

> Marshal, S. (n.d.). *The small-town jail: Myths and realities.* Retrieved from https://www.hillsboro.com/texark.asp?itemPP=20

Electronic Version of Republished Book

> Hollander, W. A. (2003). Causes of aggressive behavior in minority populations. In Y. Dearinger & J. Bowie (Eds.). *The published works of Walter Hollander* (Vol. 2, pp. 12–298). Retrieved from https://www.skinnerset.saunders.com (Original work published 1952.)

Book with DOI

> Alexander, S. (2006). *Juvenile justice in rural Tennessee.* doi:10.4211/07666642

Selection in a Multiauthor Collection

> Chapman, E. T., & Snadon, V. L. (2000). Criminal alien management in a post-9/11 world. In J. Daro, B. Palmer, & R. Palmer (Eds.), *The new age of law enforcement* (pp. 220–251). Retrieved from http://www.okresdef.org/anthol/smithson.html

Unsigned Article in a Reference Work

> Inevitable discovery rule. (1999). In P. Thomas (Ed.) *Encyclopedia of criminology and criminal justice* (4th ed., Vol. 2). Retrieved from https://www.fabenslaw.com/horizondate-71/white.html

Periodicals

Section 6.32 of the sixth edition of the *Publication Manual of the APA* (2010) explains that it is generally unnecessary to include database information in references, since the content coverage of most databases changes over time. For the same reason, it is not necessary to include information identifying such database aggregators as EBSCO, OVID, and ProQuest.

Volume numbers, issue numbers, and page numbers are often not provided for an online source, but if they are, be sure to include them.

Journal Article

If the article is an exact duplicate of a print version, as in a PDF version, give the inclusive page numbers:

> Capulet, T. J., & Finster, R. T. City attorneys as municipal problem solvers. *Community Chamber Review, 4*(2), 24–41. Retrieved from https://www.goldstar.lib.edu

Journal Article with DOI

> Lissette, A. N., & Kingsley, W. P. (2008). Volunteer support for residential watch programs. *City Law and Country Law, 14,* 193–212. doi:10.2148/ffssp.29.134.22677

Online Newsletter Article

> Cordell, T. P. (2012, October). Battered children and the criminal justice system in Texas. *Social Justice Online.* Retrieved from http://www.social/cj.net/newslettr_topic.html

Online Newspaper Article

> Squires, A. (2005, November 12). Hard times for case workers, says mayor. *El Paso Sun Times.* Retrieved from http://www.elpasosun.com/2005-12/12.html

E-Mail

According to Section 6.19 of the sixth edition of the *Publication Manual of the APA* (2010), personal communications such as e-mail messages are cited within the text but do not appear in the reference list since the data they provide are not recoverable.

Message Posted to a Newsgroup, Online Forum, or Discussion Group

Provide the message subject line, or thread, after the exact date. Place any message identifier, if there is one, in brackets after the message subject line:

> Macbeth, C. (2013, April 23). Re: Boomer crimes get serious attention [online forum content]. Retrieved from news.cyberjustice.net/agecrimes.htm

Message Posted to an Electronic Mailing List

> Barnes, P. (2010, January 14). Re: Death toll in drug war [Electronic mailing list message]. Retrieved from http://westex.elmclub/stats/message12/terminal

CD-ROM Source

> Gower, B., & Bensonhurst, P. B. (2001). Reclaiming inner-city environments: The role of the church [CD-ROM]. Humanities Omnibus.

A sample reference page follows.

REFERENCES

Alexander, S. (2006). *Juvenile justice in rural Tennessee*. doi:10.4211/07666642

Barnes, P. (2010, January 14). Re: Death toll in drug war [Electronic mailing list message]. Retrieved from http://westex.elmclub/stats/message12/terminal

Cordell, T. P. (2001, October). Battered children and the criminal justice system in Texas. *Social Justice Online*. Retrieved from http://www.social/cj.net/newslettr_topic.html

Everett, S. (1996, February 16). An entire state of illegal aliens: How Oklahomans view their "Sooner" past. *The Carrollton Tribune*, pp. D1, D4, D7–8.

Hollander, W. A. (2003). Causes of aggressive behavior in minority populations. In Y. Dearinger & J. Bowie (Eds.). *The published works of Walter Hollander* (Vol. 2, pp. 12–298). Tulsa, OK: Leesh. (Original work published 1952.)

Hunzecker, J., & Roethke, T. (2009). Reaching the revived: Rehab programs in rural communities. *Review of Recidivism, 4*, 250–262.

Marshal, S. (n.d.). *The small-town jail: Myths and realities*. Retrieved from https://www.hillsboro.com/texark.asp?itemPP=20

Yarrow, P. T., & Edgarton, S. P. (Eds.). (1987). *The Waco protocol and the prevention of violence*. New York, NY: Halley.

PART 3

HOW TO CONDUCT RESEARCH IN CRIMINAL JUSTICE

6

Organizing the Research Process

The research paper is where all your skills as an interpreter of details, an organizer of facts and theories, and a writer of clear prose come together. Building logical arguments with facts and hypotheses is the way things get done in criminal justice, and the most successful social scientists are those who master the art of research.

Students new to writing research papers sometimes find themselves intimidated by the job ahead of them. After all, the research paper adds what seems to be an extra set of complexities to the writing process. As any other expository or persuasive paper does, a research paper must present an original thesis using a carefully organized and logical argument. But a research paper often investigates a topic that is outside the writer's own experience. This means that writers of research papers must locate and evaluate information that is new to them, in effect, educating themselves as they explore the topic. A beginning researcher sometimes feels overwhelmed by the basic requirements of the assignment or by the authority of the source material.

STRATEGY FOR THE RESEARCH PROCESS

In the beginning it may be difficult to establish a sense of control over the different tasks you are undertaking in your research project. You may not know exactly in which direction to search for a thesis, or even where the most helpful sources of information might be located. If you fail to monitor your own work habits carefully, you may unwittingly abdicate responsibility for the paper's argument by borrowing it wholesale from one or more of your sources.

Who is in control of your paper? The answer must be *you*—not the instructor who assigned you the paper, and certainly not the published writers whose opinions you solicit. If all your paper does is paste together the opinions of others, it has little use. It is up to you to synthesize an original idea through the evaluation of your source material. Although at the beginning of your research project you will be unsure about many elements of your paper—you will probably not yet have a definitive thesis sentence, for example, or even much understanding of the shape of your argument—you can establish a measure of control over the process you will go through to complete the paper. And if you work regularly and systematically, keeping yourself open to new ideas as they present themselves, your sense of control will grow. Here are some suggestions to help you establish and maintain control of your paper.

UNDERSTAND YOUR ASSIGNMENT

A research assignment can fall short simply because the writer did not read the assignment carefully. Considering how much time and effort you are about to put into your project, it is a very good idea to make sure you have a clear understanding of what it is your instructor wants you to do. Be sure to ask your instructor about any aspect of the assignment that is unclear to you, but only after you have thought about it carefully. Recopying the assignment in your own handwriting is a good way to start, even though your instructor may have given the assignment to you in writing. Make sure, before you begin the project, that you have considered the following questions.

ESTABLISH YOUR TOPIC

It may be that the assignment gives you a great deal of specific information about your topic, or that you are allowed considerable freedom in establishing one for yourself. In a criminal justice class in which you are studying issues affecting the American criminal justice system, your professor might give you a very specific assignment—a paper, for example, examining the difficulties involved in locating a halfway house in a suburban community—or you may be allowed to choose for yourself the issue that your paper will address. You need to understand the terms, set up in the assignment, by which you will design your project.

SET YOUR PURPOSE

Whatever the degree of latitude you are given in the matter of your topic, pay close attention to the way in which your instructor has phrased the assignment. Is your primary job to describe a current issue in criminal justice or to take a stand on it? Are you to compare social systems, and if so, to what end? Are you to classify, persuade, survey, analyze? Look for such descriptive terms in the assignment in order to determine the purpose of the project.

DETERMINE YOUR AUDIENCE

Your own orientation to the paper is profoundly affected by your conception of the audience for whom you are writing. Granted, your number one reader is your instructor, but who else would be interested in your paper? Are you writing for the citizens of a community? a group of professionals? a city council? A paper that describes the difficulties involved in locating a halfway house in a suburban community may justifiably contain much more technical jargon for an audience of criminal justice professionals than for a citizens group made up of local business and civic leaders.

DECIDE ON YOUR KIND OF RESEARCH

In your paper you will do one or both of two kinds of research, primary and secondary. *Primary research* requires you to discover information firsthand, often through the conducting of interviews, surveys, or polls. In primary research, you are collecting and sifting through raw data—data not already interpreted by researchers—which you will study, select, arrange, and speculate upon. This raw data may be the opinions of experts or people on the street, historical documents, the theoretical speculations of a famous criminologist, or material collected from other researchers. It is important to carefully set up the method(s) by which you collect your data. Your aim is to gather the most accurate information possible, from which sound observations may be made later, either by you or by other writers using the material you have uncovered.

Secondary research uses published accounts of primary materials. While the primary researcher might poll a community for its opinion on locating a halfway house in their community, the secondary researcher will use the material from the poll to support a particular thesis. Secondary research, in other words, focuses on interpretations of raw data. Most of your college papers will be based on your use of secondary sources.

Primary Source	Secondary Source
A published collection of Thurgood Marshall's letters	A journal article arguing that the volume of letters illustrates Marshall's attitude toward the media
Material from a questionnaire	A paper basing its thesis on the results of the questionnaire
An interview with the police chief	A character study of the police chief based on the interview

The following is a list of *research approaches* commonly used to study and evaluate crime and other variables in criminal justice.

1. *Comparative research* is used to compare various explanations for crime, delinquency, and other important concerns in criminal justice. It also utilizes cross-cultural analysis. The comparative approach can help generate explanations of how something like crime develops and how society reacts to criminal behavior.

2. *Historical research* evaluates the same society at different times and looks at how a societal component like crime has changed with economic and social development.

3. *Biographical research* employs a case study approach to describe and analyze a certain type of criminal, like a serial killer. The biographical approach can help reveal the needs and motivations of the subject.

4. *Patterns of crime research* help determine where a particular kind of crime is typically committed, who commits it, who is victimized, and what the major dimensions of the criminal act are.

5. *Cohort research* examines the impact of certain cohorts on such subjects as crime and delinquency. The cohort approach is effective in delineating increases and decreases in crime rates. It attempts to isolate changes that are attributable to alterations in attitudes or behavior within an age group.

6. *Records research* uses official and unofficial records to examine such topics as how police arrest suspects, how racial discrimination affects sentencing, and how parole boards determine the release of inmates.

7. *Survey research* requires firsthand data to be gathered from prepared questions or statements and then often quantified for description or inference. This is usually done in interviews, especially with open-ended questions, or with such direct-sampling techniques as mail-outs or telephone surveys. For example, a list of statements about how police officers should and should not behave might help determine citizens' opinions concerning the role of the police in their community or society. Or in the case of interviews, the researcher might simply ask respondents the open-ended question, "How do you think police officers should behave?"

8. *Experimentation* uses direct observation and measurement to analyze the effects of different treatments on attitudes and behavior. Experiments are designed to control for the influence of outside variables.

9. *Direct observation* of social phenomena is conducted by trained observers who carefully record selected behaviors.

10. *Content analysis* is a method of analyzing written documents that allows researchers to transform nonquantitative data into quantitative data by counting and categorizing certain variables within the data. Content analysts look for certain types of words or references in the texts and then categorize them or count them.

KEEP YOUR PERSPECTIVE

Whatever type of research you are performing, it is important to keep your results in perspective. There is no way in which you, as a primary researcher, can be completely objective in your findings. It is not possible to design a questionnaire that will net you absolute truth, nor can you be sure that the opinions you gather in interviews reflect the accurate and unchanging opinions of the people you question. Likewise, if you are conducting secondary research, you must remember that the articles and journals you are reading are shaped by the aims of their writers, who are interpreting primary materials for their own ends. The farther you get from a primary source, the greater the possibility for distortion. Your job as a researcher is to be as accurate as possible, and that means keeping in view the limitations of your methods and their ends.

EFFECTIVE RESEARCH METHODS

ESTABLISH AN EFFECTIVE SCHEDULE

In any research project there will be moments of confusion, but establishing an effective procedure can prevent confusion from overwhelming you. You need to design a schedule for the project that is as systematic as possible yet flexible enough so that you do not feel trapped by it. A schedule will help keep you from running into dead ends by always showing you what to do next. At the same time, the schedule helps you to retain the presence of mind necessary to spot new ideas and new strategies as you work.

GIVE YOURSELF PLENTY OF TIME

There may be reasons why you feel like putting off research: unfamiliarity with the library, the press of other tasks, a deadline that seems comfortably far away, and so on. Do not allow such factors to deter you. Research takes time. Working in a library seems to often speed up the clock, so that the hour you expected it to take to find certain sources becomes two hours. You should allow yourself time not only to find material but to read, assimilate, and set it in context with your own thoughts.

A schedule lists the steps of a research project in the order in which they are generally accomplished. Remember that each step is dependent upon the others, and that it is quite possible to revise earlier decisions in light of later discoveries. After some background reading, for example, your notion of the paper's purpose may change, which may, in turn, alter other steps. One of the strengths of a good schedule is its flexibility. The general schedule lists tasks for both primary and secondary research; you should use only those steps that are relevant to your project. Here is a sample schedule:

Task	Date of Completion
Determine topic, purpose, and audience	_____
Do background reading in reference books	_____
Narrow your topic; establish a tentative hypothesis	_____
Develop a working bibliography	_____
Write for needed information	_____
Read and evaluate written sources, taking notes	_____
Determine whether to conduct interviews or surveys	_____
Draft a thesis and outline	_____
Write a first draft	_____
Obtain feedback (show draft to instructor, if possible)	_____
Do more research, if necessary	_____
Revise draft	_____
Correct bibliographical format of paper	_____
Prepare final draft	_____
Proofread	_____
Proofread again, looking for characteristic errors	_____
Meet deadline for final draft	_____

DO BACKGROUND READING

Whether you are doing primary or secondary research, you need to know what kinds of work have already been accomplished in your field of study. A good way to start is by consulting general reference works, though you do not want to overdo it (see following text). Chapter 7 lists specialized reference works focusing on topics of interest to criminal justice students and professionals. You might find help in such volumes even for specific, local problems, such as how to restructure a juvenile treatment program or plan an antidrug campaign aimed at area schools.

Warning: Be very careful not to rely too exclusively on material taken from general encyclopedias. You may wish to consult one for an overview of a topic with which you are unfamiliar, but students new to research are often tempted to import large sections, if not entire articles, from such volumes, and this practice is not good scholarship. One major reason why your instructor has required a research paper from you is to let you experience the kinds of books and journals in which the discourse of criminal justice is conducted. General reference encyclopedias, such as *Encyclopedia Britannica* or *Collier's Encyclopedia*, are good places for instant introductions to subjects; some encyclopedias even include bibliographies of reference works at the ends of their articles. But you will need much more detailed information about your subject to write a useful paper. Once you have learned what you can from a general encyclopedia, move on.

A primary rule of source hunting is to use your imagination. Determine what topics relevant to your study might be covered in general reference works. If, for example, you are looking for introductory readings to help you with the aforementioned research paper on antidrug campaign planning, you might look into such specialized reference tools as the *Encyclopedia of Social Work* (Edwards 1995). Remember to check articles in such works for lists of references to specialized books and essays.

NARROW YOUR TOPIC AND ESTABLISH A WORKING THESIS

Before beginning to explore outside sources, it would be a good idea for you to find out what you already know or think about your topic, a job that can only be accomplished well in writing. You might wish to investigate your own attitude toward the topic, your beliefs concerning it, using one or more of the prewriting strategies described in Chapter 1. You might also be surprised by what you know—or don't know—about the topic. This kind of self-questioning can help you discover a profitable direction for your research.

For a research paper in her criminal justice course, Blake Johnson was given the general topic of studying grassroots attempts to legislate morality in American society. She chose the topic of textbook censorship. Here is the course her thinking took as she looked for ways to limit the topic effectively and find a thesis:

General topic	**Textbook censorship**
Potential topics:	How a local censorship campaign gets started
	Funding censorship campaigns
	Reasons behind textbook censorship
	Results of censorship campaigns
Working thesis:	It is disconcertingly easy in our part of the state to launch a textbook censorship campaign.

It is unlikely that you will come up with a satisfactory thesis at the beginning of your project, but you need a way to guide yourself through the early stages of research toward a main idea that is both useful and manageable. Having in mind a *working thesis*—a preliminary statement of your purpose—can help you select material that is of greatest interest to you as you examine potential sources. The working thesis will probably evolve as your research progresses, and you need to be ready to accept such change. You must not fix on a thesis too early in the research process, or you may miss opportunities to refine it.

DEVELOP A WORKING BIBLIOGRAPHY

As you begin your research, look for published sources: essays, books, and interviews with experts in the field that may help you with your project. This list of potentially useful sources is your *working bibliography*. There are many ways to discover items for the bibliography. The cataloging system in your library will give you titles, as will specialized published bibliographies in your field. The general reference works in which you did your background reading may also list such sources, and each specialized book or essay you find will have a bibliography of sources its writer used that may be useful to you.

From your working bibliography you can select items for the final bibliography, which will appear in the final draft of your paper. Early in your research you may not know which sources will help you and which will not. It is important to keep an accurate description of each entry in your working bibliography in order to tell clearly which items you have investigated, which you will need to consult again, and which you will discard. Building the working bibliography also allows you to practice using the required bibliographical format for the final draft. As you list potential sources, include all the information about each source called for by your format, and place the information in the correct order, using the proper punctuation.

The bibliographical format of the American Sociological Association (ASA), a format required for criminal justice papers by many professional journals, is described in detail in Chapter 4 of this manual. The format of the American Psychological Association (APA) is also used in criminal justice journals and is described in Chapter 5.

WRITE FOR NEEDED INFORMATION

In the course of your research you may need to consult a source that is not immediately available to you. Working on the antidrug campaign paper, for example, you might find that a packet of potentially useful information is available from a government agency or a public interest group at the state or federal level. Maybe a needed book is not held by your university library or by any other local library. Perhaps a successful antidrug program has been implemented in the school system of a city comparable in size to yours but located in another state. In such situations as these, it may be tempting to disregard potential sources because of the difficulty of consulting them. If you ignore the existence of material important to your project, however, you are not doing your job.

It is vital that you take steps to acquire the needed material. In the first case above, you can simply write the state or federal agency; in the second, you may use your library's interlibrary loan procedure to obtain a copy of the book; and in the third, you can track down the council that manages the antidrug campaign by e-mail, mail, or telephone and ask for information. Remember that many businesses and government agencies want to share their information with interested citizens; some have employees or entire departments whose job is to facilitate communication with the public. Be as specific as possible when asking for information by mail. It is a good idea to outline your project—in no more than a few sentences—in order to help the respondent determine the types of information that will be useful to you.

Never let the immediate unavailability of a source stop you from trying to consult it. Also, be sure to begin the job of locating and acquiring such long-distance source material as soon as possible, in order to allow for the various types of delays that often occur while conducting a search from a distance.

EVALUATE WRITTEN SOURCES

Fewer research experiences are more frustrating than half-remembering something worth using from a source that you can no longer identify. You must establish an efficient method of evaluating the sources listed in your working bibliography. Here are some suggestions:

- By examining a book closely you can usually assess the quality of information presented. The preface and introduction give clues to who the author is, why the work was written, and what methodology and research tools were used in the book's preparation. If the author is an acknowledged authority in the field, this fact will often be mentioned in the preface or the foreword.
- The footnotes, in-text references, and the extent and quality of the bibliography (or in some cases, the lack of one) can also serve as clues about the reliability of the work. If few or no original documents have been used, or if major works in the field have not been cited and evaluated, you have reason to question the quality of the book.
- The reputation of the publisher or organization that sponsors a particular book or periodical says something about its value. Some publishers have rigid standards of scholarship and others do not. For example, the requirements of university presses are generally very high, and the major ones, such as Cambridge, Chicago, Michigan, and Harvard, are discriminating publishers of studies in criminal justice.
- A journal article should announce its intention in its abstract or introduction, which in most cases will be a page or less in length.

This sort of preliminary examination should tell you whether a more intensive examination is worthwhile.

Note: Whatever you decide about the source, copy the title page of the book or journal article on a photocopy machine, making sure that all important publication information (including title, date, author, volume number, and page numbers) is included. Write on the photocopied page any necessary information that is not printed there. Without such a record, later on in your research you may forget that you have already consulted a text and find yourself reexamining it.

When you have determined that a potential source is worth closer inspection, explore it carefully. If it is a book, determine whether you should invest the time it will take to read it in its entirety. Whatever the source, make sure you understand not only its overall thesis but also each part of the argument that the writer sets up to illustrate or prove the thesis. You need to get a feel for the shape of the writer's argument, how the subtopics mesh to form a logical defense of the main point. What do you think of the writer's logic and the examples used? Coming to an accurate appraisal may take more than one reading.

As you read, try to get a feel for the larger argument in which the source takes its place. Its references to the works of other writers will show you where to look for additional material and indicate the general shape of scholarly opinion concerning your subject. If you can see the source you are reading as only one element of an ongoing dialogue instead of an attempt to have the last word on the subject, then you can place the argument of the paper in perspective.

USE PHOTOCOPIES AND DOWNLOAD ARTICLES

Most colleges and universities provide online article databases, such as *FirstSearch* and *EBSCOhost,* which allow you to download or print out citations or entire articles. Many articles, however, are still not available in these databases, and you may need to photocopy them in the library.

If you do decide to copy source material from online or published sources, you should do the following:

- Be sure to follow all copyright laws.
- Determine how the library will require you to pay for photocopies. More and more libraries use copy/print card systems that will operate photocopy machines, but if your library's photocopy machines are coin operated, be sure to have the exact change for the photocopy machines. Do not trust the change machines at the library. They are usually battle-scarred and cantankerous.
- Record all necessary bibliographical information on the photocopy. If you forget to do this, you may find yourself making an extra trip to the library just to get an accurate date of publication or set of page numbers.

Important: Remember that photocopying a source is not the same as examining it. You will still have to spend time going over the material, assimilating it in order to use it accurately. It is not enough merely to have the information close at hand or even to read it through once or twice. You should understand it thoroughly. Be sure to give yourself time for this kind of evaluation.

DETERMINE WHETHER TO CONDUCT INTERVIEWS OR SURVEYS

If your project calls for primary research, you may need to interview experts on your topic or conduct an opinion survey among a select group using a questionnaire. Be sure to prepare yourself as thoroughly as possible for any primary research. Here are some tips:

- Establish a purpose for each interview, bearing in mind the requirements of your working thesis. In what ways might your discussion with the subject benefit your paper? Write down your formulation of the interview's purpose. Estimate the length of time you expect the interview to take and inform your subject. Arrive for your scheduled interview on time and dressed appropriately. Be courteous.
- Learn as much as possible about your topic by researching published sources. Use this research to design your questions. If possible, learn something about the people you interview. This knowledge may help you establish rapport with your subjects and will also help you tailor your questions. Take a list of prepared questions to the interview. However, be ready to depart from your scheduled list of questions in order to follow any potentially useful direction that the interview takes.
- Take notes during the interview. Take along extra pens. The use of a tape recorder may inhibit some interviewees. If you wish to use audiotape, ask for permission from your subject. Follow up your interview with a thank-you letter and, if feasible, a copy of the published paper in which the interview is used.

DRAFT A THESIS AND OUTLINE

Since you will never be able to find and assimilate every source pertaining to your subject, especially if it is a popular or controversial one, you should not prolong your research unduly. You must bring this phase of the project to an end—with the option of resuming it later if the need arises—and begin to shape both the material you have gathered and your thoughts about it into a paper. During the research phase, you have been thinking about your working thesis, testing it against the material you have discovered, and considering ways to improve it. Eventually, you must arrive at a formulation of the thesis that sets out an interesting and useful task, one that can be satisfactorily managed within the limits of your assignment and that effectively employs much, if not all, of the source material you have gathered.

Once you have formulated your thesis, it is a good idea to make an outline of the paper. In helping you determine a structure for your writing, the outline is also testing the thesis, prompting you to discover the kinds of work your paper will have to do to complete the task set out by the main idea. Chapter 1 discusses the structural requirements of the formal and the informal outline. (If you have used note cards, you may want to start outlining by first organizing your cards according to the headings you have given them and looking for logical connections among the different groups of cards. Experimenting with structure in this way will lead you to discoveries that further improve your thesis.)

No thesis or outline is written in stone. There is always time to improve the structure or purpose of your paper even after you have begun to write your first draft or, for that matter, your final draft. Some writers actually prefer to do a first draft of the paper before outlining, then study the draft's structure in order to determine what revisions need to be made. *Stay flexible*, always looking for a better connection and a sharper wording of your thesis. The testing of your ideas goes on the entire time you are writing.

WRITE A FIRST DRAFT

Despite all the preliminary work you have done on your paper, you may feel resistance to beginning your first draft. Integrating all your material and ideas into a smoothly flowing argument is a complicated task. It may help to think of this first attempt as only a *rough draft*, which can be changed as necessary. Another strategy for reducing reluctance to starting is to begin with the part of the draft that you feel most confident about instead of with the introduction. You may write sections of the draft in any order, piecing the parts together later. But however you decide to start writing—*start*.

OBTAIN FEEDBACK

It is not enough that you understand your argument; others have to understand it, too. If your instructor is willing to look at your rough draft, you should take advantage of the opportunity and pay careful attention to any suggestions for improvement. Other readers may be of help, though having a friend or a relative read your draft may not be as helpful as having it read by someone who is knowledgeable in your field. In any event, be sure to evaluate carefully any suggestions you receive for improvement. Always remember: The final responsibility for the paper rests with you.

AVOID PLAGIARISM

You want to use your source material as effectively as possible. This will sometimes mean that you should quote from a source directly, whereas at other times you will want to express such information in your own words. At all times, you should work to integrate the source material skillfully into the flow of your written argument.

WHEN TO QUOTE

You should quote directly from a source when the original language is distinctive enough to enhance your argument, or when rewording the passage would lessen its impact. In the interest of fairness, you should also quote a passage to which you will take exception. Rarely, however, should you quote a source at great length (longer than two or three paragraphs). Nor should your paper, or any substantial section of it, be merely a string of quoted passages. The more language you take from the writings of others, the more the quotations will disrupt the rhetorical flow of your own words. Too much quoting creates a choppy patchwork of varying styles and borrowed purposes in which your sense of your own control over the material is lost.

Quotations in Relation to Your Writing

When you do use a quotation, make sure that you insert it skillfully. According to the fourth edition of the *ASA Style Guide* (2010:25), quotations of fewer than 50 words should be integrated into the text and set off with quotation marks:

> "In the last analysis," Alice Thornton (2009) argued that "we cannot afford not to embark on a radical program of fiscal reform" (p. 12).

Quotations of 50 words or longer should begin on a new line, be indented from the left margin, and *not* be set off with quotation marks:

> Blake's (2010) outlook for the solution to the city's problem of abandoned buildings is anything but optimistic:
>> If the trend in demolitions due to abandonment continues, the cost of doing nothing may be too high. The three-year period from 2007 to 2010 shows an annual increase in demolitions of roughly twenty percent. Such an upward trend for a sustained period of time would eventually place a disastrous hardship on the city's resources. And yet the city council seems bent on following the tactic of inaction. (p. 8)

Acknowledge Quotations Carefully

Failing to signal the presence of a quotation skillfully can lead to confusion or choppiness:

> The U.S. Secretary of Labor believes that worker retraining programs have failed because of a lack of trust within the American business culture. "The American business community does not visualize the need to invest in its workers" (Winn 2004:11).

The first sentence in this passage seems to suggest that the quote that follows comes from the Secretary of Labor. Note how this revision clarifies the attribution:

> According to reporter Fred Winn, the U.S. Secretary of Labor believes that worker retraining programs have failed because of a lack of trust within the American business culture. Summarizing the secretary's view, Winn (2004) writes, "The American business community does not visualize the need to invest in its workers" (p. 11).

The origin of each quote must be indicated within your text at the point where the quote occurs as well as in the list of works cited, which follows the text.

Quote Accurately

If your transcription of a quotation introduces careless variants of any kind, you are misrepresenting your source. Proofread your quotations very carefully, paying close attention to such surface features as spelling, capitalization, italics, and the use of numerals.

Occasionally, in order to make a quotation fit smoothly into a passage, to clarify a reference, or to delete unnecessary material, you may need to change the original wording slightly. You must, however, signal any such change to your reader. Some alterations may be noted by brackets:

> "Several times in the course of his speech, the attorney general said that his stand [on gun control] remains unchanged" (McAffrey 2009:2).

Ellipses indicate that words have been left out of a quote:

> "The last time voters refused to endorse one of the senator's policies...was back in 1982" (Laws 2009:143).

When you integrate quoted material with your own prose, it is unnecessary to begin the quote with ellipses:

> Benton raised eyebrows with his claim that "nobody in the mayor's office knows how to tie a shoe, let alone balance a budget" (Williams 2008:12).

HOW TO PARAPHRASE

Your writing has its own rhetorical attributes, its own rhythms and structural coherence. Inserting several quotations into one section of your paper can disrupt the patterns of your prose and diminish its effectiveness. Paraphrasing, or recasting source material in your own words, is one way to avoid the choppiness that can result from a series of quotations.

Remember that a paraphrase is to be written in your language; it is not a near-copy of the source writer's language. Merely changing a few words of the original does justice to no one's prose and frequently produces stilted passages. This sort of borrowing is actually a form of plagiarism. To integrate another's material into your own writing fully, use your own language.

Paraphrasing may actually increase your comprehension of source material, because in recasting a passage you will have to think very carefully about its meaning—more carefully, perhaps, than if you had merely copied it word for word.

Avoid Plagiarism when Paraphrasing

Paraphrases require the same sort of documentation as direct quotes. The words of a paraphrase may be yours, but the idea belongs to someone else. Failure to give that person credit, in the form of references within the text and in the bibliography, may make you vulnerable to a charge of plagiarism.

Plagiarism is the use of someone else's words or ideas without proper credit. Although some plagiarism is deliberate, produced by writers who understand that they are guilty of a kind of academic thievery, much of it is unconscious, committed by writers who are not aware of the varieties of plagiarism or who are careless in recording their borrowings from sources. Plagiarism includes:

- Quoting directly without acknowledging the source
- Paraphrasing without acknowledging the source
- Constructing a paraphrase that closely resembles the original in language and syntax

One way to guard against plagiarism is to keep careful notes of when you have directly quoted source material and when you have paraphrased—making sure that the wording of the paraphrases is yours. Be sure that all direct quotes in your final draft are properly set off from your own prose, either with quotation marks or in indented blocks.

What kind of paraphrased material must be acknowledged? Basic material that you find in several sources need not be documented by a reference. For example, it is unnecessary to cite a source for the information that Franklin Delano Roosevelt was elected to a fourth term as president of the United States shortly before his death, because this is a commonly known fact. However, Professor Smith's opinion, published in a recent article, that Roosevelt's winning of a fourth term hastened his death is not a fact but a theory based on Smith's research and defended by her. If you wish to use Smith's opinion in a paraphrase, you need to credit her, as you should all judgments and claims from another source. Any information that is not widely known, whether factual or open to dispute, should be documented. This includes statistics, graphs, tables, and charts taken from sources other than your own primary research.

7

Information Sources

CRIMINAL JUSTICE ONLINE

The number of criminal justice sources on the Internet is bewildering. Your task as a student is to find high-quality information, so here are some places to start.

Try this first: The National Criminal Justice Reference Service (NCJRS). Also browse the Web sites of organizations such as the following:

- The American Criminal Justice Association
- The National Criminal Justice Association
- World Criminal Justice Library Network
- The U.S. Department of Justice.

Also be sure to check out your own college's criminal justice department Web site. The *John Jay College of Criminal Justice's* Web site, for example, features excellent criminal justice resource pages. Each features topical links that bring you to sites that give you just about everything you might want to know in order to write a typical term paper.

LIBRARY RESEARCH

Truth be known, many college students never enter their college libraries. They miss a lot. For one thing, they waste a lot of time googling. Ever notice how many googled sites are not worth opening? Googling is easy if you want to find a short biography of Barack Obama, but if you need, instead, to research the nesting habits of the White-faced Whistling Duck (*Dendrocygna viduata*) or the founding of Fort Sill, Oklahoma, or the myriad connotations behind the use of the pronoun "it" in seventeenth century metaphysical poetry, you can spend a great deal of time trying to find accurate, detailed information. Sometimes—in fact, very often—such information can be easier to find in a library than on a computer. Just walk in the door, tell the reference librarian what you want, and he or she will show you rows of volumes of information that you can scan many times faster than you can go through the dozens of entries produced by a Google search.

Now, if your first library adventure actually produces results, you may want to hang around a bit and browse through the astounding array of information resources, including the following:

1. *Finding aids* help you locate publications that contain information on your topic. Finding aids include bibliographies and periodical indexes.

2. *Content reference works* contain the type of factual information you are looking for about a particular topic or topics. Content reference works include handbooks, yearbooks, subject dictionaries, and subject encyclopedias.

3. *Guides to the literature* are books or articles that list—and usually describe—reference works that fit in one or both of these two categories. Some guides include discussions of various types of research materials, such as government publications, while others include lists of important book-length studies on topics in a subject field. Researchers can identify criminal justice reference publications by consulting a guide that covers a wide spectrum of fields related to their areas of interest.

Libraries contain information, old and new, that hasn't yet been converted to electronic files. And here's another fact worth bearing in mind: searching for material in an actual hard-copy book, one you can hold in your hands, is different from searching for material in an online file, and sometimes that difference rewards the student who goes hunting in the library rather than on the computer.

PART 4

BRIEF AND APPLIED WRITING ASSIGNMENTS IN CRIMINAL JUSTICE

Chapter

8

Reaction Papers

The purpose of this assignment is to develop and sharpen your critical thinking and writing skills. Your objective in writing this assignment is to define an issue clearly and to formulate and clarify your position on that issue by reacting to a controversial statement.

Completing this assignment requires accomplishing the following six tasks:

1. Select a suitable reaction statement.
2. Explain your selection.
3. Clearly define the issue addressed in the statement.
4. Clearly state your position on the issue.
5. Defend your position.
6. Conclude concisely.

SELECT A SUITABLE REACTION STATEMENT

Your first task is to find or write a statement to which to react. Reaction statements are provocative declarations. They are controversial assertions that beg for either a negative or a positive response. Your instructor may assign a reaction statement, you may find one in a newspaper or on the Internet or hear one on television, or you may construct one yourself, depending on your instructor's directions. The following statements may elicit a polite reply but will probably not stir up people's emotions. They are, therefore, not good reaction statements:

- It's cold out today.
- Plants are beautiful.
- Orange is not green.
- Saturday morning is the best time to watch cartoons.

The following statements, however, have the potential to be good reaction statements because when you hear them you will probably have a distinct opinion about them:

- Abortion is murder.
- Capital punishment is necessary.
- Government is too intrusive.

Such statements as these are likely to provoke a negative or positive reaction, depending on the person who is reacting to them. While they may be incendiary, they are also both ordinary and vague. If your instructor assigns you a statement to which to react, you may proceed to the next step. If you are to select your own, select or formulate one that is provocative, imaginative, and appropriate to the course for which you are writing the paper.

Consider the following examples of reaction statements for criminal justice classes:

- Automatic weapons should be banned.
- DNA samples should be collected from people who are merely suspected of committing crimes.
- Juveniles who commit heinous crimes should be certified and tried as adults.
- People exonerated from crimes they did not commit should be paid substantial restitution.
- The Supreme Court acted politically in securing the election of George W. Bush.
- Surveillance of some domestic telephone calls is necessary to ensure homeland security.

Where do you find good reaction statements? A good way is to think about subjects that interest you. When you hear something in class that sparks a reaction because you either agree or disagree with it, you know you are on the right track. Be sure to write your statement and ask your instructor for comments on it before beginning your paper. Once you have completed your selection, state it clearly at the beginning of your paper.

EXPLAIN YOUR SELECTION

After you have written the reaction statement, write a paragraph that explains why it is important to you. Be as specific as possible. Writing "I like it" does not tell the reader anything useful, but sentences like the following are informative: "Innocent people are being shot down by violent gangs in the inner city. We must crack down on gang violence in order to make the inner city safe for all who live there."

CLEARLY DEFINE THE ISSUE ADDRESSED IN THE STATEMENT

Consider this statement: "Marijuana should be legalized." What is the most important issue addressed in this statement? Is it the idea that use of marijuana may lead to use of more dangerous drugs? Or is it the question of whether or not taxpayers should pay to incarcerate nonviolent individuals who enjoy a widely popular habit? Perhaps some aspects of the statement are more important. As you define the issue addressed in the statement, you provide yourself with some clarification of the statement that will help you state your position.

CLEARLY STATE YOUR POSITION ON THE ISSUE

In response to the marijuana legalization statement, you might begin by saying, "Many future deaths spawned by illegal marijuana production and distribution can be avoided if marijuana is legalized. Furthermore, money saved from abandoning the war on drugs could be returned to taxpayers in the form of tax cuts or used to reduce the national debt." The reader of this response will have no doubt about where you stand on this issue.

DEFEND YOUR POSITION

You should make and support several arguments to support your stand on the issue. When evaluating your paper, your instructor will consider the extent to which you do the following:

- Identify the most important arguments needed to support your position. (When arguing for the legalization of marijuana, did you cite examples of how this has worked efficiently in Portugal or the Netherlands?)
- Provide facts and information, when appropriate. (When arguing that drug war expenditures are too high, you should state the actual amounts of recent expenditures and how the money was used in a wasteful manner.)

- Introduce new or creative arguments to those traditionally made on this issue. (When arguing for legalization, you could list new tactics by drug smugglers that have made the war on drugs more costly and dangerous to pursue.)
- Present your case accurately, coherently, logically, consistently, and clearly.

CONCLUDE CONCISELY

Your concluding paragraph should sum up your argument clearly, persuasively, and concisely. When writing this assignment, follow the format directions in Chapter 3 of this manual. Ask your instructor for directions concerning the length of the paper, but in the absence of further directions, your paper should not exceed five typed, double-spaced pages.

A SAMPLE REACTION PAPER

The following sample reaction paper was written for a criminal justice class at the University of Central Oklahoma. Read it and assess its strengths and weaknesses. How well does it meet the criteria just outlined?

A Negative Response to the Reaction Statement: "Prisons Should Be Run by the Private Sector."

by

Scott M. Houck

For
Innovations in Corrections 4773, Section 3623
Professor Gary Steward

University of Central Oklahoma
October 2009

Privatization of prisons is a mistake. Almost all private-sector industries and corporations are motivated toward the goal of making a profit. Private-sector management is mostly, if not totally, concerned with reducing overhead and increasing profit margin. In the prison setting, it would be too much of a temptation to cut overhead to such an extent that it violates the civil rights of offenders and/or threatens the health and safety of employees, offenders, and the community.

Although the current system is certainly not perfect, government-run prisons are not designed to make a profit for an individual or a group of individuals. A tax cut to the constituency is the main selling point of privatization. However, no matter what you do, it will still cost a lot of money to keep a person incarcerated. That inmate is still entitled to certain rights and liberties that have been granted by the Constitution and upheld in various court decisions. In general, the provisions of many of the rights granted by the Constitution require some form of funding. A profit-based company will test the very limits of humane incarceration by cutting costs on primary and secondary services and necessities provided to inmates. Services such as health programs, food necessities (quantitative and qualitative), treatment programs, vocational training, education, and religious provisions would be cut to increase the profit margin.

In the never-ending struggle for increased profits, personnel expenditures are the first items to be cut back. The result is lower salaries for entry-level employees, lack of or decreased in-service training events, decreased promotional opportunities, short staffing of shifts, increased potential for sick leave abuse, lack of or decreased health and retirement benefits, and reductions in other various personnel benefits.

The problem will begin in the recruitment process. Currently, it is very difficult to recruit qualified people into this thankless profession while paying a modest salary. The correctional officer position is one of the least respected, most underpaid, and most important job classifications in the prison environment. Not only must he supervise offender activity, maintain facility security, update or create reports, communicate with offenders, and defuse potentially violent situations but also try to maintain some form of a family and personal life. It is very difficult to maintain a decent family life when shift work constantly interferes with holidays, birthdays, weekends, and anniversaries. Compound that with minimal financial compensation that is given for this often unrewarding job and it's easy to see the difficulty in attracting qualified people. Private-sector prison management's

(continued)

concern with profit will make prison life even more demanding on everyone by employing just about anyone who applies for a job for as little as possible.

Another major consideration or argument against privatization of prisons is health care provisions. Due to the fact that a privatized prison is a profit-based organization, it is very likely that basic and preventative health care would be drastically reduced. Such procedures or items that are unnecessary to the survival of the offender would not be implemented. If they were provided, the cost would certainly be passed back to the taxpayer. Usually, if not always, when a contract is written by a private company with the government, certain items are included in the basic contract for the housing of the offender, such as bed space, clothing, sundry items, and food. Other items that are not included, but provided at the cost of the state, are things like major surgery, kidney dialysis, some minor surgeries, emergency room costs, and other medical items that possibly come up during a person's incarceration. These "extras" add up quickly to be a major expense, one that is not included in the original contract.

There is much more to privatization of prisons than what meets the eye. On the surface it seems to sound great. However, once one reads "the fine print" of private-sector prisons, it will probably cost the taxpayer more in the long run, while jeopardizing the rights of inmates. Privatization of prisons is a mistake; no one but the company will benefit!

9

Article Critiques
and Book Reviews

ARTICLE CRITIQUES

An article critique evaluates an article published in an academic journal. A good critique tells the reader what point the article is trying to make and how convincingly it makes this point. Writing an article critique achieves three purposes: First, it provides you with an understanding of the information contained in a scholarly article and a familiarity with other information written on the same topic. Second, it provides an opportunity to apply and develop your critical thinking skills as you attempt to critically evaluate the work of a criminal justice professional. Third, it helps you to improve your own writing skills as you attempt to describe the selected article's strengths and weaknesses so that your readers can clearly understand them.

CHOOSING AN ARTICLE

The first step in writing an article critique is to select an appropriate article. Unless your instructor specifies otherwise, select an article from a scholarly journal (such as *Justice Quarterly*, *Criminology*, *Justice Professional*, or *Journal of Criminal Justice*) and not a popular or journalistic publication (such as *Time* or *National Review*). Your instructor may also accept appropriate articles from academic journals in other disciplines, such as history, political science, or sociology.

Three other considerations should guide your choice of an article. First, browse article titles until you find a topic that interests you. Writing a critique will be much more satisfying if you have an interest in the topic. Hundreds of interesting journal articles are published every year.

The following articles, for example, appeared in a 1997 issue (Volume 10, Number 1) of *Justice Professional*:

- "Scamming: An Ethnographic Study of Workplace Crime in the Retail Food Industry"
- "A Writing-Intensive Approach to Criminal Justice Education"
- "Future Trends in Terrorism"
- "Problem-Oriented Policing: Assessing the Process"
- "The Legal Ramifications of Student Internships"
- "Retiring from Police Service: Education Needs and Second Career Planning"

The second consideration in selecting an article is your current level of knowledge. Many criminal justice studies, for example, employ sophisticated statistical techniques. You may be better prepared to evaluate them if you have studied statistics.

The third consideration is to select a current article, one written within the 12 months prior to making your selection. Much of the material in criminal justice is quickly superseded by new studies. Selecting a recent study will help ensure that you will be engaged in an up-to-date discussion of your topic.

WRITING THE CRITIQUE

Once you have selected and carefully read your article, you may begin to write your critique, which should cover the following four areas.

- Thesis
- Methods
- Evidence
- Evaluation

Thesis

Your first task is to find and clearly state the thesis of the article. The thesis is the main point the article is trying to make. In a 1997 issue (Volume 10, Number 1) of *Justice Professional*, Professors Michael Doyle and Robert Meadows of California Lutheran University's Department of Sociology and Criminal Justice published an article entitled "A Writing-Intensive Approach to Criminal Justice Education: The California Lutheran University Model." In this article, coincidentally on the importance of helping criminal justice students become better thinkers through writing, Doyle and Meadows (1997) state their thesis very clearly:

> The purpose of Criminal Justice education is to develop in students the knowledge, judgment, values, and ethical consciousness essential to becoming responsible citizens and leaders in the Criminal Justice system. Equally important is preparing students

to critically evaluate and analyze justice issues through a variety of writing assignments.... By exposing students to a number of reflective, documentary, and analytical writing assignments, a better understanding of the justice process is achieved. (p. 19)

Sometimes the thesis is more difficult to ascertain. Do you have to hunt for the thesis of the article? Comment about the clarity of the author's thesis presentation, and state the author's thesis in your own paper. Before proceeding with the remaining elements of your paper, consider the importance of the topic. Has the author of the article written something that is important for criminal justice students or professionals to read?

Methods

What methods did the author use to investigate the topic? In other words, how did the author go about supporting the thesis? In your critique, carefully answer the following two questions. First, were appropriate methods used? In other words, did the author's approach to supporting the thesis make sense? Second, did the author employ the selected methods correctly? Did you discover any errors in the way he or she conducted the research?

Evidence

In your critique, answer the following questions: What evidence did the author present in support of the thesis? What are the strengths of the evidence presented by the author? What are the weaknesses of the evidence presented? On balance, how well did the author support the thesis?

Evaluation

In this section, summarize your evaluation of the article. Tell your readers several things. Who will benefit from reading this article? What will the benefit be? How important and extensive is that benefit? What is your evaluation of the article? What suggestions do you have for repeating this study or one like it? Your evaluation might begin like the following:

> Doyle and Meadows' article entitled "A Writing-Intensive Approach to Criminal Justice Education: The California Lutheran University Model" is an excellent presentation on both the need for criminal justice students to become better writers and how a variety of writing assignments in the curriculum can enhance a "better understanding of the justice process." If they wish to ensure that students are able to "critically evaluate and analyze" important issues, those involved in criminal justice education would be well advised to consider adopting this model.

When writing this assignment, follow the directions for formats in Chapter 3 of this manual. Ask your instructor for directions concerning the length of the paper, but in the absence of further directions, your paper should not exceed five typed, double-spaced pages.

A Sample Article Critique

The sample article critique that follows was written by a student at the University of Central Oklahoma. As you read it, ask yourself how well this student followed the guidelines just described.

Critique

of

Johnson, J. D., N. E. Noel and J. Sutter-Hernandez. 2000. "Alcohol and Male Acceptance of Sexual Aggression: The Role of Perceptual Ambiguity." *Journal of Applied Social Psychology* 30(6):1186–1200.

by

Judy Garcia

for
Criminology 3633, Section 4651
Professor Tom Albert
University of North Dakota
April 10, 2014

THESIS

Studies have established that alcohol use disrupts cognitive functions, and the fact that alcohol intoxication is a factor in a significant proportion of "date rape" incidents has also been well established by prior research. This study attempts to document the relationship between the level of alcohol consumption and male acceptance of sexual aggression.

The researchers examined how the interpretation of subtle vs. explicit behavioral cues, as related to perceived sexual intent, is impacted by blood alcohol level. In this study, it was expected that the effects of alcohol consumption would be moderated by the behavior of the female, i.e. that when the female appeared receptive to the sexual advances, intoxicated male subjects would consider sexual aggression to be more acceptable than would sober subjects. If the thesis were correct, sexual aggression would be unacceptable even to intoxicated subjects, provided the female's behavior indicated a clear and consistent message of disinterest.

METHODS

Researchers recruited 118 volunteers through posters and class announcements at a medium-sized southeastern state university. The study participants included university staff and students, students' friends, and students' relatives. The study excluded those volunteers with self-reported alcohol/drug problems, alcohol-related arrests (other than one charge of DUI), and those with significant medical or psychiatric problems. Study participants were tested for blood alcohol level (BAL) at the beginning of the session and only those with an initial BAL of 0.00% were included in the study results. To minimize the probability of "demand bias," participants were told the experiment was intended to measure the effect of alcohol on visual acuity and social perceptions.

Subjects were given one of four beverages on the basis of random selection. Those in the control group received ice water, and knew they were part of the control group. The placebo group was given tonic water with 0.08-ml alcohol/kg body weight. The low-dose group received 0.33-ml alcohol/kg body weight, and the moderate-dose group received 0.75-ml alcohol/kg body weight. Drinks were served in such a way that participants, other than those in the control group, had no way of knowing what dosage they had received. Subjects were allowed 20 minutes to consume the beverage and then spent 25 minutes completing a visual-acuity task. At that point,

(continued)

the subjects were asked to participate in two social perception experiments, one of which was the videotaped interaction of a male/female couple at the beginning of a "blind date." Subjects were shown two interactions, one in which the female was enthusiastic about the upcoming date, touched the male's arm, and laughed extensively. In the second scenario, the female maintained a rigid posture, frequently checked her watch, and reminded the male of her need to end the date at the prescribed time. Both sequences ended as the couple left for the movies. Participants were than asked three questions: Should the man try to have sex with the woman, even if it means using force? Would you try to have sex with the woman, even if it meant using force? How responsible would the female be if the male forced her to have sex? Responses to the third question were rated on a 9-point scale ranging from 1 (not responsible at all) to 9 (totally responsible).

The authors of this study were diligent in structuring the experiment in a way that minimized unintended influences: (1) care was taken to ensure that participants were not influenced by their own or the researchers' expectations; (2) there were clear distinctions between the behaviors exhibited by the females in the two scenarios; and (3) variations in the experimental treatments (alcohol dosage) were consistent across experimental groups.

EVIDENCE

Researchers found a strong positive correlation between increased alcohol consumption, acceptance of sexual aggression, and attribution of responsibility to the female. As expected, study participants consistently rejected sexual aggression toward the female in the unreceptive scenario, but accepted sexual aggression toward the female in the receptive scenario, and were more accepting of that aggression as they become more intoxicated. Responsibility for the aggression was assigned to the female in the receptive scenario, to the male in the unreceptive scenario. These findings supported the thesis that unambiguous behavioral cues would be recognized and accepted even when the males were intoxicated, but that in a state of intoxication the males would attend to the most obvious behavioral cues and be more inclined to disregard other inhibitory cues (such as legal and moral sanctions against sexual aggression).

Participants' responses to the three questions indicated that BAL and the acceptance of sexual aggression increased in tandem, as did the attribution of female responsibility for the aggression, and those responses support the thesis of the experiment.

EVALUATION

This study is valuable to anyone who has occasion to be in social situations where alcohol consumption occurs. We know that males are influenced by the effects of alcohol in their interpretation of female behavior that appears to be sexually receptive. In the end, when a woman says no, it should always mean no. However, it is important to understand that this message can be obscured in a haze of intoxication from alcohol. Consequently, women need a clear understanding of how their actions may be perceived and interpreted by male companions who are under the influence of alcohol. And men need to know how alcohol influences their own perception of female sexual receptiveness, and the criminal consequences of sexually aggressive behavior when a woman says no.

In continuing the pursuit of this and related research, it would be instructive to see if these findings apply across broader economic and educational lines, and to study how female intoxication impacts the perception of sexual aggression and the attribution of responsibility for that aggression.

BOOK REVIEWS

Objectives of a Book Review

Successful book reviewers answer two questions for their readers:

- What is the book trying to do?
- How well is it doing it?

People who read a criminal justice book review want to know if a particular book is worth reading, for their own particular purposes, before buying or beginning to read it. These potential book readers want to know what a book is about, and the book's strengths and weaknesses, and they want to gain this information as easily and quickly as possible.

Your goal in writing a book review, therefore, is to help people decide efficiently whether to buy or read a book. Your immediate objectives may be to please your instructor and get a good grade, but these objectives are most likely to be met if you focus on a book review's audience: people who want help in selecting books to read. In the process of writing a review according to the guidelines given in this chapter, you will also learn about the following:

- The content of the book you are reviewing
- Professional standards for book reviews in criminal justice
- Essential steps to reviewing books that apply in any academic discipline

This final objective, learning to review a book properly, has more applications than you may at first imagine. First, it helps you to focus quickly on the essential elements of a book, to draw from a book its informational value for yourself and others. Some of the most successful professional and business people speed-read many books. They read these books less for enjoyment than to assimilate knowledge quickly. These readers then apply this knowledge to substantial advantage in their professions. It is normally not wise to speed-read a book you are reviewing because you are unlikely to gain enough information to evaluate the book's qualities fairly. However, writing book reviews helps you to become proficient in quickly locating the book's most valuable information and paring away material that is of secondary importance. The ability to make such discriminations is of fundamental importance to academic and professional success.

In addition, writing book reviews for publication allows you to participate in the discussions of the broader intellectual and professional community of which you are a part. People in law, medicine, teaching, engineering, administration, and other fields are frequently asked to write reviews of books to help others in their profession assess the value of newly released publications.

SAMPLE BOOK REVIEWS

Before beginning your book review, read the following sample. It was selected because it represents a typical academic review of a book of interest to criminal justice students and professionals. The review below was taken from Volume 102(2) of the *American Journal of Sociology* (1996). In this journal Fleisher's book is reviewed by John M. Hagedorn, of the University of Wisconsin at Milwaukee.

Fleisher, Mark S. 1995. *Beggars and Thieves: Lives of Urban Street Criminals.* Madison: University of Wisconsin Press.

With the right dominating today's politics, C. Wright Mill's admonition for social scientists to criticize "official definitions of reality" has renewed meaning. In that spirit, Herbert Gans has called for a "debunking ethnography" to dispel media stereotypes of poor people. But, given the power of the conservative revolution, are you surprised that some ethnographers are studying the poor in a manner that reinforces stereotypes? Consider Mark Fleisher's *Beggars and Thieves.*

First, Fleisher's book is devoid of structural context. Unlike Bourgeois's recent ethnography (*In Search of Respect: Selling Crack in El Barrio* [Cambridge

University Press, 1995]), which is peppered with economic and social statistics about East Harlem, Fleisher says his book "isn't about" racism or poverty (p. 4). Basically, the street criminals he studied "choose to be outlaws" (p. 16) and their lives are described with no other context than their common history of child abuse: "Their life trajectory was set in motion decades earlier in early childhood, and they can't stop it now" (p. 184). His respondents uniformly adopt a "defensive world-view" related to Hirschi and Gottfredson's low self-control.

Fleisher states that he is studying a "subpopulation" of urban criminals (p. 6), but he later implies he is generalizing to "ordinary criminals standing on street corners" (p. 259). This is especially problematic because of selectivity and lack of variation in his sample. Many refused his requests for interviews, and it was the police and prison officials, not street contacts, who helped him find his informants. He does not say whether he followed accepted practices in snowball sampling and looked for people who might, in some key respects, be "different." He also does not report how he analyzed his data, but I doubt he used analytic induction or other methods based on searching for negative cases. Are most street criminals with an abused family background similar to Fleisher's subjects? We cannot draw that conclusion from this study.

Other studies dispute many of Fleisher's findings. After an abused early childhood, Fleisher's subjects are rejected by their school mates and then form gangs. This may be plausible, but writers such as Thrasher (*The Gang* [University of Chicago Press, 1963]), Short and Strodtbeck (*Group Process and Gang Delinquency* [University of Chicago Press, 1965]), Klein (*The American Street Gang: Its Nature, Prevalence, and Control* [Oxford University Press, 1995]), and Moore (*Homeboys: Gangs, Drugs, and Prison in the Barrios of Los Angeles* [Temple University Press, 1978]) have found gang formation is less related to family factors than to ecological variables and group process. Most gang research also finds wider variation in the family background of gang members.

As Fleisher's abused subjects become adults, they stay uniformly deviant: "My informants never considered the option of getting a straight job...nor did they seriously consider asking someone to help them create a straight lifestyle" (p. 208). While there are undoubtedly some street criminals who disdain work, classic studies from Valentine (*Hustling and Other Hard Work* [Free Press, 1978]) to Bourgeois find most adult street criminals, even those

(continued)

from troubled families, go in and out of low-paying jobs and want a share of the American dream, not a deviant lifestyle.

Beggars and Thieves' view of prison may be too extreme even for some on the right. For Fleisher, who earlier had studied prisons while working as a guard, prisons are "sanctuaries," where street criminals want to be (p. 172) and are "comfortably imprisoned" (p. 179). The harried and hazardous lives of some might cause prison at times to be seen as a relief. However, the consensus from both criminals and criminologists is that U.S. prisons are brutal and overcrowded.

Finally, Fleisher never discusses why he thinks his respondents were truthful. Could his informants have told him what he wanted to hear to get the "street money" he liberally handed out? "Listen darling, you telling him bullshit?" Miss Ann asks T-Cool (p. 59). "For all they knew, I was a new associate warden or the FBI," Fleisher says (p. 59), but does not explore. Of his informants, I was most sympathetic to T-Cool, who once complained (p. 73): "I told you everything you wanted to know. You write a book about me, you get rich, and what the f**k do I get?" Fleisher said he was "annoyed" and "bored" by such questions, which I think social scientists ought to take very seriously.

This is a book avowedly aimed at influencing social policy and selectively supports the right-wing political agenda. Fleisher recommends stepped up removal of poor children from their families and creation of orphanages, called "residential homes." While he opposes incarcerating drug offenders and nonviolent criminals, he simultaneously opposed closing prisons: "Prisons are good business; they employ thousands of lawful citizens and keep violent criminals off the street" (p. 263). Neanderthal politicians can easily ignore the few spots where Fleisher says that his subjects are a small fraction of street criminals and use the book as "social science" to support their demeaning caricatures of the poor. It is not exactly what Gans meant, but I think social scientists need to be "debunking ethnographies" like *Beggars and Thieves*.

ELEMENTS OF A BOOK REVIEW

Book reviews in criminal justice and the social sciences contain the same essential elements of all book reviews. Since social science is nonfiction, book reviews within the disciplines focus less on writing style and more on content and method than reviews of works of fiction. Your book review should generally contain four basic elements, though not always in this order:

1. Enticement
2. Examination
3. Elucidation
4. Evaluation

Enticement

The first sentence should entice people to read your review. Criminal justice studies do not have to be dull. Start your review with a sentence that both sums up the objective of the book and catches the reader's eye. Hagedorn's opening paragraph portray's his view of the book's character directly and crisply.

Examination

Your book review should encourage the reader to join you in examining the book. Tell the reader what the book is about. One of the strengths of Hagedorn's review is that his first two paragraphs immediately reinforce his enticing early sentence with examples of the character of Fleisher's book.

When you review a book, write about what is actually in the book, not what you think is probably there or what ought to be there. Do not tell how you would have written the book, but instead, tell how the author wrote it. Describe the book in clear, objective terms. Tell enough about the content to identify for the reader the major points that the book's author is trying to make. One important goal that you should be careful to cultivate is objectivity. Try to be accurate about the book's point of view—a difficult goal sometimes when its point of view is very different from your own. Do you find Hagedorn's review to be objective?

Elucidation

Elucidate, or clarify, the book's value and contribution to criminal justice by defining (1) what the author is attempting to do and (2) how the author's work fits within current similar efforts in the discipline of criminal justice or scholarly inquiry in general.

The elucidation portion of a book review often provides additional information about the author. Hagedorn has not included information about Fleisher in his review, but it would be helpful to know, for example, if the author has written other books or articles on the same subject, has developed a reputation for exceptional expertise in a certain subject, or is known to have a particular ideological bias. How would your understanding of a book be changed, for example, if you knew that its author is a leader in the radical movement? Always include in your book review information about the author that helps the reader understand how the book fits within the broader picture of social science.

Evaluation

After your reader understands what the book is attempting to do, he or she will want to know the extent to which the book has succeeded. To effectively evaluate a book, you should establish evaluation criteria and then compare the book's content to those criteria. You do not need to define your criteria specifically in your review, but they should be evident to the reader. The criteria will vary according to the book you are reviewing, and you may discuss them in any order that is helpful to the reader. How well has Hagedorn constructed his review around the following criteria?

- How important is the subject matter to the study of culture and society?
- How complete and thorough is the author's coverage of the subject?
- How carefully is the author's analysis constructed?
- What are the strengths and limitations of the author's methodology?
- What is the quality of the writing in the book? Is the writing clear, precise, and interesting?
- How does this book compare with other books written on the same subject?
- What contribution does this book make to criminal justice, and more specifically, to understanding street gangs?
- Who will enjoy or benefit from this book?

When giving your evaluation according to these criteria, be specific. If you write "This is a good book; I liked it very much," you have told the reader nothing of interest or value. Notice, however, the specific character of Hagedorn's evaluative comments on Fleisher's book.

Hagedorn's review as a whole and his conclusion in particular are sharply critical of *Beggars and Thieves*. Hagedorn lists several specific deficiencies of Fleisher's book, claiming it is "devoid of structural content," and deficient in its sampling methodology. Furthermore, Fleisher's conclusions are refuted by a number of notable studies. Overall, Fleisher's work is flawed, according to Hagedorn, by being extremely ideological: it "selectively supports the right-wing political agenda." For each of these criticisms Hagedorn provides specific examples. Your review should follow Hagedorn's example in this respect.

Types of Book Reviews: Reflective and Analytical

Two types of book reviews are normally assigned by instructors in the humanities and social sciences: the reflective and the analytical. Ask your instructor which type of book review she or he wants you to write. The purpose of a *reflective* book review is for the student reviewer to exercise creative analytical judgment without being influenced by the reviews of others. Reflective book reviews contain all the elements covered in this chapter—enticement, examination, elucidation, and evaluation—but they do not include the views of others who have also read the book.

Analytical book reviews contain all the information provided by reflective book reviews but add an analysis of the comments of other reviewers. The purpose is to review not only the book itself but also its reception in the professional community. To write an analytical book review, insert a review analysis section immediately after your summary of the book. To prepare this review analysis section, use the *Book Review Digest* and *Book Review Index* in the library to locate other reviews of the book that have been published in journals and other periodicals. As you read these reviews, use the following four steps:

1. List the criticisms (strengths and weaknesses) of the book found in these reviews.

2. Develop a concise summary of these criticisms, indicate the overall positive or negative tone of the reviews, and discuss some of the most frequent comments.

3. Evaluate the criticisms of the book found in these reviews. Are they basically accurate in their assessment of the book?

4. Write a review analysis of two pages or less that states and evaluates Steps 2 and 3, and place it in your book review immediately after your summary of the book.

FORMAT AND LENGTH OF A BOOK REVIEW

The directions for writing papers provided in Part 1 of this manual apply to book reviews as well. Unless your instructor gives you other specifications, a reflective book review should be three to five pages in length and an analytical book review should be from five to seven pages. In either case, a brief, specific, concise book review is almost always preferred over one of greater length.

10
Annotated
Bibliographies

WHAT IS AN ANNOTATED BIBLIOGRAPHY?

A bibliography is, simply, a listing of written items—essays, reviews, or books—that share one or more important characteristics: they were all written by the same author, perhaps, or they all deal with the work of a particular author or else focus on a particular field of study. The sort of annotated bibliography we will be dealing with in this chapter is a listing and brief description of articles, books, or other sources on a given topic. Depending on the uses for which it is intended, the annotated bibliography may be organized in various ways. For example, if the purpose of the bibliography is to chart the growth and development of critical interest in its topic, then the listed items may appear in chronological order according to the dates when they were first published. Most frequently, however, the items listed in an annotated bibliography are simply organized alphabetically, each one placed either by the last name of its author or, if no author's name is available, by the first important word in its title.

There are usually two components to each item in an annotated bibliography:

1. The bibliographical citation, using one of the standard citation systems, such as the ASA system described in Chapter 4 or the APA system described in Chapter 5

2. The annotation, a brief description or summary (usually 100 to 250 words) of the contents of the source

Sometimes the annotation attempts to be strictly objective in nature, meaning that it only describes the contents and purpose of the source without offering an opinion as to its quality. Scholars in some disciplines refer to this type of objective annotation as an abstract. Another type of annotation offers a brief assessment or appraisal of the source in addition to a description. We'll call this type an evaluative annotation.

Annotated bibliographies are usually limited to a specific theme, area, topic, or discipline. Taken together, the annotations provide a lucid and balanced account or synopsis of the state of research on its subject.

WHY WRITE AN ANNOTATED BIBLIOGRAPHY?

The purpose for writing an annotated bibliography can differ with the audience and the assignment. It might be a project in a course you are taking or a requirement for research in the organization or agency for which you work. (Your supervisor or colleagues may wish to know more about a particular topic.) Depending on the assignment, the annotated bibliography may serve a number of purposes:

- To review the literature on a particular subject
- To illustrate the quality of your research
- To give your research historical perspective
- To illustrate the types of sources available in a given area
- To describe other items relating to a topic of interest to the reader
- To explore a particular subject for further research

WHO USES ANNOTATED BIBLIOGRAPHIES?

One of the great benefits of an annotated bibliography is that it saves time for those who consult it. Since extensive and scholarly annotated bibliographies provide a comprehensive overview of material published on a topic, they can give both researchers and practitioners a swift impression of the types of research already conducted on that topic, as well as a notion of the types of research left to do. An annotated bibliography can make researchers aware of articles or books they should read to advance their own research. Practitioners can scrutinize annotated bibliographies rapidly in order to see what new research their colleagues have conducted or what new practices have been developed in their fields and whether it would be worth their time to locate and read the entire article or book annotated.

There is another important use for annotated bibliographies written by students—there are few ways of developing the descriptive and analytical skills needed in most scholarly disciplines more effectively than by compiling and writing an annotated bibliography. By summarizing and evaluating articles on a particular topic you are both learning valuable information about that topic and gaining confidence in assimilating and connecting facts the way scholars do. You are learning mastery of the material and the mental processes that comprise your discipline.

WHAT IS THE CONTENT OF AN ANNOTATED BIBLIOGRAPHY?

The specific structure and approach to writing an annotated bibliography may vary with the professional community for which you are writing it. For example, in some situations an annotated bibliography may have an introductory paragraph or two in order to define its audience, purpose, rationale, and topic. In other situations, it may not. The following sections provide a list and a description of the most commonly found elements of an annotated bibliography.

INTRODUCTION

In addition to defining your audience and expressing your purpose, your introduction should also describe the scope of your bibliography (the specific areas or types of works upon which you are focusing) and explain the reasons why you have limited your exploration to these parameters. It is also important to let your reader know clearly what kind of annotations you are providing, whether objective or evaluative. If you say your annotations are objective, then you are telling your reader that every opinion or theory expressed in each annotation belongs to the source and its author. If, however, the annotation is evaluative, then at least some of the material in it expresses *your* opinion about the quality of the source—an opinion that the writer might not share. You must not let your reader think that every opinion or theory expressed in the annotation belongs to the source when, in fact, that is not the case.

CITATIONS

Like a regular (unannotated) bibliography or a works-cited page at the end of a research paper, an annotated bibliography provides a full bibliographic entry for each source it lists. Make sure you follow a bibliographical format approved by your instructor or by the publication for which you are writing. Chapters 4 and 5 of this manual give guidelines for the ASA and APA systems of bibliography, respectively.

ANNOTATIONS

For most annotated bibliographies, the annotations should be one or two paragraphs that together range from about 100 to 250 words. To some extent the conventions of the professional community in which you are writing will dictate the contents of your annotations, as well as your specific purpose and audience. If you are writing your annotated bibliography for a course, your instructor will provide guidelines. It can be helpful to your reader if you establish a consistent form for your annotations, perhaps beginning each time with a clear statement of the source's thesis, then a brief description of the argument used to prove or justify that thesis, followed, if required, by your evaluation of the work's value and achievement.

To Quote or Not to Quote?

How much of your annotation should be direct quoting as opposed to your own wording? This is an important question to address, and one whose answer depends to a large extent on the uses you project for your bibliography. Importing the thesis sentence directly from the source, for example, may help you to be accurate about the source's purpose—but it may also establish a tone or a level of complex reasoning that the rest of a brief annotation cannot sustain. You do not want to give the impression that you are merely pasting together passages from the source without having thoroughly understood them yourself. Remember: while the style and tone of the source belong to the source's author, the style and tone of the annotation belong to you. You want your annotation, though it is small, to have the coherence and confidence of a well-made paragraph.

Depending on your project or assignment, your annotations may provide one or more of the following.

Summation

As stated earlier, while *some* annotations offer evaluative comments, *most* annotations summarize the source. Here is a tip about summarizing: Although it is logical, when summarizing, to ask yourself what the source is about, it is rarely a good gambit to begin a brief annotation with the phrase, "This source is about…" Why not? Because a sentence beginning with these words cannot help but end with a generalization about the source's subject that will be vaguer than a simple restatement of the source's thesis.

Here are introductory sentences from two objective annotations of the same source. Which sentence more effectively sets up the rest of the annotation?

1. Rafelson's article is about racial profiling and how it is misused in school counseling programs.
2. Rafelson argues that racial profiling should be prohibited in school counseling programs because it results in preferential treatment for certain minorities at the expense of others.

Sentence one establishes the *topic* of the source, but sentence two establishes the *thesis*, which is a more comprehensive and necessary task.

After relating the thesis of the source, you might describe such elements as methodology, results, and conclusions. The required length of the annotations will determine how detailed your summary should be.

EVALUATION

Your assignment may require you to include a brief critique or appraisal in each annotation. If you are writing evaluative annotations, ask yourself the following questions: What is the overall goal of this source? Does the source achieve its goal? Do you find the contents of the source useful in relation to your own research? How does the source compare with other sources in your bibliography? Is the information reliable? How biased is it?

REFLECTION

If you are compiling this annotated bibliography in order to facilitate your own research project, you will probably want to examine the perspective taken in each source to ascertain how it fits into your research on the topic. The perspective could be a political one (liberal or conservative), a subject-matter perspective (sociological, psychological, medical, etc.), or some other perspective. It might help to point out similarities or contradictions between sources. For example, you might say, "Like Munson, Eversol approaches racial profiling from a sociological perspective. However, while Munson focuses on how law enforcement has used racial profiling to increase the probability of arrests, Eversol analyzes the practice of businesses profiling Blacks to apprehend shoplifters." You might then want to reflect on how this source has changed how you think about your topic and how it fits into your research project.

SAMPLE ANNOTATED BIBLIOGRAPHIES

The following sample short-version annotated bibliographies are fictitious. They describe articles that might be written on racial profiling. The annotations in this example are like abstracts, since they are summative and contain no evaluative component.

Annotated Bibliography

Racial Profiling

Jones, William B. 2010. "Targeting Blacks in Shoplifting Surveillance: Unjust and Inaccurate." *Social Issues* 26(2):37–45.

> Jones argues that while racial profiling of shoplifters by major department stores is an unjust practice, the process also fails to target those most

likely to shoplift. No data exists that supports the probability that blacks are more likely to shoplift than other racial groups. Targeting blacks in surveillance procedures only increases the opportunity to catch those blacks that shoplift and improves the chances of success for whites that shoplift.

Monroe, Victor G. 2012. "Using Racial Profiling to Impede the Trafficking of Illicit Drugs." *Drug Enforcement Bulletin*, August 14, pp. 42–45.

Using racial profiling to impede drug trafficking, contends Monroe, is not a good way to decrease the flow of illicit drugs in the United States. Race should never be a factor in probable cause, and the harm done from this practice far outweighs any perceived benefit. He supports applying legal sanctions to those practicing racial profiling to catch drug traffickers.

Arnold, Eugene H. 2013. "Terrorism and Racial Profiling." *Journal of International Terrorism* 17(3):510–518.

Arnold believes that the use of racial profiling to help control terrorist activities is both justified and necessary. Applying a random intervention policy wastes precious time investigating those with little potential for terrorism, while allowing those most likely to put others in harm's way—middle eastern, Muslim males between 15 and 29 years of age—to avoid careful examination.

Here are some sample entries for the same sample articles taken from a longer, abstract-type bibliography.

Annotated Bibliography

Racial Profiling

Jones, William B. 2010. "Targeting Blacks in Shoplifting Surveillance: Unjust and Inaccurate." *Social Issues* 26(2):37–45.

Jones argues that while racial profiling of shoplifters by major department stores is an unjust practice, the process also fails to target those most likely to shoplift. No data exists that supports the probability that blacks are more likely to shoplift than other racial groups. Targeting blacks in surveillance procedures only increases the opportunity to catch those blacks that shoplift and improves the chances of success for whites that shoplift. Jones takes issue with Elsner and Squires, whose study published in the

(*continued*)

June 2009 *Journal of Crime and Criminology* supports racial profiling on the basis of its cost-effectiveness. While Jones concedes that targeting a single race reduces the cost to businesses by allowing them to streamline their security operations, he argues that this cost-effectiveness is offset by the increase in whites shoplifting. Instead of using racial profiling, Jones recommends that businesses invest in more extensive human relations training for security personnel.

Monroe, Victor G. 2012. "Using Racial Profiling to Impede the Trafficking of Illicit Drugs." *Drug Enforcement Bulletin*, August 14, pp. 42–45.

Using racial profiling to impede drug trafficking, contends Monroe, is not a good way to decrease the flow of illicit drugs in the United States. Race should never be a factor in probable cause, and the harm done from this practice far outweighs any perceived benefit. Monroe supports this argument by discussing recent, disastrous attempts of government agencies in six different countries to base a drug interdiction policy on data regarding race. While two of the six countries, the Netherlands and Luxembourg, reported a slight drop in the importation of marijuana and cocaine during their interdiction campaigns, all six of the countries eventually abandoned racial profiling for two reasons: the legal tangle it caused in the courts and the negative effect such profiling had on race relations within each country. Monroe provides information charting the effects of racially based drug policing programs on morale and social and economic development among minority populations in the United States. A former state attorney general, Monroe concludes with an argument supporting the application of legal sanctions against those practicing racial profiling to catch drug traffickers.

Arnold, Eugene H. 2013. "Terrorism and Racial Profiling." *Journal of International Terrorism* 17(3):510–518.

Arnold believes that the use of racial profiling to help control terrorist activities is both justified and necessary. Applying a random intervention policy wastes precious time by focusing on those with little potential for terrorism, while allowing those most likely to put others in harm's way—middle eastern, Muslim males between 15 and 29 years of age—to avoid careful examination. Arnold constructs a three-part defense of his position, establishing first the legal argument for racially geared antiterrorist policies, then the economic argument and, finally, what he calls the moral argument. Borrowing heavily on scripture from both the Old Testament and the Koran in the last third of the article, Arnold defines a religious imperative for racial profiling that, he admits, will not be to everyone's taste but that may provide direction and control for a problem that threatens to spiral out of control.

11

Writing a Police Report

WHAT IS A POLICE REPORT?

Police officers investigate a variety of incidents, from minor traffic violations to multiple homicides, on which they must write reports. A police report is a record of the incident being investigated. Remember that many different readers will probably need to read the report and understand the information preserved in it (Marta 2004:16). In his book *Painless Police Report Writing*, Joseph Davis (2004) gives a concise definition of the police report:

> Traditionally, a report meant a "police report" or narrative you have to write after completing an investigation. But, actually, reports take many different forms. A report is defined as the following: any documentation recorded on a departmental form, or other approved medium (computer disks), and maintained as a permanent record. (p. 2)

Prior to the use of computers to store and retrieve data, all the pertinent information (who, what, where, when, why, and how) comprising a police report was contained in the *narrative*—the story of what happened. Using the computer to store and retrieve data has radically altered the traditional police report format. Most of the information is now categorized at the front of the report to facilitate cross-referencing and data retrieval. The narrative is a much shorter section of the overall report than in the past. Many past and present police administrators believe that the need to categorize details for computer access has caused the "storytelling" component of the typical police report to decline in precision, objectivity, and accuracy. So officers who show they can write good reports, especially narratives, are highly valued and much more likely to move up in rank.

WHY WRITE POLICE REPORTS?

Few elements of police work are more important than the ability to write reports that others can understand and use to make judgments. According to the San Francisco Office of Budget Analyst, "Report writing deficiencies are…one of the factors contributing to the high number of cases turned down for prosecution by the DA's office" ("Police Report Writing" n.d.).

As in reports produced in such professions as the law, medicine, and business management, it is essential that a police report record the circumstances and events that occur in an opportune, precise, and comprehensible manner. Timeliness is a crucial factor, too. Think of the last time you went to the doctor. Remember the questions that either the doctor or the doctor's assistant asked you, and the obvious care with which he or she wrote down your answers? The sooner you can record your information, the less likely you are to leave out something important. Whether you like it or not, writing reports goes with the territory, and part of being a good officer is being a good report writer.

WHO USES POLICE REPORTS?

The courts, law enforcement personnel, insurance companies, and the media all use police reports regularly to make judgments that affect people's lives. Yet important as it is that officers produce coherent, accurate reports, the sad fact is that in most police departments throughout the country police report writing is the most poorly performed aspect of police work. The sheer cost of ineffective police reports, not only in financial terms but also in emotional terms, is staggering (Ross and Plant 1977:9).

TIPS FOR WRITING EFFECTIVE POLICE REPORTS

Using proper grammar and sentence structure is essential in writing good police reports. These writing components are reviewed in Chapter 2 of this manual, and we strongly recommend that you read this chapter carefully and incorporate what you learn there into your report writing. Remember that what you write in your report is not just for someone else to read but will also allow you to recall fully what actually occurred. So what you write and how you write it are vital in communicating to yourself as well as to others. All other components of the job become easier once a police officer becomes a good report writer.

Here are three fundamental tips for making the sentences in your report as effective as possible.

PUT THE SUBJECT FIRST

Writing simple, understandable sentences is an important part of good report writing. People want to know what happened, and how you phrase this information, sentence by sentence, influences their ability to understand actions and events, human behavior and motivations. Don't clutter your sentences with unnecessary prepositional phrases, and always work to put the subject first in the sentence. Check the following sentences for problems with these guidelines:

1. After hitting the storeowner, the suspect ran west down the street in front of the building.
2. If you wish to fulfill the entrance requirements, you must pass a vision test.
3. Because of the glare of the flames that were engulfing the building, the officer had to cover her eyes with both hands.
4. With blood dripping from two gunshot wounds in her leg, the victim rolled under an automobile parked in front of the building.
5. Eager to see the dog, as it was reported to roam the neighborhood often, I drove slowly around the block.

If you read these sentences carefully—and you must read slowly and carefully to understand their meaning—you discover that each is muddled with introductory elements that obstruct the noun or pronoun subject, requiring the reader to backtrack in order to understand the meaning.

Looking at the first sentence, we find a four-word prepositional phrase blocking our access to the thing that the sentence is actually about—its subject—which is the *suspect*. Here is a way to rewrite this sentence that puts the subject first:

The suspect struck the storeowner and then ran west down the street in front of the building.

Now, before looking at the rewrites that follow, reconstruct the remaining four sentences so that they read more clearly and understandably. Do your sentences look anything like the following sentences?

- You must pass a vision exam in order to satisfy the entrance requirements.
- The officer had to cover her eyes with both hands because of the intense flames engulfing the building.
- The victim was bleeding from two gunshot wounds in her leg while she rolled under a car parked in front of the building.
- I drove slowly around the block looking for the dog that was reported to often wander the neighborhood.

Putting the subject first makes the meaning of the sentence easier to ascertain. It also makes the sentence easier to write. It's almost impossible to get confused about what you're trying to communicate when you begin with the subject of the sentence. On the other hand, beginning a sentence with an introductory word group can cause you to lose your grip on the point you are trying to make (Ross and Plant 1977:127).

Be Careful with Pronouns

How you use pronouns—words such as *he, she, it, him, her, they,* and *them* that substitute for nouns—is very important in describing the events accurately and understandably. The fundamental rule for using a pronoun is that it (the pronoun) must always *agree* with the noun for which it is substituting. Since both nouns and pronouns can be singular or plural, you must always use a singular pronoun to substitute for a singular noun and a plural pronoun for a plural noun. To break this rule is to confuse anyone who reads your report.

Another important thing to remember about using a pronoun is that it must only refer to the noun for which it is substituting, which is usually the noun immediately preceding it. Not following this proximity principle can be very confusing to the reader. See if you can determine how these principles are misapplied in these four examples:

1. The suspect pulled a gun and demanded money from the victim. He ran down the street and into an alley.
2. The men called for help. He was losing a great deal of blood.
3. The patrol car pursued the speeding car. They were intercepted at the first stop light.
4. The victim approached the suspect. She says she was terrified by the gun.

Careful examination of the first example reveals a breakdown in the proximity principle which, if applied here, suggests that it was the *victim* who fled down the street and into an alley. How can the sentences in the first example be rewritten to indicate clearly that it was the suspect, and not the victim, who fled?

Rewrite the remaining examples to correct the pronoun reference problems.

Use Active Verbs

The next item of grammar to consider in your quest to build strong, clear sentences is the relationship of the subject to the verb. The easiest sentences to write and to understand are usually those in which the subject performs the action described in the sentence. But it is easy to muddy the meaning in even a relatively simple construction. Compare the following two sentences:

1. The suspect pulled a gun.
2. A gun was pulled by the suspect.

Which sentence is sharper, cleaner, more energetic? Clearly the first one. The verb in the first sentence—"pulled"—is an *active voice* verb, meaning that it conveys an action that the subject performs. The verb in the second sentence—"was pulled"— is a *passive voice* verb, which means it conveys an action that is done to the subject. Notice that the second sentence, the one with the passive voice verb, reverses the order in which the first sentence claims our attention. The first sentence draws our attention immediately to the actor, the suspect. The second sentence focuses our attention on the object, the gun. The second sentence, in a sense, disconnects the action from the actor. These two sentences are both simple and understandable, but when you are trying to convey more complicated actions and behaviors, a reliance on passive voice verbs in a lengthy sentence can obscure meaning.

Let's recap. The first focus in most of your sentences should be the *subject*. The next focus should be *what the subject does*.

Examine these three examples and rewrite them to make the verb, and thereby the sentence, active:

1. The median was crossed by the truck.
2. The gun was fired by the female suspect.
3. The victim was hit by a foul ball.

Notice that the use of active verbs usually saves both time and space. Generally it takes fewer words to report what happened in a direct and active manner. Sentences constructed with passive verbs take longer to write and longer to read. Since you want the meaning you communicate to be as precise as possible, make sure that the person or thing about which you are reporting has actually said or done something—and show that action with your verb.

EMPLOY A CLEAR WRITING STYLE

Unlike creative writers who must use all the resources of the language to create interest in what they write or else lose their audience, a police officer is only required to report what happened and what he or she did. You might say that the officer has a captive audience, and no sell is necessary. So the major goals of a police report are accuracy and readability. Every sentence should follow the same grammatical precedent—subject first, followed by the verb, and then by other information that adds to the overall clarity of what actually occurred, with special care to keep pronouns correctly aligned with the proper nouns. The style should never vary; always use direct statements that are easy to read and understandable. According to Ross and Plant (1977):

> If you master these simple rules through practice and deliberate effort, you will find that the whole writing process becomes simpler and faster. One of the major difficulties with reporting is that the officer so often feels under some sort of compulsion to dress up his reports. Resist that feeling! A police report is not the place for the creative ebb and flow of majestic or mood inspiring language. You're not writing to entertain or to stimulate your readers. You're not conveying emotion or editorializing on the actions you are reporting. Confine yourself to just what happened. Concentrate on WHO DID WHAT TO WHOM AND WHY. (p. 23)

ASSEMBLE MEANINGFUL INFORMATION

Police report writing begins when the officer arrives at the scene of an investigation, which may be the location of an accident, a robbery, a homicide, or some other type of incident. Officers gather information about the incident in a variety of ways, using direct observation, interviews, and forensic data.

When possible, police officers begin taking notes as soon as they arrive at the investigation scene. Note-taking is pretty much an individual activity and can be accomplished in a variety of ways. What's important is that these notes, along with other data, must allow the officer to recreate the incident accurately and clearly when he or she writes the report. We recommend that you take your notes in a loose-leaf notebook because you may need to rearrange the information when writing the report. The final report will be much easier to write if you maintain good organization in the note-taking process.

Standard report forms listing prompts for various kinds of information, like date, time, place, type of incident, type of vehicle, etc., are available in most jurisdictions. These report forms are commonplace in most police departments, but they don't contain prompts that cover all the different types of information you might uncover. So good note-taking is essential, and while the final report should be short and concise, it's best to take everything down at the scene for possible later reference.

Police officers often must testify in court and answer questions from the prosecutor, the defense, and the judge. Recollection of specific details can be difficult, and reference to detailed, thorough notes taken in the field can be very helpful in testifying.

It is vital to gather and record information as systematically as possible in order to cover a crime scene comprehensively. This is why police officers, as they gather data for a report, make use of a tried-and-true organizational formula, a set of questions known generally as the five Ws and an H—WHO, WHAT, WHERE, WHEN, WHY, and HOW. It's important to remember that these six questions are not as elementary as they seem but are, in fact, starting points for other, more detailed questions (Marta 2004:16). The following listings from Ross and Plant (1977:31–34) document the multiple dimensions of each:

- WHO
  - a. Discovered the crime?
  - b. Reported the crime?
  - c. Saw or heard anything of importance?
  - d. Had a motive for committing the crime?
  - e. Helped the one committing the crime?
  - f. Committed the crime?
  - g. Associated with the subject?
  - h. Is associated with or is known to the witness?
- PHYSICAL DESCRIPTION
  - a. Height
  - b. Weight

    c. Nationality

    d. Complexion

    e. Eyes (alert—normal—droopy); eye color

    f. Glasses (if any)

    g. Visible scars, marks, tattoos

    h. Age

    i. Hat (if any)

    j. Hair (color and cut)

    k. Beard, moustache, sideburns

    l. Shirt

    m. Necktie or scarf

    n. Jacket or coat

    o. Trousers or dress

    p. Shoes

    q. Weapons (what kind and how used)

- METHOD OF ESCAPE

    a. Direction

    b. License

    c. Vehicle description

    d. Additional remarks

- WHAT

    a. Happened?

    b. Crime was committed?

    c. Are the elements of the crime?

    d. Were the actions of the suspects?

    e. Do the witnesses know about the case?

    f. Evidence was obtained?

    g. Was done with the evidence?

    h. Tools were employed?

    i. Weapons were used?

    j. Knowledge, skill, or strength was necessary to commit the crime?

    k. Means of transportation was used in the commission of the crime?

    l. Was the motive?

    m. Was the method of operation?

- WHERE

    a. Was the crime discovered?

    b. Was the crime committed?

    c. Were the suspects seen?

    d. Were the witnesses during the crime?

    e. Was the victim found?

    f. Were the tools and weapons obtained?

    g. Did the suspect live?

    h. Did the victim live?

    i. Did the suspect spend his or her leisure time?

    j. Is the suspect now?
    k. Is the suspect likely to go?
    l. Was the suspect apprehended?

- WHEN
    a. Was the crime committed?
    b. Was the crime discovered?
    c. Was notification received?
    d. Did the police arrive at the scene?
    e. Was the victim last seen?
    f. Was the suspect apprehended?

- WHY
    a. Was the crime committed?
    b. Was a particular type of tool used?
    c. Was the particular method employed?
    d. Was a witness reluctant to talk to you?
    e. Was the crime reported?

- HOW
    a. Was the crime committed?
    b. Did the suspect get to the scene?
    c. Did the suspect get away?
    d. Did the suspect get the information necessary to enable him or her to commit the crime?
    e. Was the crime planned?
    f. Did the suspect secure the tools and weapons?
    g. Were the tools and weapons used?
    h. Much damage was done?
    i. Much property was stolen?
    j. Much knowledge, skill, or strength was necessary to commit the crime?

Answers to these questions constitute the vital elements of a police report, but only if they are accurate and objective. Good note-taking assembles only the facts. That way when an opinion is called for in the narrative section of the report, as it usually will be, it can be labeled opinion and not presented as factual.

WHAT IS IN THE NARRATIVE OF A GOOD POLICE REPORT?

The narrative section of the report tells what happened by linking the information that has already been assembled in the five Ws and an H into an accurate and meaningful story. Since the event has already happened, you should write the narrative using the past tense. Follow the writing suggestions listed in the preceding sections, especially those explained in the section "Tips for Writing Effective Police Reports." Remember that your vocabulary must be precise, objective, and accurate.

SAMPLE NARRATIVE POLICE REPORTS

We now provide three examples of police reports retrieved from a small police department in a municipality contained within a large metropolitan area. For each report you will find the following:

1. The report as originally filed
2. A marked-up copy of a revision of the report
3. An un-marked copy of the revised report

To gain the most from these examples, read the original report for each one first. As you read these original reports, imagine that you have written them yourself and that you are now in court, being cross-examined by attorneys for both sides in a case that has arisen from the incident reported. Notice how seemingly insignificant inaccuracies in reporting can lead to misinterpretations of what actually occurred. Writing police reports, you will discover, is all about accuracy—clearly and unambiguously explaining what happened. After reading the original reports, carefully examine the edited revisions, and then read the revised versions.

As you complete this task you will discover many ways to make your reporting more accurate.

Incident Report 1—Original

Springfield Police Department
Narrative Information

Smith, Tom

On 05-02-2012 at approximately 0240 hours, I was on patrol in the 6600 of Lowe Ave. When I noticed a red pick-up truck driving through the yard of 6612 Lowe Ave and then across into the yard of 6606. I was able to get behind the vehicle in the drive way of 6606 Lowe, then the vehicle went out on to Lowe Ave. I engaged my emergency lights, the vehicle then run up on the curb in front of 6604 Lowe. The vehicle then drove up driveway of 6604 Lowe and stopped. I exited my patrol vehicle and when I got up to the drivers side window, I noticed the driver reaching under his seat for something. I opened the drivers door and advised him not to move at the point the driver kept reaching under the seat, I re-holstered my weapon and grab the drivers lift arm and pulled him out of the vehicle and layed him on the ground. Once he was hand chuffed, I went back to the vehicle and did not find any weapon under or around the seat. The driver who was identified

(continued)

---

as Roberto Gonzales had a strong odor of alcohol and urine about his person. Once I got him up on his feet I noticed that his eyes were bloodshot and his speech was slurred and was unsteady on his feet, and was weaving. Once in the patrol vehicle I read the implied consent law, and Mr. Gonzales advised "NO" to the test. Superior Towing arrived to pick up the vehicle. I drove back to check the yards that he had drove through to find any damages that he might have done and found nothing. I transported Mr. Gonzales to the Springfield Police Department to fill out the necessary paper work. Mr. Gonzales was charged with Driving Under the Influence of Alcohol. I transported Mr. Gonzales to Springfield County Jail. At approximately 0339 hours I released Mr. Gonzales to Springfield County, E.O.R

Incident Report 1—Revisions*

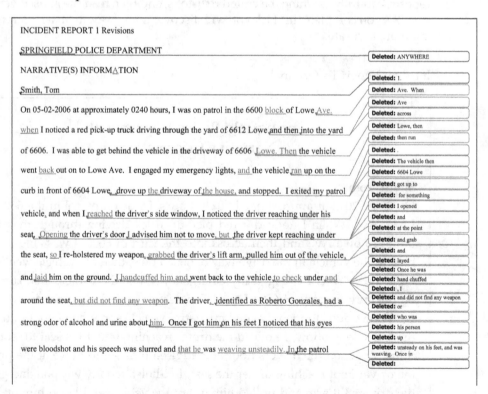

* This and succeeding samples have been taken from Microsoft® Word Student and Teacher Edition 2003 for PCs, version 11.0.5960.0. The concepts and theory being taught are applicable in other, similar versions of software.

vehicle I read <u>Mr. Gonzales</u> the implied consent law, and <u>he answered</u> "NO" to the test. Superior

| | Deleted: Mr. Gonzales advised |

Towing arrived to pick up the vehicle. I drove back to check the yards that he had <u>driven</u>

| | Deleted: drove |

through to find any damage<u>,</u> that he might have done and found nothing. I transported Mr.

| | Deleted: s |

Gonzales to the <u>Springfield</u> Police Department<u>, where I filled</u> out the necessary paper work. Mr.

| | Deleted: Anywhere |
| | Deleted: to fill |

Gonzales was charged with Driving <u>under</u> the Influence of Alcohol. I transported Mr. Gonzales

| | Deleted: Under |

to <u>the</u> <u>Springfield</u> County Jail. At approximately 0339 hours I released Mr. Gonzales to

| | Deleted: Anywhere |

<u>Springfield</u> County. E.O.R.

| | Deleted: Anywhere |

Incident Report 1—Final Report

Springfield Police Department
Narrative(s) Information

Smith, Tom

On 05-02-2012 at approximately 0240 hours, I was on patrol in the 6600 block of Lowe Ave. when I noticed a red pick-up truck driving through the yard of 6612 Lowe and then into the yard of 6606. I was able to get behind the vehicle in the driveway of 6606 Lowe. Then the vehicle went back out on to Lowe Ave. I engaged my emergency lights, and the vehicle ran up on the curb in front of 6604 Lowe, drove up the driveway of the house, and stopped. I exited my patrol vehicle, and when I reached the driver's side window, I noticed the driver reaching under his seat. Opening the driver's door I advised him not to move, but the driver kept reaching under the seat, so I re-holstered my weapon, grabbed the driver's lift arm, pulled him out of the vehicle, and laid him on the ground. I handcuffed him and went back to the vehicle to check under and around the seat but did not find any weapon. The driver, identified as Roberto Gonzales, had a strong odor of alcohol and urine about him. Once I got him on his feet I noticed that his eyes were bloodshot and his speech was slurred and that he was weaving unsteadily. In the patrol vehicle I read Mr. Gonzales the implied consent law, and he answered "NO" to the test. Superior Towing arrived to pick up the vehicle. I drove back to check the yards that he had driven through to find any damage that he might have done and found nothing. I transported Mr. Gonzales to the

(continued)

Springfield Police Department, where I filled out the necessary paper work. Mr. Gonzales was charged with Driving under the Influence of Alcohol. I transported Mr. Gonzales to the Springfield County Jail. At approximately 0339 hours I released Mr. Gonzales to Springfield County. E.O.R.

Incident Report 2—Original

Springfield Police Department
Narrative Information

Jones, Greg

On 05-02-12 at approximately 0240 hrs Officer Smith advised that he was pursuing a driver that he believed was drunk. Officer Smith advised that they were traveling south bound in the 6600 blk of Lowe. Upon arrival I noticed that Officer Smith and the suspect was parked in the driveway of 6604 N. Lowe. The suspect was later identified as Mr. Roberto Gonzales. When I exited my patrol car I saw Mr. Gonzales on the ground laying on his stomach. Mr. Gonzales was also laying on both of his arms and Officer Smith on the side of him attempting to handcuff him. Officer Smith was giving Mr. Gonzales verbal commands such as "place your hands behind your back" and "quiet resisting". Upon approach I could smell a strong odor of alcohol coming from Mr. Gonzales. I grabbed Mr. Gonzales's' left arm and placed it behind his back while Officer Smith placed handcuffed both of his wrist. When Officer Smith finished pat searching Mr. Gonzales I noticed that Mr. Gonzales had urinated on himself because of the odor of urine that I could smell coming from Mr. Gonzales and the wet spot on the front of his pants. Officer Smith escorted Mr. Gonzales to his patrol car and placed him in the backseat. Officer Smith and I began to inventory Mr. Gonzales's vehicle which the only things that he had was some paper towels that had been written on that was in his glove compartment and 1 Bud Light beer can that was empty and in the back of the truck bed. When Officer Smith touched the can he advised that it was still cold to the touch as if Mr. Gonzales had recently consumed the continents. I waited for the wrecker while Officer Smith transported Mr. Gonzales to the station to complete all of the necessary paperwork. Superior towing arrived and took possession of the vehicle and I returned to my normal patrol duties. EOR

Incident Report 2—Revisions

INCIDENT REPORT 2 Revisions

SPRINGFIELD POLICE DEPARTMENT

NARRATIVE(S) INFORMATION

Jones, Greg

> Deleted: 2

On 05-02-06 at approximately 0240 hrs Officer Smith advised that he was pursuing a driver that

he believed was drunk. Officer Smith reported that they were traveling southbound in the 6600

> Deleted: advised
> Deleted: blk
> Deleted: was
> Deleted: laying

block of Lowe. Upon arrival I noticed that both Officer Smith's patrol car and the suspect's

vehicle were parked in the driveway of 6604 N. Lowe. The suspect was later identified as Mr.

> Deleted: . Mr. Gonzales was also laying on both of his arms and

Roberto Gonzales. When I exited my patrol car, I saw Mr. Gonzales on the ground lying on his

> Deleted: on the side of him
> Deleted: attempting

stomach and his arms as Officer Smith attempted to handcuff him. Officer Smith was giving Mr.

> Deleted: place
> Deleted: quiet

Gonzales verbal commands such as "Place your hands behind your back" and "Quit resisting."

> Deleted: .
> Deleted: grabbed

Upon approach I could smell a strong odor of alcohol coming from Mr. Gonzales. I placed Mr.

> Deleted: '
> Deleted: and placed it

Gonzales's left arm behind his back, and Officer Smith handcuffed his wrists. When Officer

> Deleted: while
> Deleted: placed
> Deleted: both of

Smith finished pat searching Mr. Gonzales, I noticed from the odor of urine coming from him and

> Deleted: because of the odor of urine that I could smell coming from Mr. Gonzales and the wet spot on the front of his pants

the wet spot on the front of his pants that Mr. Gonzales had urinated on himself. Officer Smith

> Deleted: egan to inventor
> Deleted: which the only things that he had was

escorted Mr. Gonzales to his patrol car and placed him in the backseat. Officer Smith and I

> Deleted: that was

inventoried Mr. Gonzales's vehicle, finding only some paper towels that had been written on in

> Deleted: I
> Deleted: that was empty and

his glove compartment and one empty Bud Light beer can in the back of the truck bed. Officer

> Deleted: When
> Deleted: touched
> Deleted: he advised that it

Smith noticed the can was still cold to the touch, as if Mr. Gonzales had recently consumed the

> Deleted: continents

contents. I waited for the wrecker while Officer Smith transported Mr. Gonzales to the station to

complete the necessary paperwork. Superior Towing arrived and took possession of the vehicle,

> Deleted: all of

and I returned to my normal patrol duties. EOR

> Deleted: ¶
> Jones, Greg #661

Incident Report 2—Final Report

Springfield Police Department
Narrative(s) Information

Jones, Greg
On 05-02-12 at approximately 0240 hrs Officer Smith advised that he was pursuing a driver that he believed was drunk. Officer Smith reported that

(continued)

they were traveling southbound in the 6600 block of Lowe. Upon arrival I noticed that both Officer Smith's patrol car and the suspect's vehicle were parked in the driveway of 6604 N. Lowe. The suspect was later identified as Mr. Roberto Gonzales. When I exited my patrol car, I saw Mr. Gonzales on the ground lying on his stomach and his arms as Officer Smith attempted to handcuff him. Officer Smith was giving Mr. Gonzales verbal commands such as "Place your hands behind your back" and "Quit resisting." Upon approach I could smell a strong odor of alcohol coming from Mr. Gonzales. I placed Mr. Gonzales's left arm behind his back, and Officer Smith handcuffed his wrists. When Officer Smith finished pat searching Mr. Gonzales, I noticed from the odor of urine coming from him and the wet spot on the front of his pants that Mr. Gonzales had urinated on himself. Officer Smith escorted Mr. Gonzales to his patrol car and placed him in the backseat. Officer Smith and I inventoried Mr. Gonzales's vehicle, finding only some paper towels that had been written on in his glove compartment and one empty Bud Light beer can in the back of the truck bed. Officer Smith noticed the can was still cold to the touch, as if Mr. Gonzales had recently consumed the contents. I waited for the wrecker while Officer Smith transported Mr. Gonzales to the station to complete the necessary paperwork. Superior Towing arrived and took possession of the vehicle, and I returned to my normal patrol duties. EOR

Incident Report 3—Original

Springfield Police Department
Narrative Information

Mix, Frank

On 05/02/12 it was discovered through the booking process at Springfield County Jail that the subject who identified himself to the arresting officer as Roberto Gonzales had previously been booked under the name Mr. Jesus Lucas Gonzales. This identification was made through comparison of fingerprints on file with Springfield County Jail. A record check using the name Jesus Gonzales revealed an outstanding warrant out of Springfield County Jail for a prior driving under the influence charge. It was also discovered that

Mr. Gonzales had prior conviction for driving under the influence charge. It was also discovered that Mr. Gonzales had prior conviction for driving under the influence in Chuckalucka County. An interstate records check was completed using the name Jesus Lucas Gonzales. It was discovered that Jesus Lucas Gonzales is an alias for Juan Ramon. This record check revealed Juan Ramon had convictions in two other states including two driving under the influence convictions with the last ten years in the state of Oregon.

Incident Report 3—Revisions

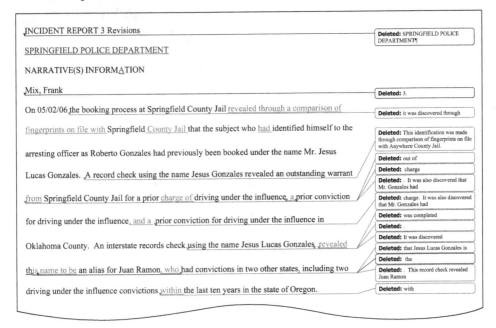

Incident Report 3—Final Report

Springfield Police Department
Narrative(s) Information

Mix, Frank

On 05/02/12 the booking process at Springfield County Jail revealed through a comparison of fingerprints on file with Springfield County Jail

(continued)

that the subject who had identified himself to the arresting officer as Roberto Gonzales had previously been booked under the name Mr. Jesus Lucas Gonzales. A record check using the name Jesus Gonzales revealed an outstanding warrant from Springfield County Jail for a prior charge of driving under the influence, a prior conviction for driving under the influence, and a prior conviction for driving under the influence in Oklahoma County. An interstate records check using the name Jesus Lucas Gonzales revealed this name to be an alias for Juan Ramon, who had convictions in two other states, including two driving under the influence convictions within the last ten years in the state of Oregon.

12

Writing Probation and Parole Reports

WHAT ARE PROBATION AND PAROLE REPORTS?

Probation is a suspension of incarceration. In other words, someone who is on probation has been convicted of a crime but is allowed to go free—but with restrictions imposed by the court and under the supervision of a corrections department (probation) officer. People on probation may or may not have served time in jail. Parole is the release of a prisoner, under specific requirements and supervision (a parole officer), before his or her full time in jail has been served.

Probation and parole officers write a variety of different kinds of reports. Some are written for administrative purposes, that is, to inform other officers or corrections department supervisors of their activities. Perhaps the two most important types of reports they write—because they directly affect people's lives—are *violation reports* (VRs) and *presentence investigation reports* (PIRs). VRs explain to corrections department supervisors, judges, and other court officials that someone has violated the terms and conditions of his or her probation or parole, evaluate the nature and severity of the violation, and suggest appropriate responses to the violation on the part of the corrections system. PIRs are written to provide judges with information they need to give a person convicted of a crime an appropriate sentence.

TIPS FOR WRITING EFFECTIVE PROBATION AND PAROLE REPORTS

Much of what Chapter 11 says about producing effective police reports is also true about the requirements of reports written by probation and parole officers. The most important of these requirements is that the report must communicate necessary information as clearly and simply as possible. Unfortunately, good writing is as hard to find in probation and parole reports as in police reports, and for the same reasons, foremost among them lack of proper grammar and sentence structure. The better writer you are, the more effective a probation and parole officer you are likely to become. As you work to master the requirements of writing probation and parole reports, we urge you to study the basic grammar and usage rules elaborated in Chapter 2 of this manual and to remember the three fundamental tips for effective sentences discussed in Chapter 11 and summarized here.

1. *Put the subject first.* Identify the subject of each sentence clearly and quickly. Do not encumber the sentence with a beginning prepositional phrase, as in this unwieldy example:

   • After minor collisions with two parked cars, the probationer drove west down the street in front of the Neighborhood Walmart.

   Instead, name the subject of the sentence immediately:

   • The probationer drove west down the street in front of the Neighborhood Walmart after minor collisions with two parked cars.

2. *Be careful with pronouns.* It is easy to confuse readers by misusing pronouns—words such as *he, she, it, him, her, they,* and *them* that substitute for nouns. The problem is that you, the writer, already know whom you are referring to in your writing. *You* know, for example, that in this pair of sentences the *He* at the beginning of the second sentence refers to the *suspect:*

   • The suspect pulled a gun and demanded money from the victim. He ran down the street and into an alley.

   You know this because, as the writer, *you already know the facts before you begin to write;* in your mind you move from *idea* to *words.* But the reader of these sentences may well know nothing about the incident before reading your account; the reader moves from *words* to *idea* and so bases his or her understanding of your sentences on the fundamental rules of writing—which, in the case of these two sentences, requires that the *He* of sentence two refer to the *victim,* not the suspect.

   For your reader's sake, you've got to be absolutely clear in your use of pronouns.

   Chapter 11 offers additional examples of sentences in need of more effective pronoun references. We encourage you to practice revising these sentences.

3. *Use active verbs.* This third rule becomes much easier to follow if you pay attention to the first rule. Naming the subject first in the sentence usually leaves you no place to go except to the verb—the word that tells what it

is the subject does. Note the difference between these two sentences. It is a difference in *feeling* as much as in *clarity*:

- Monday's hearing was attended by Officer Michaels.
- Officer Michaels attended Monday's hearing.

The sentences say the same thing, but the second sentence feels stronger, energized by its greater brevity and clarity, mainly because the subject of sentence two—*Officer Michaels*—is performing the action that the sentence names—*attending the hearing*. A verb like the one in sentence two—*attended*, indicating that the subject accomplishes the action of the sentence—is called an *active voice* verb. Now look at sentence one. Note how its verb—*was attended*—actually separates the performer of the action—*Officer Michaels*—from the act. A verb that breaks the line of activity like this is called a *passive voice* verb, and it robs the sentence of much of its sense of forward motion.

While the improvement that active voice verbs make in short sentences like our example is relatively slight, it becomes very important in longer, complex sentences, and especially in groups of sentences making up paragraphs. Take another look at the examples given in Chapter 11 of sentences becalmed by passive voice verbs. Can you strengthen them by changing their verbs from passive to active voice?

THE DAILY JOURNAL

Probation and parole officers need to keep a detailed daily record of their experiences. This may be a notebook or a journal, or a special record format provided by their department. As a probation or parole officer, you need to write a daily journal for two reasons. First, you rarely know exactly when an ordinary experience you have in the course of your duties may later be important to a judge or another corrections system officer. Second, no matter how good your memory may be, if you do not maintain a daily and detailed account of your activities you will undoubtedly forget a detail or two that may turn out to be highly important to the parolees, probationers, or corrections systems officials you serve.

Probation and parole officers have many duties. They not only advise judges and their superiors of the activities of parolees and probationers but also provide a wide variety of other services as well. They find resources, such as jobs, job training, and places to live, for the people they are monitoring or supervising. They help parolees and probationers relate to their communities in a positive way, providing counseling and practical advice. On a daily basis probation and parole officers are called upon to report many of their activities using a wide array of standard forms provided by the states, cities, or counties in which they work. Standard report forms normally list prompts for various kinds of information (date, time, place, type of incident, status of parolee, etc.). A clearly written, detailed daily journal enables officers to provide the accurate information necessary to compile an effective report. Furthermore, probation and parole officers often must testify in court and answer questions from the prosecutor, the defense, and the judge. In such a situation, having recourse to detailed, thorough notes taken in the field and recorded in a daily journal can help officers with the difficult task of remembering the specifics of a particular case.

VIOLATION REPORTS

Parole and probation violations may be minor, such as showing up to work late, or they may be major, like possessing a firearm. In any case, when reporting a specific violation you will be describing a particular incident, and it is therefore wise to gather information in the same manner that police officers do for their incident reports (described in Chapter 11 of this manual). As in police reports, you need to record information on the five Ws and an H—WHO, WHAT, WHERE, WHEN, WHY, and HOW. You may want to make a list of examples like the following, based on the list from Ross and Plant (1977:31–34) used in Chapter 11, and copy it into the notebook in which you keep your daily journal.

- WHO
  a. Committed the violation? List the elements of the violator's personal information (address, phone number, date of birth, citizenship, occupation, record of incarcerations, etc.)
  b. Discovered the violation?
  c. Reported the violation?
  d. Was the victim?
  e. Saw or heard anything of importance?
  f. Helped the person committing the violation?
  g. Else was involved: doctor, nurse, ambulance driver?
- WHAT
  a. Prompted you to report the violation?
  b. Violation was committed?
  c. Happened in the course of the violation?
  d. Was the motive for the violation?
  e. Is the attitude of the violator?
  f. In the violator's history is relevant to this violation?
  g. Special circumstances are involved?
  h. Efforts were made to gain the compliance of the offender?
  i. Is the ability of the offender to comply with the requirements of his or her probation or parole?
  j. Is the willingness of the offender to comply with the requirements of his or her probation or parole?
  k. Risk did this violation pose to the community?

    l. Risk does the offender pose to the community?
    m. Evidence was obtained?
    n. Was done with the evidence?
- WHERE
  - a. Did the violation occur?
  - b. Was the violation discovered?
  - c. Was the violator seen?
  - d. Were the witnesses during the violation?
- WHEN
  - a. Was the *specific* violation committed?
  - b. Was the violation discovered?
  - c. Was notification delivered or received?
  - d. Did police arrive at the scene?
- HOW
  - a. Specifically was the violation committed?
  - b. Was the violation planned?
  - c. Did the violator secure tools or weapons?
  - d. Were tools and weapons used?
  - e. Was damage done?
- WHY
  - a. Was the violation committed?
  - b. Was the violation reported?

Remember that the answers you compile must be as objective as possible, free of bias and presupposition.

As mentioned previously, much of the information presented here may be provided on a standard required form. In addition to including spaces to fill in for specific prompts like those above, the form may provide an area for a general narrative description. When you write these narratives, be sure to be concise and accurate and clearly distinguish between what you consider to be fact and what your personal opinion or recommendation is.

PRESENTENCE INVESTIGATION REPORTS

PIRs often require much if not all of the information provided in VRs; so if you are prepared for your VR you will have much of what you need for your PIR. The PIR, however, will require more specific information, some of which will call for your own good judgment. Remember, you will very probably submit your PIR as part of your *testimony in court*. Providing clear, accurate information, in your written report and your oral testimony, is your surest way to success in helping judges come to the best conclusion for the violator, for the community, and for the department you serve.

Perhaps the main difference between a VR and a PIR is that a PIR is more likely to require you to write a definite recommendation concerning the action to be taken with respect to the specific violation at hand. In order to provide a solid recommendation, you will need to carefully consider the following factors:

1. What are the options in this particular case? Dismissal of the case? A lecture to the violator by the judge? Incarceration? Fine? Community service? Work release? Medical or emotional treatment? Inpatient or outpatient services? What are the costs and benefits of these options?

2. What is the objective of judicial action? What should the criminal justice system be trying to accomplish in this case? What is in the interest of the community? The violator? Friends and family of the violator?

3. What can realistically be achieved, under any of the available options?

4. What is the most logical thing to do, given the circumstances and severity of this particular violation?

Your PIR should be carefully written in a series of concise paragraphs. Once you have edited it and it is suitable for submission, you will be able to answer the questions asked of you in court. Be honest and confident. Provide clear and concise answers, and do not go beyond what you know and what you are asked.

Included below are a complete sample VR and the paragraph from a PIR that offers a parole officer's investigative recommendation.

Sample Violation Report

ALLISON COUNTY COMMUNITY SENTENCING
1300 W. Jimpson, Suite 406, Squires, OK 76767

VIOLATION REPORT

DATE: _____07/09/2013_____   DISTRICT JUDGE: Honorable Judge Joe Llano

NAME: Mr. James C. D. Gooch-Ross   CASE NO. _____CL00-1300_____

CRIME: Ct. 1: <u>Driving under the influence of alcohol</u>   ELIGIBLE _x_ NOT ELIGIBLE FOR FUNDS

DATE SENTENCED: _11/29/2012_   SENTENCE LENGTH/TYPE: _3 yrs. S/S_

OFFENSE: The offender has violated the following terms and conditions of his probation:

__x__ Failure to Report as Directed

__x__ Left the State without Permission

___x___Violation of Law

_____Positive Test for Drug Use

_____Association with Felons

_____Failure to Notify Change of Address

___x___Failure to Provide Truthful Information

_____Carrying a Concealed Weapon

_____Possession of a Firearm

_____Failure to Pay Court Ordered Fees, Fines, and Restitution

___x___Failure to Maintain Lawful Employment

_____Failure to Perform Community Service

___x___Possession and/or Consumption of Alcohol or Illegal Substances

_____Failure to Comply with Court Ordered Directives

SPECIFIC RULE VIOLATIONS:

Mr. Gooch-Ross has violated the terms and conditions of his supervised probation by failure to report as directed, leaving the state without permission, violation of a law, failure to provide truthful information, failure to maintain lawful employment, and possession and consumption of alcohol.

Mr. Gooch-Ross failed to report for a scheduled office visit on 05/11/2013. He did not respond to three attempted telephone calls or to an attempted home visit on 05/15/2013. Mr. Gooch-Ross failed to report that he had quit his job at Ryman's Feed and Grain on 05/10/2013.

On 05/17/2013 Texas State Highway Patrol Officer Patricia Swofford stopped Mr. Gooch-Ross on Interstate 40 two miles south of Exit 78, driving west. Officer Swofford reported that Mr. Gooch-Ross had been driving recklessly and at a speed in excess of 80 mph. The officer discovered an open container of alcohol in the front floorboard of Mr. Gooch-Ross' car and, upon administration of a breath alcohol test, found that Mr. Gooch-Ross registered a blood alcohol concentration in excess of 0.15 percent. Officer Swofford ascertained that Mr. Gooch-Ross was in violation of Section 49.04 of the Texas State Penal Code and was DWI. The officer arrested Mr. Gooch-Ross and drove him to the Texas Department of Public Safety lock-up in Amarillo. The TDPS contacted Mr. Gooch-Ross' parole officer on 05/19/2013.

Mr. Gooch-Ross was transferred to the OK County Jail on 05/21/2013, where he remains pending adjudication of his probation violation.

Eliot W. Kneff
Probation Officer
Telephone: 974-xxxx

PIR Recommendation Paragraph

The PIR will have its own standard form and will allow you to rehearse much of the information given in the violation report. But the PIR will also give you an opportunity to submit a recommendation concerning the action to be taken regarding the violation. Here is the sort of recommendation paragraph that the parole officer might include in the PIR concerning Mr. Gooch-Ross' probation violation:

Investigative Recommendation

Reinstatement of probation is not recommended. Mr. Gooch-Ross has violated the terms of his probation twice now. Both violations involved driving while intoxicated and leaving the state without permission. Mr. Gooch-Ross has been unable during his probation to prevent himself from becoming a danger to the public. I therefore recommend that he serve the remainder of his sentence.

Chapter

13

Criminal Justice Agency Case Studies

WHAT IS A CASE STUDY?

A case study is an in-depth investigation of a social unit, such as a police department, a group of prisoners, or a juvenile detention agency, undertaken to identify the factors that influence the manner in which the unit functions. Case studies have been used effectively for several decades, and although the topics they address may change, the principles that govern how they should be written have not. Following are some examples of case studies:

- Evaluation of the comparative effectiveness of behavior modification methods in maximum-security facilities
- Study of management practices at Arkansas State Penitentiary
- Study of the personality types of juvenile justice officers

Case studies have long been used in law schools, where students learn how the law develops by reading actual court case decisions. Business schools began to develop social service agency case studies to help students understand actual management situations. Courses in social organization, public administration, and social institutions adopt the case study method as a primary teaching tool less often than business or law schools, but case studies have become a common feature of many courses in these areas.

Psychologists have used the case histories of mental patients for many years to support or negate a particular theory. Criminologists and sociologists use the case study approach to describe and draw conclusions about a wide variety of subjects, such as labor unions, police departments, medical schools, gangs, public and private bureaucracies, religious groups, cities, and social class (Philliber, Schwab, and Sloss 1980:64). The success of this type of research depends heavily on the open-mindedness, sensitivity, insights, and integrative abilities of the investigator. Case studies fulfill many educational objectives in the social sciences. As a student in a criminal justice course, you may write a case study in order to improve your ability to do the following:

- Analyze information carefully and objectively.
- Solve problems effectively.
- Present your ideas in clear written form, directed to a specific audience.

In addition, writing a case study allows you to discover some of the problems you will face if you become involved in an actual social situation that parallels your case study. For example, writing a case study can help you understand these areas:

- Some potential benefits and problems of society in general
- Operation of a particular cultural, ethnic, political, economic, or religious group
- Development of a particular problem, such as crime, alcoholism, or violence, within a group
- Interrelationships, within a particular setting, of people, structures, rules, politics, relationship styles, and many other factors

USING CASE STUDIES IN RESEARCH

Isaac and Michael (1981:48) suggest that case studies offer several advantages to the investigator. For one thing, they provide useful background information for researchers planning a major investigation in the social sciences. Case studies often suggest fruitful hypotheses for further study, and they provide specific examples by which to test general theories. Philliber et al. (1980:64) believe that through the intensive investigation of only one case the researcher can gain more depth and detail than might be possible by briefly examining many cases. Also, the depth of focus in a single case allows investigators to recognize certain aspects of the object being studied that would otherwise go unobserved. For example, Becker et al. (1961) noticed that medical students tend to develop a slang, which the researchers called "native language." Only after observing the behavior of the students for several weeks were the researchers able to determine that the slang word *crocks* referred to those patients who were of no help to the students professionally because they did not have an observable disease. The medical students felt the crocks were robbing them of their important time.

Bouma and Atkinson (1995:110–114) call attention to the exploratory nature of some case studies. Researchers, for example, may be interested in what is happening within a juvenile detention center. Before beginning the project, they may not know enough about what they will find in order to formulate testable hypotheses. The researchers' purpose in doing a case study may be to gather as much information as possible in order to help in the formulation of relevant hypotheses. Or the researchers may intend simply to observe and describe all that is happening within the case being studied. Or as is the case in our juvenile detention study in this chapter, the intention may be to observe, describe, and measure certain behaviors in order to test predetermined hypotheses statistically.

LIMITATIONS OF THE CASE STUDY METHOD

Before writing a case study you should be aware of the limitations of the methods you will be using in order to avoid drawing conclusions that are not justified by the knowledge you acquire. First, case studies are relatively subjective exercises. When you write a case study, you select the facts and arrange them into patterns from which you may draw conclusions. The quality of the case study will depend largely upon the quality of the facts you select and the way in which you interpret those facts.

A second potential liability to the method is that every case study, no matter how well written, is in some sense an oversimplification of the events that are described and the environment within which those events take place. To simplify an event or series of events makes it easier to understand but at the same time distorts its effect and importance. It can always be argued that the results of any case study are peculiar to that one case and, therefore, offer little as a rationale for a general explanation or prediction (Philliber et al. 1980:65).

A third caution about case studies pertains strictly to their use as a learning tool in the classroom: Remember that any interpretations you come up with for a case study in your class, no matter how astute or sincere, are essentially parts of an academic exercise and therefore may not be applicable in an actual situation.

TYPES OF CASE STUDIES WRITTEN IN CRIMINAL JUSTICE

Criminal justice cases usually take one of two basic forms. The first might be called a *didactic case study*, because it is written for use in a classroom. It describes a situation or a problem in a certain setting but performs no analysis and draws no conclusions. Instead, a didactic case study normally lists questions for the students to consider and then answer, either individually or in class discussion. This sort of case study allows the teacher to evaluate student analysis skills, and if the case is discussed in class, to give students an opportunity to compare ideas with other students. The second form, an *analytical case study*, provides not only a description but an analysis of the case as well. This is the form of case study most often assigned in a criminal justice class, and it is the form described in detail in this chapter.

Criminal justice professionals conduct case studies for a variety of specific purposes. An *ethnographic case study*, for example, is an in-depth examination of a group of people or an organization over time. Its major purpose is to lead the researchers to a better understanding of human behavior through observations of the interweaving of people, events, conditions, and means in natural settings or subcultures.

Ethnographic case studies examine behavior in a community or, in the case of some technologically primitive societies, an entire society. The term *ethnography* means "a portrait of a people," and the ethnographic approach was historically an anthropological tool for describing societies whose cultural evolution was very primitive when compared to the "civilized" world (Hunter and Whitten 1976:147). Anthropologists would sometimes live within the society under scrutiny for several months or even years, interviewing and observing the people being studied. The in-the-field nature of ethnographies has caused them to be referred to occasionally as field studies.

HOW TO CONDUCT A CRIMINAL JUSTICE AGENCY CASE STUDY

Unlike an ethnographic study, which looks at a community or a society as a whole, a *service agency case study* focuses on a formal organization that provides a specific service or set of services either to a section of a society or society as a whole. A service agency case study usually describes and explains some aspect of a service agency's operation. Case studies do not attempt to explain everything there is to know about the organization. To conduct a service agency case study, you should undertake the following tasks:

1. Select a particular service agency to study.
2. Formulate a general goal, for example, to better understand how the agency works.
3. Describe in general terms the agency and how it operates.
4. Describe the structure, practices, and procedures of the agency.
5. Select a specific objective, for example, to discover the responsiveness to the agency's programs of the people the agency serves.

6. Describe your methodology, that is, the procedures you will use to conduct your investigation.
7. Describe the results of your study, the observations you have made.
8. Draw conclusions about your findings.

The specific goal of your case study is to explain the effectiveness or ineffectiveness of some aspect of the agency's operation. This focused inquiry will, in turn, contribute to a general understanding of how the selected agency works. You may select any service agency, such as the United Way, the Social Security Administration, the American Red Cross, or your state's Department of Human Services. Its personnel, however, should be directly accessible to you for interviews.

Once you have chosen a service agency to examine, you then need to focus on a specific topic related to the agency—some characteristic procedure or situation—and write a description of how that topic has developed within the agency. For example, if your agency focus is a county health department and your topic focus is recruitment problems, you might choose to describe how the recruitment problems evolved within the overall operations of the department.

Most social service agency case studies assigned in criminal justice classes are not fictional. They are based on your investigation of an actual current or recent situation in a public or private agency.

SELECTING A TOPIC

In seeking a topic, you are looking for a situation that is likely to provide some interesting insights about how social service agencies affect people's lives. There are two ways to begin your search. The first is to contact an agency involved with a matter that interests you and then inquire about recent events. If, for example, you are interested in the court system, you would contact a local court administrator's office. Tell the secretary who answers the phone that you are a student who wants to write a college term paper about the agency and ask to talk to someone who can explain the organization's current programs. Ask for an appointment for an interview with the person to whom you are referred by the secretary. When you arrive for the interview, tell the agency official to whom you are speaking that you are interested in doing a case study on some aspect of the agency's operations and that your purpose is to understand better how government agencies operate. Then ask a series of questions aimed at helping you find a topic to pursue. These questions might include the following:

- What recent successes has your agency had?
- What is the greatest challenge facing your agency at the moment?
- What are some of the agency's goals for this year?
- What are some of the obstacles to meeting these goals?

You should follow up these questions with others until you identify a situation in the agency appropriate for your study. There will probably be many. Consider the following examples:

- The agency faces budget cuts, and the director may have to decide among competing political pressures which services she must reduce.
- The agency faces a reorganization.
- The agency is criticized by the people it serves.
- The agency has initiated a controversial policy.

Another way to select a topic is to find an article of interest in your local newspaper. The successes, failures, challenges, and mistakes of government and private agencies are always in the news. The benefit of finding a topic in the newspaper is that when you contact the agency involved, you will already have a subject to discuss; the disadvantage is that agency officials may be reluctant to provide detailed information on some publicized topics.

THE IMPORTANCE OF INTERVIEWS

The goal of your first interview is to obtain enough information to request a series of other interviews. The answers to questions you pose in these interviews will allow you to understand the course of events and the agency interactions that have resulted in the situation you are studying. Remember that you are writing a story, but the story you are writing is accurate and factual. Do not accept the first version of a course of events that you hear. Ask several qualified people the same basic questions.

Take notes constantly. It's best not to record interviews because recorders tend to inhibit people from giving you as much information as they would without one present. At every interview ask about documents relevant to the case. These documents may include committee reports, meeting minutes, letters, or organizational rules and procedures. Sort out facts from appearance. When the facts are straight, you will be ready to organize your thoughts first into an outline and then into a first draft of your paper.

ELEMENTS OF THE CASE STUDY PAPER

CONTENTS

Your case study should consist of four basic parts:

1. Title page
2. Executive summary

3. Text

4. Reference list

The title page, executive summary, text, and references should all conform to the directions in Part I of this manual.

TEXT

The text of a service agency case study includes the following elements:

- Facts of the case
- Environment, context, and participants of the case
- Topic analysis of the case
- Conclusions about the case

Although the content of the text should adhere to this general order, elements will overlap. Ask your instructor for the assigned length of the paper. In general, case studies should be brief and concise. They may include material from numerous interviews and documents—but only material essential to understand the case. A case study can be any length, but a paper of about 15 pages, double-spaced, is usually adequate to describe and analyze a case situation accurately.

Facts

The facts of the case that you will reveal include a description of the events, the major actors and their relationships with one another, and the external and internal agency environments and contexts within which the events of the situation you are describing developed.

Environment, Context, and Participants

In your account, consider the following aspects of a situation and relate to your readers those items that are relevant to the case at hand:

- The law under which the agency operates
- Political and economic factors of the agency's internal environment (e.g., power and influence, budget constraints, agency structure, rules, role, and mission)
- Other factors of the agency's internal environment (e.g., style, tone, preferences, and procedures)

Without altering the essential facts of the course of events, alter or delete the names of the actors and the agencies for which they work. Accuracy of facts in a case study is essential for a correct interpretation, but the actual identities of the individuals involved are irrelevant, and people may want their privacy protected. Any change of facts for this purpose should be done in a manner that does not alter the content of the story of the case at hand.

A well-written criminal justice agency case study will reveal much about how public and private agencies conduct business in the United States and even more about the agency selected for study. Public and private administrators face many of the same problems: They must recruit personnel, establish goals and objectives, account for expenditures, and abide by hundreds of rules and regulations. In several important respects, however, public agencies are very different from private businesses. A public administrator will often serve several bosses (governor, legislators) and have several competing clienteles (interest groups, the general public). Public officials are more susceptible than private businesses to changes in political administrations. They also face more legal constraints and are held accountable to higher ethical standards. In addition, public administrators are more likely to be held under the light of public surveillance, and so they are held accountable to a different bottom line.

The goal of most businesses is, first and foremost, to earn profits for their owners. The amount of these profits is normally easy to quantify. The success of public agencies, however, can be hard to measure. Criteria used to evaluate public programs, such as effectiveness and efficiency, often contradict one another. For example, America's space program has accomplished some remarkable achievements, but not many people commend the program's economic efficiency.

Topic Analysis

Your analysis should explore and explain the events in your selected situation, concentrating upon the strategies and practices used by the primary actors at the social service agency. Your analysis should answer questions such as the following:

- How did the situation or problem at the heart of the case arise?
- What were the important external and internal factors that directed what transpired?
- What were the major sources of power and influence in the situation, and how were they used?
- What social service agency styles and practices were employed, and were they effective and appropriate within the situation described?
- How did relationships within the organization affect the conduct of other public or private programs?

Conclusions

To the fullest extent possible your conclusions should use what you have learned about the nature of administrative practices to explain causes and effects, summarize events and their results, and interpret the actions of administrators. One major purpose of a social service agency case study is to give its readers an opportunity to benefit from the successes and mistakes of others. In your conclusion, tell the reader what you have learned from this situation, what you would imitate in your own social service agency practice, and what you would do differently if you found yourself in a similar situation.

A SAMPLE CASE STUDY

The following sample case study, which addresses the topic of how incidents of negative behavior affect program implementation in a juvenile detention center, was taken from a professional juvenile detention journal. Therefore, it has no table of contents and executive summary. Notice how it accomplishes the following goals:

1. The problem being investigated is introduced along with a rationale for doing the case study.
2. The professional literature is reviewed to see what is already known about the issue or problem.
3. The design of the study is explained: data collection and analysis procedures.
4. The results and conclusions are given: limitations of the study, interpretation of the results, discussion of how this interpretation affects the detention center, suggestions or recommendations for future studies.

Sample Case Study

An Analysis of Negative Behavior Incidents and Their Impact on Program Implementation at the Oklahoma County Juvenile Detention Center

Johnson, William A. and Richard P. Rettig. 1990.
Journal for Juvenile Justice and Detention Services 5(2):13–20.

INTRODUCTION

Over the past twenty years there has been a major effort within the juvenile justice system to treat delinquent offenders within confined settings from the fundamental assumptions of the rehabilitation model. Here the major

(continued)

assumption about juvenile offenders is that they are experiencing one or more acute problems, i.e., emotional distress, conflicts with other family members, difficulties in school, underdeveloped social skills, low ability to cope with failure or stress, or lack of job skills. Furthermore, it is also assumed that any assistance in meeting these needs, whether the juvenile offender is detained, confined or in the community, might prevent him or her from committing more delinquency in the future (Glaser 1969). Gendreau and Ross (1987:395) feel that offender rehabilitation has had many successes in the past and will continue to be successful in the future. However, there have been a number of significant attacks on this perspective (Lipton, Martinson and Wilks 1975; Martinson 1974:181; Rubin 1979:280).

From a different perspective Schwartz (1988) argues that the "get tough" policy of the Reagan years has infiltrated the juvenile court principally through the judges who are "either incompetent or ill-suited for the job," and tend to disregard or violate the rights of children in making detention decisions, as well as in all other segments of the juvenile court process.

The youth who come before the Oklahoma County Juvenile Court and are considered for preventive detention are either adjudicated delinquent or are alleged to have committed an offense which would be a felony were they an adult. Additionally, they usually fall into two broad categories: (1) those who are no longer subject to the guidance or effective control of their parents or guardians, and (2) those who have no custodians at all. These conditions have contributed to their delinquency to the extent that the court often must exercise a substitute form of protective control. In some sense these youth are victims. But it is also clear that sometimes they are the perpetrators of homicides, robberies, burglaries, assaults and rapes which seriously threaten our communities.

The argument here is that there is in fact a legitimate basis for treating juveniles differently from adults with respect to openness of the courts, privacy of records, length of incarceration, right to treatment and presumption of release. Therefore, it should be clearly recognized that there are valid reasons for detaining them when detention is in the best interest of society or the particular juvenile involved.

If the detention authorities are to provide a socially and psychologically healthy climate, and discharge their responsibilities to the youth and the community, then several opportunities for furthering the youth's growth and development must be made available; the nature and quality of the detention experience rather than its limited or extended duration must be the prime consideration.

Rettig (1980) maintains that when the detention community is fulfilling its philosophy and stated purposes in helping adolescents, the following contributions are possible:

1. A system of controls or limits to protect both the child and the community while insuring the child's legal rights.

2. A life experience which enables the child to be studied in his physical, social, emotional, and spiritual dimensions.

3. Resources such as program, personnel, and facilities especially equipped and oriented to meet both the normal and special physical, social and emotional needs during a time of crisis in the child's life.

4. A sociological climate conducive to working on the problems of the detained child through understanding, acceptance, consistency, limits, structure, and individual and group counseling which together provide emotional security and first aid enabling the child to have constructive experiences contributing to personality growth.

5. A sound and integrated detention program outlining and specifying the limited treatment goals for each detainee. (p. 453)

Among juvenile justice practitioners detention refers to pretrial and predispositional confinement (Rubin 1979:86). Norman (1960) states that "the detention of children awaiting juvenile court disposition has been a problem ever since juvenile courts were established" (p. 1). The U.S. Department of Justice defines the detention center as "a short-term facility that provides custody in a physically restricting environment pending adjudication or, following adjudication disposition, placement, or transfer" (Office of Justice Programs 1989:4).

The development of residential short-term programs for juvenile offenders is among the most challenging problems confronting juvenile justice administrators today. Detention programs around the country range from very inadequate custodial arrangements, like "boob-tube therapy," to very complex and sophisticated intervention strategies, such as behavioral management (Whitehead and Lab 1990:244–256).

During the 70s and 80s the courts repeatedly affirmed the rights of juveniles to services at the pretrial level. All juveniles in custody must now have

(*continued*)

clear access to educational, recreational, and other therapeutic services while in detention care. This has been supported by both case law and national standards, and any program which can be construed as punitive in and of itself is no longer acceptable in any juvenile facility.

Presently, the juvenile justice system is involved in an era of accelerated change in response to rapidly advancing juvenile case law, federal and local legislation, improved standards of practice, more sophisticated training, increasing experience in the field, and modifications in the juvenile population itself. For example, the preventive detention of juvenile offenders awaiting court disposition is now reserved for more serious offenders (Bynum and Thompson 1989:413), while truants, runaways, and out-of-parental-control youth—status offenders—are often diverted away from detention. Statistics show that youth referred for violent offenses are twice as likely to be detained as youth charged with non-violent offenses (Juvenile Justice Bulletin 1989:1).

Therefore, the population at detention facilities has come to assume a more serious character than in the past. Young felons and serious misdemeanants, overrepresented by blacks and Hispanics, now comprise a much larger percentage of the detention population (Office of Justice Programs 1989:1). Distribution of detainees by race is a critical variable. While white youths make up the vast majority of all arrestees (74.9 percent) and all Part 1 property offenses (72.1 percent), personal offenses, i.e., murder, rape, robbery and aggravated assault, are committed more by black juveniles (52 percent) than any other racial group. This overrepresentation of blacks in violent offenses is dramatic, in that blacks comprise only 15 percent of the youthful U.S. population (Uniform Crime Reports 1987:183).

Despite an ongoing decline in detention rates, the average length of stay is increasing; many juveniles are remaining in detention longer, and the same young people are being admitted more often than in the past (Juvenile Justice Bulletin 1989). Overcrowding, which places a strain on all resident, staff, and facility resources, has in many jurisdictions become critical.

These problems continue to be manifested in the detention environment, leading some youth to display disruptive and sometimes violent behavior consistently. This not only affects the ongoing program but also results in personal injury and the destruction of property. Staff often spend an inordinate amount of time and resources contending with young people who are in detention because some of them don't understand that their abusive actions have consequences. If this highly volatile situation could to some extent be remediated, detention programming would be positively affected (Askeland 1989).

Therefore, when residents act out violently they must be restricted or confined to their rooms until the situation can be resolved. Room restriction is used as a cooling-off time for minor infractions for a time not to exceed one hour. Room confinement is used as a last resort for major infractions "after all other techniques and resources have failed and only when [there is] a danger to self, others, property or to prevent escape . . . or the inciting of others" (OCJJDC Policies and Procedures Manual 1989).

One way that a juvenile detention program can be characterized as successful or unsuccessful is by monitoring the process of discipline applied when youth seriously misbehave—room restriction and/or confinement. While some degree of insubordination and conflict is normative in this environment, the focus of this paper reflects our attempt to study what occurs when youth commit serious behavioral infractions and must be disciplined by the use of room confinement.

DESIGN

This study was designed to measure negative behavior incidents that occur within a detention facility for juveniles awaiting disposition and/or placement. Data were collected from the daily incident reports, room confinement records, daily log and resident files over a seven month period beginning June 1, 1988, and ending December 31, 1988. The following variables were operationalized (turned into numbers): race, gender, age, type of infraction, chargeable offense, time of day infraction occurred, location of incident, disciplinary hearing, injury, disciplinary action taken, length of assigned confinement, actual time in confinement, precautionary warning code (suicidal, violent, etc.), behavioral level, prescore (daily behavioral evaluation before confinement for infraction), postscore (daily behavioral evaluation after confinement for infraction), and number of times held at this detention facility.

The average length of stay at this detention center is eight days. Some juveniles are there for as long as six months, others for as short as a few hours. During the seven months in which the data were collected, 103 residents committed 236 behavioral infractions that were "written up." While there were numerous minor incidents that resulted in a brief room restriction (less than one hour), almost all (191) of the 236 infractions were considered

(continued)

serious enough to receive a one-hour or greater confinement penalty. Those infractions that were "written up" during this seven-month period comprise the data being analyzed in this study.

RESULTS AND CONCLUSIONS

Any conclusions that we draw will be limited by several problems encountered while collecting the data. The Oklahoma County Juvenile Detention Center is a relatively new facility; the program has only been on line for about three years. Problems, such as the ones listed below, are gradually being worked out. Many have been solved since the data for this study were collected. With the recent addition of a state-of-the-art computer system, future data collection should encounter few, if any, of these problems: (1) some days no incidents were reported, but records showed that several incidents occurred; (2) several incident reports were not documented in the daily restriction log; the incident was written up but there was no record of any time served; (3) dates on the incident reports often did not correspond with the actual date in the restriction log. Sometimes this was because the room confinement occurred the day after the incident, but there was no record keeping that allowed the researcher to ascertain if this was the case; (4) times and dates were sometimes not entered, especially for release from confinement, making it impossible to determine the actual length of time in detention; (5) on several occasions there was more than one incident committed by the same person during a given day, but only one was written up. Since the written up incidents were not coded as such, it was difficult, if not impossible, to compare sentence with actual length of time in confinement; (6) the pre/post comparison was lost in cases where individuals were released from the facility before obtaining a postscore; and finally, (7) the limited access to important information (gender, race, age, length of employment) about those who "write up" residents and impose sanctions restricted our ability to analyze the results fully. If race is a meaningful variable in determining who is most likely to be written up and confined for a particular incident, what role does the racial composition of the staff play in influencing this outcome? Gender? Length of employment?

With these limitations in mind, the following conclusions utilize those variables and variable relationships that best explain negative behavior incidents at this particular detention facility.

Prescore and Postscore

While there are many significant findings in this study, perhaps the most meaningful one tends to confirm the room confinement process itself as workable. Administrators and staff sometimes question the functional viability of this type of behavior modification because of the high standards of fairness and legality they have imposed on themselves by requesting accreditation by the American Correctional Association.

Detention officers score the behavior of each resident at the close of the morning and evening shift. Training is provided in this behavior rating process and unit supervisors regularly check for reliability and validity. Scores are assigned on a scale of 10 (negative) to 100 (positive). The average prescore (assigned the day prior to incidents for which room confinement was given) was 50.98. The average postscore (assigned the day after room confinement was served) was 73.60. This finding was extremely significant.

Under very controlled conditions room confinement is used as negative reinforcement to increase the likelihood of reasonably conforming behavior and the extinction of violent, abusive behavior. In learning theory terms, negative reinforcement involves the application of an aversive stimulus (temporary withdrawal of program privileges and room confinement) contingent upon the occurrence of a desired behavior (the cessation of the problem behavior). The aversive stimulus (room confinement) is terminated if the desirable behavior (obedience to the rules) occurs, thereby increasing the likelihood of this desired behavior continuing. Our data clearly show that the program is at least achieving success in regulating the behavior of certain residents. Due to the limitations of our study we cannot determine to what extent, if any, the program is successful in permanently altering attitudes and behavior patterns.

Dominant Offenders

Another compelling finding would seem to be important for program development. Seventeen percent (17 percent) of all incidents during this seven month period were instigated by three male residents. Twenty-seven percent (27 percent) of all incidents were instigated by six male residents. To be clear, while 103 residents committed 236 infractions serious enough to earn them room restriction or confinement, only six residents were responsible for 64 infractions. It is difficult to determine how many

(continued)

other incidents were stimulated because of the chronic negative influence of these few offenders.

One implication from this finding is that negative incidents might be reduced by as much as 25 to 50 percent over time by the differential treatment of chronic program disrupters. Perhaps specified juveniles could be "flagged" for special treatment. For example, upon the commission of the second violent or serious offense while in detention, the juvenile could be selected into a special program planned and staffed to address obvious behavioral problems; one that clearly segregates him from others. A special program of this type would be enriched by a much higher staff-to-resident ratio so that more moment-by-moment attention, communication, and feedback could be effected by staff to meet the intense needs of residents. Caution must be used to ensure that in no way would this program be considered or interpreted as punitive. Since the inception of this study, individualized treatment plans have been implemented for several dominant offenders. While no follow-up study has been done to confirm this, staff members feel that there has been some significant success in the overall reduction of negative behavior.

We take our cue from the adult criminal justice literature on selective incapacitation (Greenwood 1982), which seeks to identify those offenders who are most likely to commit future crimes. Our research showing that a disproportionate amount of serious incidents are committed by a minority of offenders supports the idea that selectively treating those few would result in less program disruption. Not only could a special program be developed to meet the needs of chronic disrupters, but the existing program, using room confinement as necessary, should run more efficiently.

Race

A number of interesting findings emerge when the racial composition of detention (Fiscal Year 1988) is compared with the number of infractions committed by each group. Black youth comprised 47.3 percent of the population while whites comprised 41.9 percent. But Blacks were charged with 58.5 percent of the infractions, while white youth committed 34.3 percent. The discrepancy between their respective number in the population and their reported infractions is significant ($p < .01$). This may reflect the extent to which violence is more normative in the black youth subculture than among the white youth. Some might contend that these statistics reflect less toleration by staff when confronted by black youth acting out in the program, but this position would seem to be contradicted by observation and by the fact that many of the detention officers are black.

Recidivism was significantly (p = .0008) related to race, with American Indians, others, and blacks detained at this facility more often than whites. Recent examination of detention practices in the United States noted that black and Hispanic youth constitute well over 50 percent of the youth being confined in detention, and that this proportion has been increasing through the 70s and 80s (Schwartz et al. 1987:219–235). In Oklahoma urban areas, such as metropolitan Oklahoma City, the percentage of blacks detained (47.3) is much higher when compared to whites (41.9). Askeland (1989) reports that juveniles detained from rural Oklahoma counties are predominately white, while juveniles detained from metro Oklahoma City are predominately black. Other minorities make up about 11 percent of the population at the Oklahoma County Juvenile Detention facility. It is possible that if we controlled for poverty, a factor differentially permeating the black and Hispanic cultures when compared with white culture, race might diminish as a meaningful variable. Hopefully, any follow-up studies might be able to examine poverty as a possible contributing factor.

Behavioral level and race were significantly (p = .0283) related, with blacks having a lower behavioral level than whites prior to the infraction. The differential acting out activity we have noted among the black and white cohorts in detention appears to correlate quite well with the differential arrest rates of juveniles by racial groups. As indicated by 1986 data (Uniform Crime Reports 1987:183), the probability of young blacks being arrested for crimes of violence is higher than for young whites.

It is not likely that any inherent connection between racial background and delinquent behavior exists. The high incidence of antisocial behavior may be related more to the poor socioeconomic circumstances of inner-city minority groups than to the biology of race (Bynum and Thompson 1989:111).

If blacks are differentially arrested and differentially detained, perhaps they are differentially disciplined while in detention. This disturbing question is raised by a recent study on factors affecting the detention decision. Using a sample of 55,000 cases from one state, Frazier and Bishop (1985) found that neither relevant legal variables (offense severity and prior record) nor sociodemographic characteristics had much impact on detention decisions. One possible conclusion of this line of research is that the entire

(continued)

detention decision "process is idiosyncratic, causing some juveniles to suffer significant deprivations of liberty based on considerations that are irrelevant to the approved purposes of detention" (p. 1151).

The question at least needs to be asked, if data exists to seriously question decisions to arrest and detain by race, is it possible that decisions to discipline within detention are also affected by the racial variable? A follow-up study might address this issue, among others. We have no way of analyzing staff activity in these incidents. Perhaps the age, sex, and race of staff influence the various transactions with residents leading up to decisions to institute sanctions such as room confinement.

Sex

Males comprised 87 percent of the detention population, while females comprised 13 percent (FY 1988). However, males were responsible for 95 percent of the infractions (p < .001), as compared to 4.2 percent for females. Perhaps females present significantly less of a threat to staff and therefore are not "written up" as often, or the infraction does not result in room confinement as often because their behavior can be de-escalated through mediation, whereas male behavior during these incidents tends to escalate and often ends in violent confrontation. This conclusion is somewhat supported by the results of the prescore and sex hypothesis. Females scored significantly (p = .017) higher than males on their daily evaluation prior to an incident. Even if an incident occurs, it is usually not precipitated by an ongoing barrage of negative behavior where females are concerned. Simply speaking, it would appear that dealing with the behavior problems of males, especially those few that seem to be consistently causing disruption, is a much greater concern in the implementation of program guidelines.

DISCUSSION

While there were other significant findings in this study, the ones presented above proved to be the most meaningful for program development and implementation. To summarize, there were two principal findings in this study that relate significantly to program modifications. One had to do with the comparison of prescores and postscores recorded on each resident that received the negative reinforcement of room confinement. The second had to do with the relatively high number of offenses meriting room confinement committed by chronic program disrupters or dominant offenders.

The prescore/postscore finding supports the existing method of dealing with negative behavior incidents within this detention setting. The implication is that the program is successful and should be continued. Some professionals feel that any confinement that exceeds one hour may be counterproductive. Our finding does not support this conclusion. The possibility exists that the postscoring process was biased, that staff rated the behavior of residents higher after room confinement to prove to themselves that the program worked, or because they felt sorry for the resident. Staff report that the opposite reaction is more tenable; it is more likely that residents are monitored closely after release from confinement, and staff have to be especially careful to practice discretion so as not to rate them lower.

We suggest that the room confinement process remain in place as it is for now. Since there are already several meaningful modifications to the existing procedures at this facility, i.e., individualized programming for problem residents, computerized intake and information retrieval, and more could occur after this evaluation is completed, any follow-up study should carefully reevaluate the room confinement process, with special attention given to the prescore/postscore comparison.

Another compelling finding has to do with chronic program disrupters. These dominant offenders committed over one-quarter of all serious offenses in detention, and their negative presence could extend to as many as half of the incidents.

Detained offenders are almost always male. They are more often nonwhite (usually black at this facility), of low socioeconomic status, have experienced more family disruption and school discipline problems, completed fewer grades in school, and measure lower on intelligence tests. Studies have shown that expressions of violence are part of the norms of the lower socioeconomic classes and are a learned response to pressures of survival. Young males, often black, particularly from female-headed households in socially deprived areas, tend to develop norms of violence or disruption as a means of achieving status among their peers. They are frustrated in their search for self-esteem, lack of success, and desire for material goods. Therefore, their violence may not be rooted in psychological disorder as much as it is normatively prescribed: violence that is goal-oriented behavior, normal for that group.

(continued)

It is reasonable to assume that chronic program disrupters in detention have characteristics similar to these chronic juvenile offenders. Their
control and treatment in the short-term detention setting is a serious challenge. Space limitations usually will not permit the physical isolation and
separation of these dominant offenders. We recommend the continued uti-
lization of the individualized programming (maybe one-on-one if possible)
that began after this study was initiated. Since dominant offenders tend to
come to detention more often and stay longer, it makes sense for staff to continue to develop highly individualized programs for these residents oriented
around their special needs. This should be coupled with a group dynamic
approach that challenges and confronts these individuals, one that provides
them opportunities to examine and re-evaluate their life experiences, handi-
caps, deficiencies and strengths. The use of group counseling, positive peer
culture, reality therapy, role playing sessions, and token self-government programs are all aimed at getting troubled youth to assume the role of responsible people so that they might better understand why they act out their
frustrations, and to convince them that ultimately they must assume part of
the responsibility for solving their own problems.

Hopefully, this will facilitate some meaningful attitude changes.
Realistically, it at least serves to isolate these disruptive influences from the
larger group. As we see it, this process contains three potentially positive
outcomes: (1) the chronic disrupter is isolated from the major group in a way
that reduces his opportunity for negative behavior, (2) this reduces the "rip-
ple" effect from his chronic disruption, and (3) it enhances the probability
that both he and all the others in the detention environment can receive the
greatest benefits from the rehabilitation effort.

Any program additions and modifications should also consider some
of the other findings from this study. The most important of these results
primarily centers around race and gender. The residents at this facility are
predominantly minority (most often black) males. Since the inception of
this study the composition has moved even further in this direction. For
the most part this is due to the infiltration of drug-related gangs into the
metropolitan area. Greater emphasis is being placed on controlling the negative influence of these gangs on the communities, and consequently, more
arrests are occurring from the sector most likely to participate—young, black
males. Many bring with them the norms associated with aggression and
violence we discussed earlier. Race is highly associated with recidivism and

behavioral level, and those returning often and behaving negatively tend to be black males. Any program modifications should consider the changing nature of the detention population and target the rehabilitation of the young black male as a high priority.

If this study is replicated in the near future, and we feel that it should be, most, if not all, of the limitations outlined at the beginning of the design section will have been corrected. The computer system described earlier should significantly reduce the error associated with the data collection process and also help in the measurement of other variables connected to the system of controlling negative behavior incidents, especially those concerning staff input. Also, an individualized instruction program for chronic program disrupters was already set in motion at this facility before the findings from this study were reported.

We believe that this facility represents a model program for dealing with juvenile offenders awaiting trial or placement. The entire organization is oriented toward helping those young people who find themselves in trouble with the system. Many people have written them off as hopeless, but the philosophy at this facility is one of hope through help. Administrators and staff continue to pursue the idea that one positive experience can make a difference, and every youth detained should have a chance to change.

Many of these delinquent youth will go on to become career criminals. Some will spend the majority of their lives behind bars. Those who act out violently in the detention setting, particularly the chronic offenders, will probably continue to act out violently in the community, becoming more and more dangerous with each encounter with a punitive judicial and correction system. To paraphrase the director, if they somehow can become aware of the consequences of their actions and shown that what they think and feel matters, maybe the experience they have in this environment might help to prevent them, when pointing a gun at someone, from pulling the trigger.

REFERENCES

Askeland, Dean. 1989. Director of Detention, Oklahoma County Juvenile Justice Center. Interview. August.

Bynum, Jack E. and William E. Thompson. 1989. *Juvenile Delinquency: A Sociological Approach*. Boston, MA: Allyn and Bacon.

(continued)

Frazier, C. E. and D. M. Bishop. 1985. "The Pretrial Detention of Juveniles and Its Impact on Case Dispositions." *Journal of Criminal Law and Criminology* 76:36–44.

Gendreau, P. and R. R. Ross 1987. "Revivification of Rehabilitation: Evidence from the 1980's." *Justice Quarterly* 4:349–407.

Glaser, D. 1969. *The Effectiveness of a Prison and Parole System*. Indianapolis, IN: Bobbs-Merrill.

Greenwood, P. W. 1982. *Selective Incapacitation*. Santa Monica, CA: Rand.

Juvenile Justice Bulletin. 1989. OJJDP Update on Statistics. NJC 115338. January.

Lipton, Douglas, Robert Martinson and Judith Wilks. 1975. *The Effectiveness of Correctional Treatment*. New York: Praeger.

Martinson, Robert. 1974. "What Works? Questions and Answers about Prison Reform." *The Public Interest*. Spring.

Norman, Sherwood. 1960. *Detention Practice*. New York: National Probation and Parole Association.

Office of Justice Programs. 1989. *Fact Sheets on Children in Custody*. Washington, D.C.: U.S. Department of Justice.

Oklahoma County Juvenile Justice Detention Center (OCJJDC). *Policy and Procedures Manual*. Chapter 3: Rules and Discipline Policy 14.4:2–3.

Rettig, Richard P. 1980. "Considering the Use and Usefulness of Juvenile Detention: Operationalizing Social Theory." *Adolescence*. 25.

Rubin, H. Ted. 1979. *Juvenile Justice: Policy, Practice and Law*. New York: Random House.

Schwartz, I. M., G. Fishman, R. Rawson Hatfield, B. A. Krisberg and Z. Eisikovits. 1987. "Juvenile Detention: The Hidden Closets Revisited." *Justice Quarterly*. 4.

Schwartz, Ira M. 1988. In *Justice for Juveniles: Rethinking the Best Interests of the Child* as quoted in a comprehensive review in *Child Protection Report*. 14 (November).

Uniform Crime Reports. 1987. *Crime in the United States: 1986*. Washington, D.C.: United States Government Printing Office. Table 38:183.

Whitehead, John T. and Steven P. Lab. 1990. *Juvenile Justice: An Introduction*. Cincinnati, OH: Anderson.

SUMMARY

In this chapter we have introduced you to the importance of the case study in criminal justice. Completing a case study will help improve your ability to do the following:

- Design and implement a plan to study a specific case.
- Collect and analyze information carefully and objectively.
- Solve problems effectively.
- Present your ideas and recommendations in clear, written form, directed to a specific audience.

Doing a study of this type allows you to discover some of the issues you will face if you become involved in an actual social situation that parallels your case study. This mode of research provides the criminal justice student or professional with a powerful tool to describe and a wide variety of topics within the discipline.

14

Criminal Justice Policy Analysis Papers

LEARN THE BASICS OF POLICY ANALYSIS

WHAT IS POLICY ANALYSIS?

President Obama's re-election in 2012 gave him little time to celebrate. Long-standing problems like widespread unhappiness over immigration laws, belligerent actions by the leaders of Syria, North Korea, and Iran, and the nation's aging infrastructure were enough to keep any chief executive busy. Solutions to these problems waited while Congress focused on a series of scandals. A quarter of the armed services' women had been sexually harassed or assaulted, yet less than one percent of the reported cases had been successfully prosecuted. The Internal Revenue Service had been excessively scrutinizing conservative organizations' applications for tax exemptions. The National Security Agency fought charges of collecting information on thousands of American citizens and spying on Chinese corporations. Spurred by the killing of 20 children and six adult staff members at the Sandy Hook Elementary School in Newtown, Connecticut, and other mass murders, the President's most visible efforts with respect to criminal justice centered on violence prevention in general and restrictions on gun ownership in particular.

Governments address problems by formulating *policies*, which are sets of principles or rules that guide government agencies in creating and running programs aimed at solving the problems. Like all presidents before him, President Obama's administration developed and proposed to Congress sets of policies to address many issues, some of which were eventually passed and became law.

Policy analysis is the examination of a policy to determine its *effectiveness* (how well it solves the problem it was designed to solve) and its *efficiency* (the extent to which the cost of implementing the policy is reasonable, effi-

considering the size and nature of the problem to be solved). Every day at all levels of government, analysts, sometimes called policy wonks, are writing policy analysis papers. Legislators at the state and national levels hire staff people who continually investigate public policy issues and seek ways to improve legislated policy. The United States Department of Justice develops policy proposals for presidents, and state governors receive policy analyses from their own staffs and corrections departments.

Public officials are constantly challenged to initiate new policies or change old ones. If they have a current formal policy at all, they want to know how effective it is. They then want to know what options are available to them, what changes they might make to improve current policy, and what the consequences of those changes will be. Policies are reviewed under a number of circumstances. Policy analyses are sometimes conducted as part of the normal agency budgeting processes. They help decision makers determine what policies should be continued or discontinued. By mastering the art of policy analysis you add to your resume skills that are needed by thousands of government agencies, non-profit organizations, and business corporations.

In writing a criminal justice (or any other) policy analysis paper, you should:

1. Select and clearly define a specific government policy. Since national-level policy issues, like the interstate highway system, are most often vastly complex, it is wise to select a policy of a state or local government agency.

2. Carefully define the social, governmental, economic, or other problem which the policy is designed to solve.

3. Describe the economic, social, and political environments in which the problem arose and in which the existing policy for solving the problem was developed.

4. Evaluate the effectiveness of the current policy or lack of policy in dealing with the problem.

5. Identify alternative policies that could be adopted to solve the selected problem, and estimate the economic, social, environmental, and political costs and benefits of each alternative.

6. Provide a summary comparison of all policies examined.

Successful policy analysis papers all share the same general purpose: to inform policymakers about how public policy in a specific area may be improved. A policy analysis paper, like a position paper, is an entirely practical exercise. It is neither theoretical nor general. Its objective is to identify and evaluate the policy options that are available for a specific topic.

WRITE A POLICY ANALYSIS PAPER

THE CONTENTS OF A POLICY ANALYSIS PAPER

Policy analysis papers contain six basic elements:

1. Title page
2. Executive summary
3. Table of contents, including a list of tables and illustrations
4. Text (or body)
5. References to sources of information
6. Appendixes

PARAMETERS OF THE TEXT

Ask your instructor for the number of pages required for the policy analysis paper assigned for your course. Such papers at the undergraduate level often range from 20 to 50 typed, double-spaced pages in length.

Two general rules govern the amount of information presented in the body of the paper. First, content must be adequate to make a good policy evaluation. You must include all the facts necessary to understand the significant strengths and weaknesses of a policy and its alternatives. If your paper omits a fact that is critical to the decision, a poor decision will likely be made.

Never omit important facts merely because they tend to support a perspective other than your own. It is your responsibility to present the facts as clearly as possible, not to bias the evaluation in a particular direction.

The second guideline for determining the length of a policy analysis paper is to omit extraneous material. Include only the information that is helpful in making the particular decision at hand. If, for example, you are analyzing the policy by which a municipal government funds a museum dedicated to the history of fishing in area lakes, how much information do you need to include about the specific exhibits in the museum?

THE FORMAT OF A POLICY ANALYSIS PAPER

Title Page

The title page for a policy analysis paper should follow the format provided for title pages in Chapter 3.

Executive Summary

A one-page, single-spaced executive summary immediately follows the title page. The carefully written sentences of the executive summary express the central concepts to be explained more fully in the text of the paper. The purpose of the summary is to allow the decision maker to understand, as quickly as possible, the major facts and issues under consideration. The decision maker should be able to get a clear and thorough overview of the entire policy problem and the value and costs of available policy options by reading the one-page summary.

Table of Contents

The table of contents of a policy analysis paper must follow the organization of the paper's text and should conform to the format shown in Chapter 3.

Text

The structure of a policy analysis paper's text may be outlined as follows.

I. **Description of the policy currently in force**
   A. A clear, concise statement of the policy currently in force
   B. A brief history of the policy currently in force
   C. A description of the problem the current policy was aimed at resolving, including an estimate of its extent and importance

II. **Environments of the policy currently in force**
   A. A description of the *physical* factors affecting the origin, development, and implementation of the current policy
   B. A description of the *social* factors affecting the origin, development, and implementation of the current policy
   C. A description of the *economic* factors affecting the origin, development, and implementation of the current policy
   D. A description of the *political* factors affecting the origin, development, and implementation of the current policy

III. **Effectiveness and efficiency of the current policy**
   A. How well the existing policy does what it was designed to do
   B. How well the policy performs in relation to the effort and resources committed to it

IV. **Policy alternatives**
   A. Possible alterations of the present policy, with the estimated costs and benefits of each
   B. Alternatives to the present policy, with the estimated costs and benefits of each

V.   Summary comparison of policy options

Most public policy analysis textbooks describe in detail each of the policy analysis components listed in the above outline. The following sections of this chapter, however, provide further information with respect to the above-mentioned points. Be sure to discuss the outline with your instructor to ensure that you understand what each entails.

References

You must be sure to cite properly all sources of information in a policy analysis paper. Follow the directions for proper citation in Chapters 4 and 5.

Appendixes

Appendixes can provide the reader of policy analysis papers with information that supplements the important facts contained in the text. For many local development and public works projects, a map and a diagram are often very helpful appendixes. You should attach them to the end of the paper, after the reference page. You should not append entire government reports, journal articles, or other publications, but feel free to include selected charts, graphs, or other pages. The source of the information should always be evident on the appended pages.

ANALYSIS OF A CRIMINAL JUSTICE POLICY

Let's suppose you are interested in current problems in Oklahoma's criminal justice system. You have recently read a report entitled "Action Items for Oklahoma: Criminal Justice: Increase Safety and Savings with Smart on Crime Reforms," written by Gene Perry for the Oklahoma Policy Institute. The introduction to this report says in part:

> Oklahoma's criminal justice system is in a crisis. The state ranks 1st in the nation for incarceration of women per capita and 4th for men. From FY 1996 to FY 2011, the number of inmates in Oklahoma prisons increased by 30 percent, going from 19,968 to 25,977. (i) This increase in prisoners was double the state's overall population growth over that same period (15 percent). All of this incarceration is not paying off in public safety, either—in 2011, the violent crime rate in Oklahoma was 18 percent higher than the national average. (ii) At the same time, the corrections system has become overwhelmed with non-violent drug offenders serving long sentences. From FY 2005 to FY 2010, non-violent drug offenders made up 31 percent of new prison admissions, compared to just 29 percent who were violent offenders. (iii) State budgets have not kept pace with inmate growth, and the corrections system has become severely understaffed. The Department of Corrections now employs 871 fewer full-time workers than it did in FY 2008 and has been operating at between 67 and 75 percent staffing capacity for several years. (iv) This puts both inmates and corrections officers in serious danger. There

are signs of hope. The 2012 justice reinvestment bill showed a new willingness to make progress on this issue. New models of corrections like drug courts and the Women in Recovery program are gaining bipartisan support. Some in Oklahoma are taking a different mentality towards criminal justice—one that doesn't pursue punishment for its own sake, but instead looks for what works to protect public safety in the most cost-effective way. However, we have more work to do. The implementation of already passed corrections reforms are faltering due to lack of funding and inadequate coordination and leadership. We continue to follow counterproductive policies that push Oklahomans who are trying to escape addiction and contribute to society into a downward spiral, and the problem is growing more costly to taxpayers every year. This report details concrete steps Oklahoma can take to address the financial and moral crisis in our criminal justice system. (Perry 2013)

Since this report discusses a substantial array of problems, you decide to find out why Oklahoma incarcerates more women than any other state in the country, and try to decide if the state's policies leading to this situation are adequate or in need of change. Following the outline suggested in this chapter for writing criminal justice policy analyses papers, you construct your own initial outline in which you ask a series of questions that you will need to answer in order to write an informative paper.

I. **Description of the policy currently in force**

    A. A clear, concise statement of the policy currently in force:
       What policy or policies result in so many women being incarcerated?

    B. A brief history of the policy currently in force:
       How did these policies come to be adopted?

    C. A description of the problem the current policy was aimed at resolving, including an estimate of its extent and importance:
       What was the purpose of the relevant policies (to teach people a lesson? to reduce the use of drugs? to lower the general crime rate?)?

II. **Environments of the policy currently in force**

    A. A description of the *physical* factors affecting the origin, development, and implementation of the current policy: Is there anything about the geography, climate, or natural resources of Oklahoma that contribute to the incarceration of women?

    B. A description of the *social* factors affecting the origin, development, and implementation of the current policy: Do patterns of social class, religion, or ethnicity contribute to the high rate of incarceration of women?

    C. A description of the *economic* factors affecting the origin, development, and implementation of the current policy: Is poverty a contributing factor? Unemployment?

    D. A description of the *political* factors affecting the origin, development, and implementation of the current policy: Do conservative or liberal values tend to increase the incarceration rate?

III. **Effectiveness and efficiency of the current policy**

   A. How well the existing policy does what it was designed to do? Does increased incarceration decrease crime or drug use?

   B. How well the policy performs in relation to the effort and resources committed to it: How expensive is it to maintain current incarceration policies?

IV. **Policy alternatives**

   A. Possible alterations of the present policy, with the estimated costs and benefits of each: Can small changes in current policies make significant changes in policy outcomes?

   B. Alternatives to the present policy, with the estimated costs and benefits of each: Are there one or more ways of approaching the "women and crime problem" that reduce incarceration and still achieve Oklahoma's goals?

V. **Summary comparison of policy options**

Conclude your paper by comparing available options and recommending the one or ones you believe will be most beneficial for the State of Oklahoma. Cite references properly (as described in Chapter 4 of this Manual) and attach appropriate appendixes.

A SAMPLE POLICY ANALYSIS PAPER

The following policy analysis paper was written by a student at the University of Central Oklahoma. Does the paper make its point clearly? Does it convince you?

An Analysis of the Death Penalty in the State of Oklahoma

by Markus Smith

for

Public Policy Analysis
PLTSC 4413
Dr. Gregory M. Scott
University of Central Oklahoma
December 2, 2005

EXECUTIVE SUMMARY

Oklahoma is one of 38 states that have a death penalty statute. Title 21, chapter 701.9, of the *Oklahoma Statutes* states, "A person who is convicted of or pleads guilty or *nolo contende* to murder in the first degree shall be punished by death, by imprisonment for life without parole or by imprisonment for life" (3573). Although the implementation of the death penalty was enacted to deter crime and punish murderers, many Oklahoma citizens have serious doubts about the viability of the death penalty.

Just last year, questions raised by forensic experts and the courts about the work of Oklahoma City Police Department chemist Joyce Gilchrist resulted in Gilchrist's suspension and then dismissal from the department (Hamilton 2001:1A). It was later discovered that Gilchrist's inaccurate testimony in cases spanning her 21-year career resulted in innocent individuals being incarcerated and sent to death row.

The total number of murders committed in Oklahoma from 1999 to 2001 was 263, an average of about one murder every four days. As of March 22, 2002, Oklahoma was ranked number one in executions per capita in the United States. Also, Oklahoma falls second in the total number of executions from 1999 to 2002, with a total of 35, of which 18 were carried out in 2001 alone. To compound the problem, Oklahoma ranks third in the nation among states that have released innocent people from death row, with a total of seven. The innocents in Oklahoma have spent an average of seven years in prison from the time they were convicted until they were exonerated and released ("Innocents Released from Death Row by State" 2001).

It is apparent that Oklahoma needs to come up with alternatives to the death penalty. Right now there are 116 people on death row, some of whom may be innocent. The only person who could clear them of a crime they did not commit is the OCPD's chemist. And as we witnessed in the case of Joyce Gilchrist, the chemist's findings may not be reliable.

Oklahoma spent approximately $50 million on 18 executions in 2001 alone, averaging $2.8 million per person. This total amount compares to a Life without Parole (LWOP) cost of $11.25 million over the next 40 years, which would save Oklahoma and taxpayers $2.2 million per execution.

Before Oklahoma executes another inmate, the state should address two issues. First, there should be a moratorium and a full investigation of the individuals currently on death row, whether by DNA testing or some other

(*continued*)

means, to ensure that Oklahoma does not continue to execute innocent victims. And second, the state should consider the benefits of doing away with the death penalty altogether.

TEXT

Oklahoma is one of 38 states that have a death penalty statute. Title 21, chapter 701.9, of the *Oklahoma Statutes* states, "A person who is convicted of or pleads guilty or *nolo contende* to murder in the first degree shall be punished by death, by imprisonment for life without parole or by imprisonment for life" (3573).

Also, at least one of eight statutorily defined aggravating circumstances has to be in conjunction with the murder for the perpetrator to be sentenced to death. These circumstances are:

(1) The defendant was previously convicted of a felony involving the use or threat of violence to the person; (2) The defendant knowingly created a great risk of death to more than one person; (3) The person committed the murder for remuneration or the promise of remuneration or employed another to commit the murder for remuneration or the promise of remuneration; (4) The murder was especially heinous, atrocious, or cruel; (5) The murder was committed for the purpose of avoiding or preventing a lawful arrest or prosecution; (6) The murder was committed by a person while serving a sentence of imprisonment on conviction of a felony; (7) The existence of a probability that the defendant would commit criminal acts of violence that would constitute a continuing threat to society; or (8) The victim of the murder was a peace officer as defined by Section 99 of Title 21 of the Oklahoma Statutes, or guard of an institution under the control of the Department of Corrections, and such person was killed while in performance of official duty. (*Oklahoma Statutes* 3573)

Inspired by the use Britain made of the death penalty for centuries, America established its own death penalty mainly to deter capital offenses and to punish individuals who committed heinous crimes. The original death penalty law in Oklahoma called for executions to be carried out by electrocution. From 1915 to 1966, Oklahoma executed 82 individuals by electrocution and 1 by hanging. But in 1972 the United States Supreme Court ruled in *Furman v. Georgia* (408 U.S. 238) that death by electrocution was unconstitutional ("Capital Punishment: Legal Background of Death Penalty in South Carolina" 2002).

So, in 1977, Oklahoma became the first state to adopt lethal injection as a means of execution. The first lethal injection execution in Oklahoma took place on September 10, 1990, claiming the life of Charles Troy Coleman, who in 1979 was convicted of first-degree murder in Muskogee County ("Capital Punishment" 2001).

The method requires the insertion of two intravenous tubes into each arm. Then, one at a time, the drugs sodium thiopental, which causes unconsciousness, pancuronium bromide, which stops respiration, and potassium chloride, which stops the heart, are injected by syringes into the intravenous tubes ("Capital Punishment" 2001).

Although some states abolished the death penalty in the mid-1800s, the first half of the 1900s marked the Progressive Period of reform in the United States. From 1907 to 1917, six states completely prohibited the death penalty, but many others continued to use it, Oklahoma being one of them. As long as Oklahoma has had the death penalty there have been many organizations that have striven to prevent further executions. One of the most recognized anti-death penalty organizations in Oklahoma is the Oklahoma Coalition to Abolish the Death Penalty. Founded in 1987, it consists of individuals, human rights groups, churches, and other religious-based organizations ("About the Coalition" 2002).

Oklahoma's Governor Frank Keating is an advocate for the death penalty. In an article from *Human Events*, Keating makes five assertions about capital punishment, some dealing primarily with his state, some with the nation as a whole. First, says Keating, Oklahoma is not a "kill happy" state. Second, Oklahoma is not in a hurry to execute inmates. In fact, the average length between sentencing and execution is more than 12 years. Third, claims of racial bias in death penalty cases are simply untrue. Of the 68 inmates executed across the nation in 1998, 48 were white and 18 black. Fourth, capital punishment is a deterrent to homicide. And lastly, Keating asserts that capital punishment is justice. Take someone's life and you have to forfeit yours (Keating 2000:1).

Although the implementation of the death penalty was enacted to deter crime and punish murderers, many Oklahoma citizens have serious doubts about the viability of the death penalty. In October of 2001, the Oklahoma City Police Department fired its chemist of 21 years, Joyce Gilchrist, because of questions raised by forensic experts and the courts about the accuracy of her work. It was later alleged that her inaccurate testimony resulted

(continued)

in innocent individuals being incarcerated and even sent to death row. Gilchrist's analyses had a powerful influence on judges and juries when determining whether or not an individual was sent to death row. Gilchrist was responsible for working on approximately 3,000 cases; 23 cases involved defendants who were either sentenced to death, have been executed, or still remain on death row. And 11 of those defendants were executed during the past two years, despite strong doubts as to their guilt because of Gilchrist's testimony ("Innocents Released from Death Row by State" 2001).

The total number of murders committed in Oklahoma from 1999 to 2001 was 597, which is an average of one murder every other day. As of March 22, 2002, Oklahoma was ranked number one in executions per capita in the United States. Also, Oklahoma falls second in the total number of executions from 1999 to 2002, with a total of 35. Eighteen of those executions were carried out in 2001 alone, ranking Oklahoma number one in total executions for that year. And to compound the problem, Oklahoma ranked third in the nation among states who have released innocent people from death row, with a total of seven. The innocents in Oklahoma have spent an average of seven years in prison from the time they were convicted until they were exonerated and released (DPIO website).

Taking no action to abolish or qualify the use of the death penalty could cause more innocent individuals to be sent to death row, costing taxpayers millions of dollars because of the expenses involved in trying capital cases in court. And, more importantly, inaction could result in the high possibility that innocent individuals would be executed. Solving problems in the state's use of the death penalty, on the other hand, could result in the exoneration of innocent individuals and save taxpayers millions of dollars per execution. Furthermore, it would give citizens the feeling that the policy that is in place is a dependable one.

One of the main arguments for the death penalty has been that it is cheaper to execute an inmate than it is to let him live the remainder of his life in prison. But in fact, the daily cost of an inmate in Oklahoma prisons is $42.36 per day, which adds up to $15,461.00 a year. Hypothetically, even if you housed an inmate for 40 years, the total cost would be approximately $618,456.00. Studies have shown that the cost for executing inmates is about four times what it would cost to house them for 40 years ("Capital Punishment" 2001).

A death penalty case is more expensive than any other criminal case, costing more than if an individual received a sentence of imprisonment for life without the possibility of parole. States that implement the death penalty pay a high price in doing so. In Texas, for instance, the cost placed on taxpayers for each death penalty case averages $2.3 million, or about three times what it would cost to imprison someone at the highest security level for 40 years. In Florida, which ranks just above Oklahoma in total executions, each execution costs the state $3.2 million. A report focusing on California estimated that abolishing the death penalty would save that state approximately $90 million a year ("Innocents Released from Death Row by State" 2001).

Reuters News Service reported that in her weekly Justice Department news briefing on January 21, 2000, United States Attorney General Janet Reno said, "I have inquired for most of my adult life about studies that might show that the death penalty is a deterrent. And I have not seen any research that would substantiate that point" ("Facts about Deterrence and the Death Penalty" 2002). The majority of studies completed on the death penalty have shown that it has not caused a deterrent effect in the states. In fact, the studies have shown that murder rates continue to rise in states that implement the death penalty compared to those in states that do not have it. Ironically, the United States is the only Western country that implements the death penalty, and yet it has the largest number of murders of all Western countries ("Facts about Deterrence and the Death Penalty" 2002).

For the past four years (1998–2001) there has not been a significant decline in the number of murders committed in Oklahoma. In 2001 there were 185, four more than the previous year. This figure comes as a surprise, especially since in 2001 Oklahoma executed more inmates in one year than ever before. In 2001 there were 92, nine more than the previous year. Since 1983, Oklahoma has averaged 75 murders per year ("Murder 1 Receptions by Year from FY 1980 to FY 2002" 2002). This fact alone is enough to show that the death penalty is not a deterrent to murder in Oklahoma.

In 25 out of the 38 states that implement the death penalty it is permissible to execute a mentally retarded or mentally ill inmate ("Mental Retardation and the Death Penalty" 2000). In the past four years Oklahoma has executed at least two inmates who had been diagnosed with serious mental illness. And there are others on death row with serious mental illnesses who are awaiting their fate ("Mental Illness and the Death Penalty" 2001).

In the final days of the 2002 Legislative Session, the House and Senate approved a bill that would have prohibited the execution of people with developmental disabilities. House Bill 2635 passed by a 53–46 vote in the

(continued)

House on May 23, 2002, and by a 25–16 vote in the Senate on May 24. Once both the House and Senate passed HB 2635, all that was left was for it to go to the governor, who could either sign it into law or veto the bill. On June 7, 2002, Governor Frank Keating vetoed HB 2635 ("Governor Keating Vetoes House Bill 2635" 2002).

Oklahoma needs to come up with alternatives for the death penalty. Right now there are 116 people on death row, and there may be a possibility that some of those individuals are innocent. The only person who could clear them of a crime that they did not commit is the OCPD's chemist, but as we witnessed in 2001, chemist Joyce Gilchrist ended up doing more harm than good. Remember, Oklahoma ranked third among all states for innocents released and first in total executions in 2001. These facts alone should be enough to alter or do away with the death penalty, because it is obvious that there are flaws in the legal system. The individuals who were later exonerated were the lucky ones. What about other innocent individuals, if any, who remain incarcerated or have already been executed?

For any type of policy to be successful, it must be viable, especially if the policy result is the execution of individuals. One possible first step in finding an alternative to the current policy could be a moratorium on the death penalty. In Illinois Governor George Ryan has imposed a moratorium on the state's death penalty. All lethal injections are to be postponed indefinitely pending an investigation into why more executions have been overturned than carried out since 1977, when Illinois reinstated the death penalty. Illinois has had 13 people who have been exonerated and 12 who have been put to death. The Governor's decision makes Illinois the first of 38 states with capital punishment to halt all executions while it reviews its death penalty procedures ("Governor Calls for Review of 'Flawed' System" 2000).

Maryland has become the second state to declare a death penalty moratorium. Governor Parris Glendening, who stayed the execution of Wesley Eugene Baker, announced a moratorium on all executions in the state pending the release of a state study that examines racial biases in capital cases (Tierney-Rust 2002). Other states are jumping on the bandwagon also. Ohio is attempting to put a moratorium on capital punishment; Representative Shirley Smith, who is the main sponsor of the legislation, believes that some of the inmates on Ohio's Death Row have been wrongfully convicted. Smith's bill would require legislative leaders to appoint a capital punishment review commission. They would have a year to determine whether the death penalty is being carried out fairly ("Ohio Bill Seeks Moratorium" 2000).

There are at least two potentially beneficial alternatives to the death penalty available to Oklahomans for consideration. The first of these is a moratorium, one benefit of which is that it would halt executions immediately, saving taxpayers and the State of Oklahoma millions of dollars. The second alternative is, simply, to do away with the death penalty altogether, sentencing those who would have been executed to life without parole instead. This course of action would also result in saving Oklahomans millions of dollars.

Benefit-Cost Analysis Summary

Alternative	Benefit	Cost
Moratorium	Stop Executions	Taxpayers/State ($0)
Do Away With Save	Taxpayers $Millions	$2.2 million/person (LWOP)

Though an economic study of Oklahoma's use of the death penalty has never been made, it is possible to analyze data from states with similar demographics. A 1992 *Dallas Morning News* study revealed that a sentence of life without parole (LWOP) generally costs the state of Texas $750,000 per person. By comparison, a capital trial, appeals, death row security, maintenance and the execution itself cost about $2.3 million per person. A North Carolina study showed execution costs two to five times greater than LWOP, about $2.1 million. Estimates based on these figures suggest that Oklahoma spent approximately $50 million on executions in 2001 alone, an average of $2.8 million per person. This amount compares to an LWOP cost of $11.25 million over the next 40 years (Fricker 2001:A1).

REFERENCES

"About the Coalition." 2002. *Oklahoma Coalition to Abolish the Death Penalty.* Retrieved November 28, 2002 (http://www.ocadp.org/index.html).

"Capital Punishment." 2001. *Oklahoma Department of Corrections Home Page.* Retrieved November 29, 2002 (http://www.doc.state.ok.us/DOCS/CapitalP.HTM).

(*continued*)

"Capital Punishment: Legal Background of Death Penalty in South Carolina." 2002. *South Carolina Department of Corrections.* Retrieved December 1, 2002 (http://www.state.sc.us/scdc/Capital%20Punishment/capital-punishment.htm).

"Facts about Deterrence and the Death Penalty." 2002. *Death Penalty Information Center.* Retrieved November 29, 2002 (http://www.deathpenaltyinfo.org/article.php?did=167&scid=12).

Fricker, Richard L. 2001. "When Is It Right for the State to Kill?" *Oklahoma Eagle,* January 19, A1–A2.

"Governor Calls for Review of 'Flawed' System." 2000. *Cable News Network (CNN),* January 31. Retrieved November 28, 2002 (http://www.cnn.com/2000/US/01/31/Illinois.executions.02/).

"Governor Keating Vetoes House Bill 2635." 2002. *Oklahoma Coalition to Abolish the Death Penalty,* June 9. Retrieved November 29, 2002 (http://www.ocadp.org/news/2002/HB2635_update.html).

Hamilton, Arnold. 2001. "Chemist's Errors Stir Fear: Did Oklahoma Execute Innocent?" *Dallas Morning News,* October 22, 1A, 11A.

"Innocents Released from Death Row by State." 2001. *Death Penalty Institute of Oklahoma,* June 4. Retrieved November 26, 2002 (http://www.dpio.org/death_row/Innocents_Released_by_State.html).

Keating, Frank. 2000. "Why I Support Capital Punishment." *Human Events,* May 19, p. 1.

"Mental Illness and the Death Penalty." 2001. *Death Penalty Institute of Oklahoma,* February 27. Retrieved November 26, 2002 (http://www.dpio.org/Issues/Mental_Illness.html).

"Mental Retardation and the Death Penalty." 2000. *Death Penalty Institute of Oklahoma,* August 14. Retrieved November 26, 2002 (http://www.dpio.org/Issues/Mental_Retardation.html).

"Murder 1 Receptions by Year from FY 1980 to FY 2002." 2002. *Oklahoma Department of Corrections.* Retrieved November 31, 2002 (http://www.doc.state.ok.us/charts/murder.htm).

"Ohio Bill Seeks Moratorium." 2000. *American Civil Liberties Union: News,* July 13. Retrieved November 31, 2002 (http://www.aclu.org/DeathPenalty/DeathPenalty.cfm?ID=7621&c=67).

Tierney-Rust, Diann. 2002. "Maryland Stays Execution and Becomes Second State to Declare Death Penalty Moratorium; ACLU Applauds Governor's Courage." *American Civil Liberties Union: News*, May 10. Retrieved December 1, 2002 (http://www.aclu.org/DeathPenalty/DeathPenalty. cfm?ID=1033.

Glossary

accountability The obligation to perform responsibly and exercise authority in terms of established performance standards.

accreditation The status achieved by a correctional program, police agency, court, or other facility when it is recognized as having met certain national standards following an on-site audit by the relevant commission on accreditation.

accusation A formal charge against a person inferring that he or she may be guilty of a punishable offense.

accusatory instrument An indictment, information, simplified traffic information, prosecutor's information, misdemeanor complaint, or felony complaint. Every accusatory instrument, regardless of the person designated therein as the accuser, constitutes an accusation on behalf of the state as plaintiff and must be titled "the people of the state of …" against a designated person, known as the defendant.

accusatory stage The investigation that occurs in police practice after suspicion has focused on one or more particular individuals as having guilty knowledge of the offense, distinguished from the investigatory stage during which the offense is the subject of general investigation before suspicion has focused on a particular accused; also, any stage in a criminal prosecution from arrest to conviction or acquittal.

accused The generic name for the defendant in a criminal case.

acquittal A legal and formal certification of the innocence of a person charged.

act of God An act occasioned exclusively by violence of nature without the interference of any human agency; an act, event, happening, or occurrence due to natural causes.

actus reus The criminal act; the act of a person committing a crime.

adaptative behavior One of the various responses through which inmates adjust to the institutional setting, including such psychological defense mechanisms as rejecting authority, projecting blame, or rationalizing.

addict One who has a physical and psychological dependence on one or more drug(s), who has built up a physical tolerance that results in taking increasingly larger doses, and who has an overpowering desire to continue taking the drug(s). A person can become addicted to illegal as well as legal drugs (such as alcohol).

adjudicate To determine finally; to adjudge.

adjudication The giving or pronouncing of a judgment or decree in a cause; also, the judgment given. It is the equivalent of "determination," the formal finding of guilt or innocence by a court of law, or the stage that would be considered a trial in the criminal justice system, which in juvenile court refers to a hearing to establish the facts of the case.

administration The act of administering, or the state of being administered; also, the management of direction of affairs, or the total activity of a manager.

administrative remedies The formal administrative mechanisms used within correctional institutions to proactively reduce litigation, such as the implementation of grievance procedures to identify and address complaints.

administrative segregation The separate confinement of inmates who, for any of a number of reasons, need closer attention or supervision than is available in the general population.

administrative sentencing model A sentencing plan in which legislatures and judges prescribe boundaries but administrative agencies determine the actual length of sentence.

adversary An opponent; the opposite party in a writ or action.

adversary proceeding A proceeding having opposing parties, as distinguished from an ex parte proceeding.

adversary process The view of criminal justice as a contest between the government and the individual.

adversary system The practice of conducting a legal proceeding as a battle between opposing parties under the judge as an impartial umpire with the outcome determined by the pleading and evidence introduced into courts; in Anglo-American jurisprudence, it includes the presumption of innocence of the accused. It is to be distinguished from the accusatory system used in continental law, where the accusation is taken as evidence of guilt that must be disproved by the accused.

advocate One who assists, defends, or pleads for another.

affidavit A written or printed declaration or statement of facts, taken before an officer having authority to administer oaths.

affirmative action The range of programs instituted by government to increase the number of minority employees in the public and private sectors.

aftercare The follow-up services and supervision provided an inmate upon release from a juvenile correctional institution, similar to parole or supervised mandatory release in the adult system.

aggravated assault An assault with intent to kill or for the purpose of inflicting severe bodily injury; assault with the use of a deadly weapon.

aggregate crime rate The number of crimes per 100,000 of the general population.

aggregate data The data on large numbers of subjects showing a common characteristic.

aggressive field investigation An investigatory model in which police consistently check out suspicious circumstances, places, and persons.

alcoholism The disease associated with abuse of legally available drugs (such as beer, wine, and/or liquor). Tendencies toward alcoholism may be inherited genetically, as well as precipitated by social and psychological factors.

alias A fictitious name; otherwise, in another manner.

alienist One who specializes in the study of mental disease.

allocution The court's inquiry of a prisoner as to whether he or she has any legal cause why judgment should not be pronounced against him or her upon conviction. *See also* right of allocution.

alternative dispute resolution A type of formal diversion in which a neutral third party attempts to reach an agreeable compromise between the victim and the offender to resolve the case outside the criminal justice system.

amicus curiae A friend of the court; also, a person who has no right to appear in a suit but is allowed to introduce argument, authority, or evidence to protect his interest.

anomie The weakening of social norms, which has been linked with crime and delinquency.

anonymity The assurance that research subjects' identities will not be disclosed.

anthropology A discipline focusing on the nature of human culture, in which field research is the primary method of study.

appeal The removal of a case from a court of inferior jurisdiction to one of superior jurisdiction for the purpose of obtaining a review and retrial.

appearance The coming into court as party to a suit.

appearance ticket A written notice issued by a public servant requiring a person to appear before a local criminal court in connection with an accusatory instrument to be filed against him or her therein.

appellant The party who takes an appeal from one court of justice to another; in criminal law, usually the defendant in the lower court.

appellant jurisdiction The right of a court to review the decision of a lower court; the power to hear cases appealed from a lower court. Appellant jurisdiction is to be distinguished from original jurisdiction.

appellee The party in a cause against whom an appeal is taken; in U.S. criminal law, usually the state or the United States.

applied research The type of research for which one of the primary purposes is that the study may have some practical use.

archival research A method of studying organizations or societies based on the collected records they have produced.

argot The unique vocabulary used in communication between inmates and street criminals.

arraign To bring a prisoner before the court to answer an indictment or information; in practice, used to refer to any appearance of the accused before a magistrate or before a trial court to enter a plea. *See also* arraignment.

arraignment The proceeding for arraignment of the accused at which he enters a plea to the charge. *See also* arraign.

arrest The taking of a person into custody to answer to a criminal charge; a detention of a suspect subject to investigation and prosecution.

arson The intentional and unlawful burning of property; at common law, the malicious burning of the dwelling or outhouse of another.

asportation The removal of things from one place to another, such as required in the offense of larceny in some states.

assault The intentional unlawful use of force by one person upon another. If severe bodily harm is inflicted or a weapon is used, the offense is aggravated assault. The lesser degree of the crime is called assault or simple assault. *See also* assault and battery and simple assault.

assault and battery A battery is an unlawful touching of the person of another. *See also* assault.

assessment A screening procedure in which a candidate's strengths and weaknesses are evaluated by a team of trained assessors on the basis of performance.

assessment center The place where screening procedure or assessment is implemented.

atavistic Having the characteristics of savages, as in early forms of human evolution.

attrition The loss of members of a sample, usually as a result of their refusal to respond or the researcher's inability to contact them.

attrition of cases The cases dropped at various stages in the criminal process.

Auburn system The approach that focused on congregate work and harsh discipline, as practiced at the correctional facility in Auburn, New York.

authority The sum of the powers and rights assigned to a position, such as a chief of police or a warden.

auto theft The act of stealing or driving away and abandoning a motor vehicle. It may exclude taking for temporary use, or the taking for temporary use may carry a smaller penalty.

backdoor strategy The reduction of a prison population by the early release of prisoners.

background forces The psychological, biological, and sociological causes of crime.

bail To procure the release of a person from legal custody by instructing that he or she must appear at the time and place designated and submit himself or herself to the jurisdiction and judgment of the court.

bail bond A bond executed by a defendant who has been arrested, together with other persons as sureties, naming the sheriff, constable, or marshal as obligee, to receive a court-specified sum on condition that the defendant must appear to answer the legal process.

bailee One to whom goods are delivered under a contract or agreement of bailment.

bailment A delivery of goods or personal property by one person to another to carry out a special purpose and redeliver the goods to the bailor.

bailor One who delivers goods under a contract or agreement of bailment.

banishment and exile (also called *transportation*) The forms of punishment in which offenders were transported from Europe to distant lands (such as the Americas and Australia).

bar graph A graph on which the categories of a variable are presented on the horizontal axis and their frequencies on the vertical axis. The height of each bar represents the frequency of each attribute of a variable. The bars have gaps between them on the scale.

basic research Any research whose primary purpose is to contribute to systematic knowledge in a discipline.

behavior modification The process of changing behavior through the conditioning power of such reinforcements as rewards and punishments.

bench warrant A process issued by the court itself, or "from the bench," for the attachment or arrest of a person; either in case of contempt, or whether an indictment has been found, or to bring in a witness who does not obey a subpoena (to bring him or her in); so called to distinguish it from a warrant issued by a justice of the peace or magistrate.

beyond a reasonable doubt A level of proof to a moral certainty, satisfying the judgment and consciences of the jury, as reasonable men and women, that the crime charged has been committed by the defendant. Moral certainty is not a requirement in some states.

bivariate table A two-variable table.

bond The money or property required to obtain release of an inmate from jail for a criminal charge in order to ensure his or her appearance at trial.

booking An administrative record of an arrest, or the clerical process involving the entry on the police blotter, or arrest book, of the suspect's name, the time of the arrest, the offense charged, and the name of the arresting officer; used in practice to refer to the police station house procedures that take place from arrest to the initial appearance of the accused before the magistrate.

brainstorming The exploration, discovery, and development of details to be used in a research study.

breach of the peace A violation or disturbance of the public tranquility and order.

breaking and entering Any unlawful entry, even if no force was used to gain entrance.

building-tender system A system in which prisoners assist officers in managing cell blocks.

burglary The act of breaking and entering with intent to commit a felony or theft, or in some states, with intent to commit any offense.

capability The range, variety, and depth of skills that a person holds in a certain job or position in the organization. It is also the sum total of the structure, process, and systems that make up the organization itself.

capacity The outside limits of a person or organization or population that determine the amount of accomplishment or production that can be done. Capacity, for example, can be increased by adding resources, restructuring the application of resources, or increasing the capability of resources within the organization. In criminal justice, population capacity is usually a matter of law.

career criminal A criminal who devotes the greater part of his or her life to crime.

career-criminal units A unit with prosecutors who specialize in the prosecution of repeat offenders.

carnal knowledge The act of sexual intercourse; the slightest penetration of the sexual organ of the female by the sexual organ of the male.

carrying concealed weapons A violation of a regulation or status controlling the carrying, using, possessing, furnishing, and manufacturing of deadly weapons.

case A general term for an action, cause, suit, or controversy in law or equity; a question contested before a court of justice.

case study The observational study of a single environment (a detention center, a police precinct, a public place). Field research is often based on a single case study.

caseload The workload of a probation (or parole) officer, usually measured by the number of cases being supervised and/or investigated.

caseload classification (also called *case management*) The act of separating cases according to the intensity of supervision needed by the client.

causation One or more variables that produce a result. *See also* independent variable.

cell The position where two categories meet in a cross-classification table (e.g., in a 2 3 3 bivariate table there will be six cells); also, an inmate's living quarters.

cell search (also called *shakedown*) A thorough examination of the structure and contents of a cell to detect and remove any contraband items. Searches may be conducted routinely, randomly, or based on suspicion, but not for harassment.

central intake (often called a *diagnostic* or *reception center*) The place where new inmates are received, processed, tested, and assigned to housing.

certification The use of a legal process to treat juveniles as adults for criminal prosecution.

certiorari To be informed of, to be made certain in regard to; the name of a writ of review or inquiry, or a writ directed by a superior court to an inferior court asking that the record of a case be sent up for review; a method of obtaining a review of a case by the U.S. Supreme Court.

change of venue The removal of an action begun in one county or district to another county or district for trial.

charge To initiate formal criminal court proceedings; to impose a burden, duty, or obligation; to claim, demand, or accuse; to instruct a jury on matters of law.

charge bargaining The process of plea negotiations over the charge the government will file.

chronic stress The stress associated with the long-term effect of experiencing continual pressures and problems in the work environment.

circumstances The attendant facts. Any fact may be a circumstance with reference to another fact.

circumstantial evidence The evidence that is of an indirect nature. The existence of a principal fact is inferred from circumstances.

citation An order to appear in court; in writing, the citation of a documentable source.

citizen One who under the Constitution and laws of the United States or of a particular state is a member of the political community.

civil liability The act of being held accountable in a civil court of law, where nominal, compensatory, and/or punitive damages can be awarded against those held liable for actions or in actions that resulted in harm, injury, or death.

civilian review board A commission set up outside the police or corrections department to hear and review citizen complaints against the police or the correctional system.

classification The separation of inmates at all levels into groups according to characteristics that they share in common.

client One who is under the care, custody, or control of a correctional agency.

closed-ended question (also called *forced-choice questions*) A question in a questionnaire that forces the respondent to select from a list of possible responses.

co-correctional institutions (also known as *coed prisons*) A correctional facility where both men and women are housed within one compound. Although they do not share living quarters in the United States, males and females interact socially and have access to the same institutional programs.

coercion Compulsion, constraint, or compelling by force.

cognitive dissonance A perceived discrepancy between what is stated to be reality and what is reality in fact.

colloquy The formal discussion between a judge and defendant to determine if the defendant has pleaded knowingly and voluntarily.

commercial bail The private business of bail bonding.

common law A custom translated into law over time and social circumstances.

communication and feedback systems The kind and amount of information flow among people, within an organization, and between an organization and people.

community policing A policing system in which citizens participate in setting police priorities and police operations.

community residential center A minimum-security community-based residential facility that typically provides such programs as work release and drug treatment as well as educational opportunities.

community service internship A field experience offering officers or students an opportunity to gain a broad perspective on crime and criminal law enforcement.

community-based supervision The services, programs, or facilities provided within the community to offenders who are not incarcerated in high-security confinement.

complaint A charge in criminal law preferred before a magistrate having jurisdiction that a person named has committed a specific offense; usually, the first document filed with a court charging the offense. In some states, the term *complaint* is interchangeable with *information*; it is also sometimes used interchangeably with *affidavit*. *See also* information.

concept A general idea in management stated in a formalized manner so that it can be communicated in a standardized fashion.

concurrent sentences Two or more sentences that run at the same time. Each day served by the prisoner is credited on each of the concurrent sentences.

conditional release The release of an offender from incarceration under certain conditions, violation of which allows for reactivation of the unserved portion of the sentence.

conditioning The expectation that a certain reaction will follow a certain stimulus, which is reinforced by repetition of the stimulus/response pattern.

conflict perspective A perspective that conflict, not agreement, is the normal state of society and that crime is the product of the power structure.

conglomerate A complex organization composed of numerous diverse functions.

conjugal visit The authorization of a visit between an inmate and a visitor that involves sexual intimacy.

consecutive sentences Two or more sentences that are served one after the other. Inmates refer to such sentences as stacked or as boxcars.

consensus perspective The general agreement on values in society.

consensus prison management A balance of control and responsibility management.

consent decree A response to a lawsuit whereby the court agrees to delay direct intervention in exchange for voluntary compliance with certain stipulated conditions.

consent search A search conducted with knowing and voluntary consent.

consistent supervisory style An approach to inmate management in which the correctional officer responds in a uniform manner whenever similar situations are encountered.

conspiracy The agreement between or among parties to commit a crime.

constructive intent The conscious or unconscious creation of risk of harm.

contact visit The authorization of physical contact (within specified limits) during visits in jails and correctional centers.

contempt A willful disregard or disobedience of a public authority.

contempt of court An act that is calculated to embarrass, hinder, or obstruct the court in the administration of justice or that is calculated to lessen its authority or dignity. Directed contempt (also called *criminal contempt*) is an act committed in the immediate view of the court (such as insulting language or acts of violence) and is punishable summarily. Constructive (or indirect) contempt arises from matters not occurring in or near the presence of the court but with reference to the failure or refusal of a party to obey a lawful decree of court.

contempt powers The power of a court to punish for contempt. A court of record has this power.

contingency contracting An agreement between parties (e.g., an inmate and the correctional administration) whereby one agrees to take specified action if the other meets certain conditions stipulated in the contract.

contraband Any item that people are not authorized to possess, or an authorized item that is altered from its original state.

contract labor The practice of using prisoners to work under contract to private industry.

control model of management A perspective of prison management emphasizing obedience, work, and education of prisoners.

controlled movement The restriction of inmates' freedom of movement to better ensure institutional security.

controlling The act of measuring and correcting activities of employees to make certain that plans succeed. Controlling is closely related to the organizational planning system.

conventional goal A socially established goal (such as money, status, and prestige) that is recognized as desirable throughout society.

conviction The result of a criminal trial that ends in a judgment or sentence that the person is guilty as charged.

corpus delicti The body of the crime; the essential elements of the crime; the substantial fact that a crime has been committed; the actual commission by someone of the offense charged.

correctional boot camps The use of shock incarceration for youthful first-time nonviolent offenders.

correlation An association, but not necessarily causal.

count The plaintiff's statement of his or her cause of action, used to specify the several parts of an indictment or information, each charging a distinct offense. It is often used synonymously with the word *charge*.

counts The periodic verification of the total number of inmates in custody.

court above The court to which a case is removed for review, whether by appeal, writ of error, or *certiorari*, in appellate practice.

court below The court from which the case is removed for review in appellate practice.

court martial A military court convened under the authority of the government and the Uniform Code of Military Justice for trying and punishing offenses committed by members of the armed forces.

court of appeal An appellate tribunal; the name given to the court of last resort in several states; the court of last resort of a particular type of case; or in some states, an intermediate appellate court below the state supreme court.

court of common pleas One of the four superior courts at Westminster in English law; in U.S. law, the name given to a court of original and general jurisdiction for the trial of issues and law. The superior court of the District of Columbia is called the court of common pleas.

court of competent jurisdiction The court having power and authority of law at the time of acting to do the particular act.

court of errors and appeals The court of last resort in the state of New Jersey. Formerly, the same title was given to the highest court of appeal in New York.

court of general sessions The name given in some states to a court of general original jurisdiction in criminal cases.

court of record A court in which appeals are heard on the record; a court whose judicial acts and proceedings are recorded and which has the power to fine or imprison someone for contempt.

court of special sessions A court of inferior criminal jurisdiction in Oklahoma whose jurisdiction is roughly equivalent to that of a justice of the peace.

court of star chamber An English court of very ancient origin. Originally, its jurisdiction extended legally over riots, perjury, misbehavior of sheriffs, and other misdemeanors contrary to the laws of the land; afterward, it stretched to the asserting of all orders of state; becoming both a court of law to determine civil rights and a court of revenue to enrich the treasury. It was finally abolished "to the general satisfaction of the whole nation."

courts of appeals A system of courts of the United States (one in each circuit) created by act of Congress, composed of three or more judges (provision also being made for allotment of the justices of the Supreme Court among the circuits) and having appellate jurisdiction as defined by statute; also called the U.S. Courts of Appeals. They were formerly called the circuit courts of appeals or U.S. Circuit Courts of Appeals.

courts of the United States The courts that comprise the Senate of the United States as a Court of Impeachment, the U.S. Supreme Court, the courts of appeals, the district courts, the court of claims, the court of customs and patent appeals, the customs court, the tax court, the provisional courts, and courts of territories and outlying possessions.

crime An act in violation of penal law; an offense against the state.

crime cleared by arrest A crime known to the police but removed from active police records.

crime control The value or goal of reducing crime, emphasizing informal discretionary decision making.

crime control model The use of values discretion to quickly sort out the factually innocent from the factually guilty.

criminal One who has committed a criminal offense, who has been legally convicted of a crime, or who has been adjudged guilty of a crime.

criminal action The whole or any part of the procedure that law provides for bringing offenders to justice.

criminal charge An accusation of crime in a written complaint, information, or indictment.

criminal court A court charged with the administration of the criminal laws and empowered to sentence the guilty person to fine or imprisonment. In New York, the criminal courts comprise the superior and local criminal courts. "Superior court" here means the supreme court or a county court. "Local criminal court" means a district court, or the New York City criminal court, a city court, a town court, a village court, or a supreme court justice sitting as a local criminal court or a county judge sitting as a local criminal court.

criminal event The commission of a specific crime.

criminal history A record of prior offenses.

criminal homicide A willful felonious homicide as distinguished from death caused by negligence.

criminal information A formal accusation of crime, differing from an indictment only in that it is preferred by a prosecuting officer instead of a grand jury.

criminal intent An intent to commit a crime; malice, as evidenced by a criminal act; an intent to deprive or defraud the true owner of his or her property.

criminal justice process The sequence of steps taken from the initial contact of an offender with the law until he or she is released back into free society.

criminal justice system A loose confederation of agencies, including police, courts, and corrections.

criminal law The branch or division of law that deals with crime and punishment.

criminal negligence The unconscious creation of a high risk of harm.

criminal procedure The law prescribing how the government enforces criminal law. A method for the apprehension, trial, prosecution, and fixing the punishment of persons who have broken the law.

criminal proceeding A proceeding instituted and conducted for the purpose of preventing the commission of crime, of fixing guilt for a crime already committed, and of punishing the offender.

criminal prosecution An action or proceeding instituted in a proper court on behalf of the public for the purpose of securing the conviction and punishment of one accused of crime.

criminal recklessness The conscious creation of a high risk of harm.

criminogenic forces The causes of crime in the society, such numerous variables as poverty, socioeconomic status, or physical or mental impairment, among many others.

cross-examination The examination of a witness, in a trial or hearing by the party opposed to the one who produced him or her, on the evidence given, to test its truth, to further develop it, or for other relevant purposes.

crowded prisoner A prisoner who must live in less than 60 square feet of floor space.

curfew offense An offense relating to violation of local curfew or loitering ordinances, which provide regulations as to when a person (usually a juvenile) may lawfully be on the streets.

curtilage The enclosed space of ground and buildings immediately surrounding the dwelling house.

custodial institution A secure physical structure where offenders are confined, with strict limitations on their access to free society.

cycle of violence The hypothesis that childhood abuse creates a predisposition to later violent behavior.

D.A.R.E. (Drug Abuse Resistance Education) The use of specially trained police officers assigned to schools to teach drug prevention.

day in court The opportunity to present one's claim before a competent tribunal.

daylight The portion of time after sunrise and before sunset, often important for assessing degree of criminal culpability. *See also* nighttime.

dealer One who buys to sell, not one who buys to keep.

decision making The process of figuring out who decides what is going to be done with the plan, how the person decides, when and how fast he or she decides, and how the decision will be put into action; also, the determination of who is going to solve problems and in what ways these problems are going to be solved.

decree The judgment of the court; a declaration of the court announcing the legal consequences of the facts found.

decriminalization The removal of status offenses from juvenile jurisdiction.

defendant The person defending or denying; the party against whom relief or recovery is sought in an action or suit. In criminal law, the party charged with a crime.

defense The answer made by the defendant to the state's case in a criminal action.

defense attorney The attorney representing the accused in a criminal action.

defense of excuse The admission to the wrongfulness of a crime but a denial of responsibility.

defense of justification The admission to a crime but the assertion that it was morally or ethically right to do it.

deferred release decision The setting of release after the determination that a prisoner has reformed and/or completed a task or judicial assignment.

deinstitutionalization A community-based noninstitutional treatment as an alternative to incarceration.

delegation The work a manager performs to entrust responsibility and authority to others and to create accountability for results (e.g., a state director of corrections delegates authority and responsibility to a warden or area superintendent).

deliberation The weighing of the evidence and the law for the purpose of determining the guilt or innocence of a defendant. In the case of jury sentencing, the deliberation may be for the purpose of fixing the sentence.

delinquency An act by a juvenile that would be criminal if committed by adults.

delinquent juvenile A person of no more than a specific age who has violated any law or ordinance or is incorrigible; a person who has been adjudicated a delinquent child by a juvenile court while of juvenile court age.

density The number of square feet of floor space per prisoner.

deprivation model A perspective of the prisonization process that maintains that it is a function of adapting to an abnormal environment that is characterized by numerous deprivations.

descriptive guidelines A sentencing range based on actual past sentencing practices.

detainer A kind of "hold order" filed against an incarcerated person by another state or jurisdiction, which seeks to take the person into custody to answer to another criminal charge or conviction whenever he or she is released from the current imprisonment.

detention center A secure, temporary holding facility, usually designated for juvenile offenders; also, a municipal jail.

diagnostic reception center A central intake location where newly arriving inmates are interviewed, tested, examined, and evaluated for classification purposes.

differential association The premise that criminal behavior depends on association.

differential response The premise that police response to routine calls differs from that to emergency calls.

diminished capacity A state of mental impairment that is less disabling than insanity.

direct evidence The means of proof that tends to show the existence of a fact in question without the intervention of the proof of any other fact. It is distinguished from circumstantial evidence, which is often called indirect.

direct examination The first interrogation or examination of a witness, on the merits, by the party on whose behalf he or she is called.

direct information A fact known by direct knowledge.

direct supervision A situation in which officers are in constant direct contact with the prisoners they supervise.

directing The guiding, overseeing, coaching, and leading of people toward goals and objectives while staying within the policies, procedures, and standards of the organization. Directing, more than any other management function, involves functional personal relationships.

discharge The removal of a client from supervision, generally as a result of satisfactory completion of the conditions of probation or parole.

discretion The ability to make decisions without formal recourse to laws and other written rules.

disorderly conduct An act or conduct against public order; sometimes used synonymously with breach of peace, although not all disorderly conduct is a breach of peace.

disposition hearing A hearing to determine what treatment and custody should follow the finding of delinquency.

district attorney A term in many states for not only a district attorney but also an assistant district attorney, the attorney general, or an assistant attorney general.

diversion The removal of a juvenile from the juvenile justice system to alternative programs or the transfer of a defendant into some alternative to criminal prosecution.

doubt An uncertainty of mind; the absence of a settled opinion or conviction; the situation in a case in which, after the entire comparison and consideration of the evidence, the minds of the jurors are in such a condition that they cannot determine with a moral certainty the truth of the charge. Upon proof that there is a reasonable doubt remaining, the accused is entitled to the benefit of an acquittal.

dual system of justice The use of two separate systems for adults and juveniles.

duces tecum A Latin phrase meaning "bring with you." A subpoena *duces tecum* requires a party to appear in court and bring certain documents, pieces of evidence, or other matters to be inspected by the court.

due process The value of formal rules and procedures to limit the power of government and protect the rights of individuals.

due process clause The guarantee of fair procedures and protection of life, liberty, and property.

due process model Emphasizes formal legal adversary process at the heart of the criminal process.

due process of law The fundamental rights of the accused to a fair trial; the prescribed forms of conducting a criminal prosecution; the safeguards and protection of the law given to one accused of a crime. In substantive criminal law, the right to have crimes and punishments clearly defined in the law. Government can act only according to rules.

due process revolution The expansion by the Supreme Court during the 1960s of the rights of criminal defendants and the application of the rights to state proceedings.

duress The act of committing a crime under coercion.

d.w.i. (driving while intoxicated) The act of driving or operating any motor vehicle while drunk or under the influence of liquor or narcotics.

effectiveness The measurement of a program, plan, or effort in terms of its result or impact and not in terms of its resource cost. A program could, therefore, be highly effective (in terms of client service) but not efficient in terms of dollars, time, or other costs. Usually, programs are best measured in terms of both effectiveness and efficiency in order to attain a favorable benefit–cost ratio. However, this is not always possible in matters of custody or treatment.

efficiency The planning in an organization and its work so that objectives can be attained with the lowest possible costs, which may mean money costs, human costs, or other resource costs.

embezzlement The misappropriation or misapplication of money or property entrusted into one's care, custody, or control.

empiricism The idea that all knowledge results from sense experience; a scientific method that relies on direct observation and the analysis of data.

equal protection of the law The rule that prevents unreasonable classifications.

et al. An abbreviation for Latin words meaning "and elsewhere" or "and others."

ethnographic study The research done through intensive field observation and interviews.

ethnography The observational description of a people or some other social unit.

evaluation research Research designed to measure the effectiveness of a social program or institution.

evidence A species of proof presented at the trial for the purpose of inducing belief in the minds of the court or jury.

ex parte A Latin phrase meaning "on one side only"; "by or for one party"; or "done for, in behalf of, or on the application of one party only."

ex post facto A Latin phrase meaning "after the fact."

ex post facto design An after-only evaluation research design where pretesting is not possible. *See also* nonequivalent control group.

ex post facto law A law passed after the occurrence of a fact or commission of an act that retrospectively changes the legal consequences or relations of such fact or deed. A retroactive law is forbidden to both the states and the federal government by the U.S. Constitution.

ex rel A Latin phrase meaning "by or on the information of"; used in case titles to designate the person at whose instance the government or public official is acting.

exclusionary rule The rule that excludes from the trial of an accused evidence illegally seized or obtained; prohibiting the use of illegally obtained evidence to prove guilt.

exclusive jurisdiction The sole authority to hear and decide cases.

executive clemency The authority of presidents and governors to eliminate a sentence. *See also* pardon.

existing statistics The statistical data that are available to researchers for analysis.

experiment A research method that seeks to isolate the effects of an independent variable on a dependent variable under strictly controlled conditions.

experimental group The group in an experiment that is exposed to the experimental treatment.

experimental mortality The loss of subjects in an experiment over time. This is a potential cause of internal validity problems.

expert evidence The testimony given in relation to some scientific, technical, or professional matter by experts (persons qualified to speak authoritatively by reason of their special training, skill, or familiarity with the subject).

expert witness A person who gives the results of a process of reasoning that can be mastered only by special scientists; one who has skilled experience or extensive knowledge in his or her calling or in any branch of learning; a person competent to give expert testimony.

express bargaining A direct meeting to decide concessions.

external validity The generalizability of an experiment to other settings, other treatments, other subjects.

face validity A form of content validity in which a careful consideration and examination of the measurement instrument is made to determine whether the instrument is measuring what it purports to measure.

face-to-face interview A method of administering a survey in which an interviewer questions an interviewee using a structured set of questions. *See also* interview schedule.

factorial design The design of an experiment in which more than one independent variable is being measured.

factual guilt A determination that a defendant has actually committed a crime, or has knowledge of guilt but not necessarily provable in court.

family crime A crime against people known to the offender.

federal question A case that contains a major issue involving the U.S. Constitution or statutes. The jurisdiction of the federal courts is governed, in part, by the existence of a federal question.

federalism The division of power between federal and state governments.

felony A serious crime punishable by one year or more in prison; a crime of a graver or more atrocious nature than those designated as a misdemeanor.

felony complaint A verified written accusation by a person, filed with a local criminal court, which charges one or more defendants with the commission of one or more felonies and which serves to begin a criminal action but not as a basis for prosecution thereof.

field experiment An experiment taking place in a real-world environment, where it is more difficult to impose controls.

field research A research method based on careful observation of behavior in a natural social environment.

focus group A small group of individuals drawn together to express views on a specific set of questions in a group environment. This method may serve a number of functions in social research; as a starting point for developing a survey, to recognize potential problems in a research design, or to interpret evidence.

follow-up research procedure The method of following up nonrespondents to mail questionnaires to increase response rate. The procedures include sending postcard reminders, sending second questionnaires and request, and telephoning to solicit cooperation or to get the responses over the telephone.

forcible rape A rape by force or against the consent of the victim.

forecasting The work a manager performs to estimate the future.

forgery The making, altering, uttering (passing), or possessing anything false that is made to appear true, with intent to defraud.

formal criminal justice The law and other written rules that determine the outer boundaries of action in criminal justice.

formalization The replacement of discretion with rules.

formative evaluation An evaluation of a program in process, information from which will be used to reform or improve the program.

frequency distribution The distribution of cases across the categories of a variable, presented in numbers and percentages.

frisk search The physical pat-down of a clothed subject to determine whether weapons or other contraband items are concealed externally within clothes, shoes, hair, mouth, and so on.

fruits of a crime The material objects acquired by means of and in consequence of the commission of a crime, and sometimes constituting the subject matter of the crime.

function The total of positions encompassing one kind of work grouped to form an administrative unit; a group or family of related kinds of management work, made up of activities that are closely related to one another and have characteristics in common derived from the essential nature of the work done.

functional unit management A decentralized approach wherein a unit manager, case manager, and counselor, along with supportive custodial, clerical, and treatment personnel, maintain full responsibility for providing services, making decisions, and addressing the needs of inmates assigned to a living unit.

fundamental fairness doctrine A due process definition focusing on substantive due process.

funnel effect The result of sorting decisions that lead to fewer individuals remaining at successive stages in the criminal justice process.

furlough The privilege granted of temporary release from confinement, with the understanding that an inmate will return to the institution at a given time.

gambling The act of promoting, permitting, or engaging in games of chance.

general deterrence The method of preventing crime in general population by threatening punishment.

general intent The intent to commit the *actus reus*.

general jurisdiction The authority to hear and decide all criminal cases.

general population inmate A prisoner without special problems.

general principles of criminal law The broad general rules that provide the basis for other rules.

goal The broadest, most long-range statement, in management terms, of the purpose or mission of an organization or unit within the organization. *See also* objective.

goal maintenance The process of working toward an established goal according to a plan, the application and guidance of resources toward the goal, and assessment of the degree and rate of progress toward attainment of the goal. It is appropriate within this process to redefine or redevelop goals as necessary.

goal setting The identification of individual or organizational purposes and intent; their specification as to time, resources needed, planning, and how to measure and report results.

good time The number of days deducted from prison terms based on good behavior of prisoners.

good-time laws The reduction of sentence length by one-third or one-half based on behavior in prison.

grand jury A jury of inquiry authorized to return indictments, made up of citizens who test the government's case and agree or disagree on prosecutable indictments.

grand larceny A larceny at the felony grade, generally expressed in dollar value of amount stolen.

gross misdemeanor A crime punishable by jail terms of 30 days to a year.

group home A relatively open community-based facility.

guided discretion statute A law requiring juries to use guidelines on mitigating and aggravating circumstances.

habeas corpus (literally, "you have the body") *See* writ of habeas corpus.

halfway house An institution in the community for parolees and probationers.

hands-off doctrine A perspective that prison management should be left to discretion of prison administrators.

Hawthorne principle The finding that creation of a new and closely watched project produces temporary positive results.

hearing A broad term for whatever takes place before a court or a magistrate clothed with judicial function and sitting without a jury. A trial is always a hearing, but not all hearings require the formalities of a trial.

hearsay The information acquired through a third person; any evidence offered by someone who does not know its truth firsthand.

home confinement A sentence to detention at home except for work, study, service, or treatment.

homicide The killing of one human being by another.

homogeneous group The stratum formed in sampling by sets of individuals who share certain characteristics (such as gender, race, age).

hung jury A jury so irreconcilably divided in opinion that it cannot agree upon any verdict.

hypothesis A conditional statement relating the expected effect of one variable on another, subject to testing.

impact evaluation The assessment of whether a program, after its implementation, has helped or not helped the group of people for whom it was intended; sometimes referred to as product evaluation.

impeachment A criminal procedure against a public officer to remove him or her from office. In the law of evidence, it is the adducing of proof that a witness is unworthy of belief.

importation hypothesis The theory that prison society has its roots in the criminal and conventional societies outside the prison.

in re A Latin phrase meaning "in the affair of, in the matter of; concerning." This is the usual method of entitling a judicial proceeding in which there are no adversaries. For this reason, it is used in the titles of cases in a juvenile court.

incapacitation The prevention of crime by incarceration, mutilation, or capital punishment.

incident report A patrol or a correctional officer's description of a crime or broken regulation, usually detailing witnesses and suspects.

incident-based reporting The reporting of each offense separately, whether part of the same event or not.

incident-driven strategies The perspective that an isolated event determines the response by officers.

incorporation doctrine A due process focusing on procedural regularity.

independent variable The variable, in an experiment or survey, that exercises an effect on a dependent variable; the cause in a cause-and-effect model. *See also* causation.

indeterminate sentence An open-ended penalty tailored to the needs of individual offenders.

index A composite measure developed to represent different components of a concept.

index crimes The crimes used by the Federal Bureau of Investigation in reporting the incidence of crime in the United States in the Uniform Crime Reports. The statistics on the Index Crimes are taken as an index of the incidence of crime in the United States.

indicator An observable phenomenon that can be used to measure the dimensions of a concept.

indictment The formal accusation of a crime by a grand jury. *See also* presentment.

indigenous theory The belief that conditions inside a prison shape prison society.

indigent defendant A defendant too poor to afford a lawyer.

inducement test A test of entrapment focusing on government actions.

infamous crime A crime that reflects infamy on the one who has committed it; a crime punishable by imprisonment in the state prison or penitentiary. At common law, all felonies were considered to be infamous crimes.

inference An accurate guess or conclusion based on evidence gathered on a relatively small probability sample, extrapolated to a much larger population.

inferential statistics The statistics that allow a researcher to draw conclusions regarding the general population from the findings of a representative sample drawn from that population; statistics that use probability in decision making; hypothesis-testing statistics.

informa pauperis A Latin phrase for "in the form of a pauper" or "as a poor person or indigent," meaning the permission to bring legal action without the payment of required fees for counsel, writs, transcripts, and the like.

information An accusation exhibited against a person for some criminal offense, without an indictment. An accusation differs from an indictment only because it is presented by a competent public officer on his or her oath of office instead of by members of a grand jury on their oath. It also means a formal accusation of a crime by a prosecutor.

informed consent The consent achieved when subjects in a research study comprehend its objectives, understand their level of confidentiality, and agree to cooperate. *See also* invasion of privacy.

informer A person who informs or prefers an accusation against another whom he or she suspects of a violation of some penal statute.

infraction The name given to any minor offense (chiefly traffic offenses) in the California Infractions Code.

initial case screening The step at which prosecutors review a case to determine whether to charge, divert, or dismiss it.

injunction A writ prohibiting an individual or organization from performing some specified action.

insanity The legal term excusing criminal liability. It is not synonymous with mental illness.

institutional review board A committee in an institution where scientific research is being carried out that reviews the research methods to be sure that the rights of human (or animal) subjects are being protected.

institutional support A system in which prisoners work in maintaining the jail to pay part of their expenses of incarceration.

instrumentality of a crime The tool or implement used to commit a crime.

intake The initial juvenile court process following a serious infraction of the law, unless preceded by diversion.

intensity structure The pattern that makes best sense of the multiple items in a scale and their interrelation.

intensive probation supervision A closely supervised probation, stressing retribution, incapacitation, and economy.

interaction effect The tendency for a third variable to interact with the independent variable, thereby altering the relationship of the independent variable to the dependent variable. This means that the relationship between the independent and dependent variables will vary under different conditions of the third variable.

intermediate appellate court A court that hears initial appeals.

intermediate punishment The range of sanctions somewhere between the extremes of incarceration and straight probation.

intermittent incarceration The incarceration of a prisoner at night and on weekends with release for school, work, treatment, or community service.

internal affairs unit A police unit created to investigate, report, and recommend with respect to civilian complaints against police officers.

internal grievance mechanism A procedure inside prisons for dealing with grievances.

internal validity The extent to which an experiment actually has caused what it appeared to cause.

interrogation The process used in questioning suspects, usually after arrest and prior to filing charges.

intersubjectivity The shared perceptions of individual observers. The greater the intersubjectivity is, the greater the validity and reliability of the observations.

intervening variable A third variable in a trivariate study that logically falls in a time sequence between the independent and dependent variables.

interview schedule A set of questions with guided instructions for an interviewer to use in carrying out an interview. *See also* face-to-face interview.

invasion of privacy A possible abuse in social research in which rights of privacy have been ignored. This must be weighed in relation to the public's right to know. *See also* informed consent.

investigatory stage The stage of investigation in police practice during which the offense is the subject of general inquiry before suspicion has focused on a particular person or persons. It is distinguished from the accusatory stage, which covers the investigation that occurs after suspicion has focused on one or more particular individuals as being guilty of the offense.

issue A single, certain, and material point, deduced from the pleadings of the parties, which is affirmed by one side and denied by the other; a fact put in controversy by the pleadings. In criminal law, an issue is a fact that must be proved to convict the accused or that is in controversy.

item analysis A test for validity of an index in which a cross-tabulation of total index scores to separate items making up the index is examined.

jail time The credit allowed on a sentence for the time spent in jail awaiting trial or mandate on appeal.

judge An officer so named in his or her commission who presides in some court.

judgment The official and authentic decision of a court of justice upon the respective rights and claims of the parties to the action or suit therein litigated and submitted to its determination.

judicial process The sequence of steps taken by the courts in deciding cases or disposing of legal controversies.

jurisdiction The power conferred on a court to hear certain cases; the power of the police or judicial officer to act; the extent of the power of a public official to act by virtue of his or her authority.

jury panel A list of jurors returned by a sheriff, to service at a particular court or for the trial of a particular case. The word may be used to denote either the entire body of the persons summoned as jurors for a particular term of court or those selected by the clerk by lot.

justice model The perspective that justice demands punishment for any crimes that are committed, with a focus on rights and rules in corrections.

juvenile delinquent A youth who has committed either a status or a delinquency offense.

labeling theory A theory stating that society's response to crime defines some people as criminals.

laboratory experiment An experiment taking place in a laboratory setting, where it is possible to maintain a large number of controls.

larceny The taking of property from the possession of another with intent of the taker to convert it to his or her own use. Depending on the value of the property taken, the offense is a felony or a misdemeanor.

law The formal means of social control that involves the use of rules interpreted and enforceable by the courts of a political community. Law is the effort of society to protect persons, in their rights and relations, guard them in their property, enforce their contracts, hold them to liabilities for their torts, and punish their crimes by means of sanctions administered by government.

leader A person who enables other people to work together to attain identified ends.

leadership The guidance and direction of the efforts of others. In management, the work of planning, organizing, directing, staffing, and controlling is performed by a person in a leadership position to enable people to work most effectively together to attain identified ends.

leadership evolution The systematic and continuing adaptation of a leader to the needs of the person, group, or organization.

leading question A question that steers a witness to a desired answer.

legal Conforming to the law; according to a law; being required or permitted by law; not being forbidden or discountenanced by law; being a good and effectual law.

legal duty An act that the law requires to be done or forborne.

legal ethics The usages and customs among the legal profession, involving their moral and professional duties toward one another, toward clients, and toward the courts.

legal guilt The proof beyond a reasonable doubt by admissible evidence.

legal provocation A provocation sufficient in law to be a defense to the act (e.g., justifiable homicide).

legalistic style A style with an emphasis on criminal law enforcement and formal rules.

legislation A rule of general application, enacted by a law-making body in a politically organized society. Included in legislation are constitutions, treaties, statutes, ordinances, administrative regulations, and court rules. Legislation should be distinguished from case law, common law, and "judge-made law."

legislative sentencing model A model in which a legislature sets penalties for offenses.

lesser included offense A crime committed in the process of committing a crime of more serious degree or grade.

lesser offense A synonym for a less serious offense or a minor offense.

level of measurement One of the four commonly defined levels for measuring variables: nominal, for distinct categories with no order; ordinal, for ordered categories; interval, for numerical scales with mathematically defined intervals between points on the scale but no true zero point; and ratio, for numerical scales with mathematically defined intervals and a true zero point.

limitation of actions The time at the end of which no action at law can be maintained. In criminal law, it is the time after the commission of the offense within which the indictment must be presented or the information filed.

limited jurisdiction A court that is limited to hearing and deciding minor offenses and preliminary proceedings in felonies.

linear relationship A relationship that shows that an increase (or decrease) in one variable is related to an increase (or decrease) in the other—indicated by a diagonal best-fit line in a scattergram.

line-up (also called a *show up*) A police identification procedure during which a suspect is exhibited, along with others, to witnesses to the crime to determine whether or not the witnesses can connect him or her with the offense.

literature review The task of canvassing publications, usually professional journals, in order to find information about a specific topic for a research project.

local criminal court *See* criminal court.

local legal culture The attitudes, values, and expectations toward law and legal practice in specific communities.

lockdown The suspension of all activities, with prisoners confined to their cells.

longitudinal data The data gathered over time.

longitudinal designs A study based on longitudinal data. Different types include trend studies, in which data are compared across time points on different subjects; cohort studies, in which data on subjects from the same age cohort are compared at different points in time; and panel studies, in which the same subjects are compared across time points.

mail survey A survey consisting of a self-administered questionnaire, instructions, and a request for participation sent out through the mail to a selected sample.

mala in se A Latin phrase for acts or crimes immoral or wrong in and of themselves.

mala prohibita A Latin phrase for crimes that are wrong because a statute defines them as wrong, although no moral turpitude may be attached, and that constitute crimes only because they are prohibited.

management by exception A feature of delegation where routine and frequently recurring matters should be handled by subordinates, allowing the manager to concentrate time and energies on exceptional and very important matters.

management development The work a manager performs to help managers and candidates for management positions to improve their knowledge, attitudes, and skills.

manager The person in the organization who may be responsible for any or all of the following: (1) the outcome of his or her job, (2) the outcomes of some other people's jobs (subordinates), (3) some of the outcomes of other people's jobs (peers, staff, and other managers), and (4) the outcomes of activities of some persons outside the organization. A professional manager is one who specializes in the work of planning, organizing, directing, staffing, and controlling the efforts of others (and does so through systematic use of classified knowledge as well as a common vocabulary and principles) and who subscribes to the standards of practice and code of ethics established by a recognized body.

mandatory minimum sentence legislation The requirement that judges must sentence offenders to a minimum time in prison.

mandatory parole release statute A law requiring the release of prisoners at specified times.

mandatory release The release of a prisoner based on good behavior and other sentence-reducing devices.

manslaughter The lowest degree of culpable homicide death caused by culpable recklessness or negligence.

matching An experimental procedure in which subjects to be placed in the experimental group are matched with subjects possessing similar characteristics in the control group.

material allegation An allegation essential to the claim of defense, which could not be stricken from the pleading without leaving it insufficient.

material fact A fact that is essential to a case, defense, or application, without which it could not be supported.

matrix question One of a set of questions in a questionnaire that uses the same set of response categories.

maximum-security prison A prison that focuses on preventing prisoners from escaping or hurting themselves or others.

measured capacity A measure of prison capacity based on one prisoner per cell.

measurement A process in which numbers are assigned according to rules of correspondence between definitions and observations.

measurement error An error unavoidably introduced into measurement in the process of observing a phenomenon. An observed measure (or score) is therefore based on the true score plus or minus the error. In social research this error may necessarily be great because of the crudity of the instruments used in measuring social phenomena.

medical model A perspective that views crimes as a disease that requires treatment to cure.

medium-security prison A prison that focuses less on security, allowing prisoners greater freedom of movement.

mens rea A Latin phrase meaning guilty mind, a guilty or wrongful purpose, a criminal intent, guilty knowledge, and willfulness.

merit system The selection of judges by a governor from a list drawn up by a commission of citizens, lawyers, and judges.

middle-range offender A person not requiring imprisonment but demanding more than ordinary probation.

minimum-security prison A prison containing prisoners who do not pose security problems that can therefore emphasize trust and a normal lifestyle.

minor A person or infant who is under the age of legal competence; someone under age 21.

Miranda warning The warning that must be given to a suspect whenever suspicion focuses on him or her. The officer must warn the suspect (1) that he or she has the right to remain silent; (2) that if the suspect talks, anything he or she says may be used against him or her; (3) that he or she has the right to be represented by counsel and the right to have counsel present at all questioning; and (4) that if he or she is too poor to afford counsel, counsel will be provided at state expense.

misdemeanor Any offense that is not a felony, punishable by one year or less in jail.

misdemeanor complaint A verified written accusation (as defined in several states) by a person, filed with a local criminal court, that charges one or more defendants with the commission of one or more offenses, at least one of which is a misdemeanor and none of which is a felony, and that serves to begin a criminal action but which may not, except upon the defendant's consent, serve as a basis for prosecution of the offenses charged therein.

mistake of fact The ignorance or an error concerning facts.

mistake of law The ignorance or a mistake concerning the law.

moot Pertaining to a subject for an argument that is unsettled or undecided. A moot point is one not settled by judicial decision.

moot case A case that seeks to get a judgment on a pretended controversy, or a decision in advance about a right before it has actually been asserted and contested, or a judgment on some matter which, when rendered, for any reason, cannot have any practical legal effect on a then-existing controversy.

moot court A court held for the arguing of moot (or pretended) cases or questions such as those posed by students in law school.

moral turpitude An act of baseness, vileness, or depravity in the private and social duties that humans owe to their kind, or to society in general, contrary to the accepted and customary rule of right and duty between person and person.

motivating work The work a manager performs to inspire, encourage, and impel people to take desired action.

murder The highest degree of culpable homicide.

narcotic A drug, such as morphine or heroin, that in medicinal doses relieves pain and induces sleep but that in toxic doses causes convulsions, coma, or death.

narcotic offense An offense relating to narcotic drugs, such as unlawful possession, sale, or use; also used to describe any substance abuse offense.

National Crime Victim Survey (NCVS) A national sample of victims surveyed about their victimization.

National Institute of Justice The research arm of the U.S. Department of Justice.

natural experiment An experiment that has not been brought about by the efforts of the experimenter but has occurred naturally in the real world and is being selected out for study by the experimenter.

negative evidence The nonoccurrence of expected events, an occurrence that is not reacted to, or one that is distorted in its interpretation or withheld from analysis in a field study.

negative (inverse) relationship A type of relationship between two variables in which cases that are low on one variable are high on the other. *See also* positive (direct) relationship.

negotiated plea A plea of guilt in exchange for a concession by the government.

negotiation A give-and-take activity that allows individuals or groups to agree in common to a set of objectives, tasks, and shared use of resources.

net widening The process of expanding jurisdiction, such as when sentencing borderline cases to intermediate punishments instead of straight probation.

new-generation jail A jail that combines architecture, management, and training to provide safe, humane confinement.

new-generation prisons A prison that combines management and architecture to provide safe, secure confinement for maximum-security prisoners.

Nighttime The period between sunset and sunrise, often important for assessing degree of criminal culpability. *See also* daylight.

nonequivalent control group A control group that was not selected on the basis of random assignment. It is usually created as a rough comparison group to participants in a social intervention program under evaluation. *See also ex post facto* design.

null hypothesis A logical assumption that there is no relationship between the two variables being studied in the population. This assumption can be tested with inferential statistics.

objective A specific time-framed behavioral expression of some end result or end product that is reasonably attainable yet sufficiently challenging. Objectives can be long range (several years) or very short range (a day or less). *See also* goal.

occupancy The number of prisoners for each unit of confinement as set by federal and state statutes.

occupational crime A crime committed in the course of employment.

operating work The work a manager performs other than the planning, organizing, directing, staffing, and controlling work that logically belongs to that position.

opportunity theory The belief that criminal behavior depends on the available criminal opportunities, on noncriminal behavior, and on noncriminal opportunity structure.

order of bail A securing order fixing the amount of bail.

order of recognizance A securing order releasing a principal on his or her own recognizance.

organization Any group of people formally associated to plan, implement, or evaluate a program or idea. The organization can be a group of people in need of a program, an agency or office to meet a need, or any other group formed to help meet a need.

organization chart A schematic representation of organization structure, authority, and relationships.

organization crime A crime committed to benefit organizations illegally.

organization structure The pattern that work assumes as it is identified and grouped to be performed by people.

organize To establish a system for performance toward stated goals and objectives; to put the organization into a desired structure and order.

original jurisdiction The authority to initiate proceedings; jurisdiction in the first instance; jurisdiction to take cognizance of a case at its inception, impanel a jury, try the case, and pass judgment on the law and facts. Original jurisdiction is to be distinguished from appellate jurisdiction. *See also* trial jurisdiction.

pardon An act of grace, proceeding from the power entrusted with the execution of the laws, that exempts the person on whom it is bestowed from the punishment the law inflicts for the crime committed. *See also* executive clemency.

parens patriae (literally, "father of his country") The doctrine that the juvenile court treats the child as "a kind of loving father" and that government acts as parent.

parole A conditional release from prison; the release of a prisoner from imprisonment, but not from legal custody of the state, for rehabilitation outside prison walls under such conditions and provisions for disciplinary supervision as the parole board or its agents may determine. Parole is an administrative act and follows incarceration.

parole board A panel of civilians and experts that determines the release from prison to parole.

particularity The detailed description in a warrant of the object of a search.

pendulum swing The alternating emphasis on crime control and due process in the history of criminal justice.

per curiam A Latin phrase meaning "by the court," referring to an opinion of the court that is authored by the justices collectively.

per se A Latin phrase meaning "by himself, herself, or itself; taken alone."

performance appraisal A formal program comparing employees' actual performance with expected performance.

persons arrested A statistic on a wide variety of serious and minor offenses reported in raw numbers.

petit jury A trial jury as distinguished from a grand jury; an ordinary jury of 12 people (or fewer) for the trial of a civil or criminal action.

petit larceny A larceny of the grade of misdemeanor.

petty misdemeanor A crime punishable by a fine or up to 30 days in jail.

plain view search A search that discovers an object of seizure inadvertently where an officer has a right to be.

plan A predetermined course of action in management.

planning The selection of one from several alternative courses of future action; the determination of goals to be accomplished as well as how and when they are to be achieved.

plea of guilty A confession of guilt in open court.

plea of *nolo contendere* (literally, "no contest") A plea of neither guilty nor not guilty of a charge in criminal court that has the same effect in a criminal action as a plea of guilty but does not bind the defendant in a civil suit for the same wrong.

plea of not guilty A plea denying the guilt of the accused for the offense charged and putting the state to the proof of all the material elements of the offense.

podular design A design that allows greater security and opportunity for surveillance of fewer numbers of prisoners.

police academy A training school where police socialization begins.

police corruption A form of occupational crime in which officers use their authority for private gain.

police defensiveness The distrust of outsiders, who may not understand the law enforcement policies and procedures.

police depersonalization The treatment of violence and other unpleasant experiences as matter of fact.

police misconduct A range of illegal behavior, including brutality, constitutional violations, corruption, and unfair treatment of citizens.

police stress The negative pressures associated with police work.

police working personality The character traits of police officers revealed in their work as usually identified by sociologists and psychologists.

police–prosecutor team A team of police officers and prosecutors working together from investigation to conviction.

policy A standing decision made to apply to repetitive questions and problems of significance to an organization as a whole.

political community A community using forcible maintenance of orderly dominion over a territory and its inhabitants.

population The collection of all elements (either known or unknown) from which a sample is drawn. In a probability sample, the population consists of the elements in the sampling frame.

position The work tasks grouped for performance by one person.

positive (direct) relationship A type of relationship between two variables in which cases that are high on one variable tend to be high on the other, and cases that are low on one variable tend to be low on the other. *See also* negative (inverse) relationship.

positivist A person who strives to accumulate facts as the sole means of establishing explanations.

posttraumatic stress syndrome The mental impairment caused by stress during battle or some other traumatic event.

precedent An adjudged case or decision of a court of justice considered as furnishing an example of authority for an identical or similar case afterward arising on a similar question of law. *See also stare decisis.*

precoded questionnaire The coding information that is included on the questionnaire instrument itself and that facilitates transferring the data to a computer.

preemptory challenge A self-determined, arbitrary challenge requiring no cause to be shown. As applied to selection of jurors, peremptory challenges are allowed by law to both the state and defense to remove a prospective juror without cause from the panel of jurors.

preliminary hearing The examination of a person charged with a crime before a magistrate.

preliminary jurisdiction The jurisdiction of a criminal court over an offense, regardless of whether it has trial jurisdiction, when a criminal action for such an offense may be begun there and when the court may conduct proceedings that may or may not lead to prosecution and final disposition of the action in a court having the trial jurisdiction.

preponderance of the evidence A greater weight of evidence. The preponderance of the evidence rests with the evidence that produces the stronger impression and is more convincing as to its truth when weighed against the evidence in opposition.

prescriptive guideline A sentencing range prescribing new practices.

presentment The initial appearance by the accused before the magistrate after arrest; also, a written notice taken by a grand jury of any offense, from their own knowledge or observation, without any bill of indictment laid before them at the suit of the government. *See also* indictment.

presumption of fact An inference affirmative or disaffirmative of the truth or falsehood of any proposition or fact. Presumptions of fact are not the subject of fixed rules but are merely natural presumptions such as those that appear from common experience to arise from the particular circumstances.

presumption of innocence The treatment of an individual as innocent until proven guilty according to legally correct proceedings.

presumption of law A rule of law stating that courts and judges shall draw a particular inference from a particular fact, or from particular evidence, unless and until the truth of such inference is disproved; an inference that the court will draw from, the proof of which no evidence, however strong, will be permitted to overcome. Presumptions of law come from the part of the system of jurisprudence to which they belong and are reduced to fixed rules. Presumptions are evidence or have the effect of evidence.

preventive detention The detention of defendants prior to trial to protect public safety.

preventive patrol The movement of police patrols through the streets to intercept and prevent crime.

prima facie case A case developed with evidence that will suffice until contradicted and overcome by other evidence.

prima facie evidence The evidence good and sufficient on its face. Such evidence, in the judgment of the law, is sufficient to establish a given fact (or a group or chain of facts) constituting the party's claim or defense, and if it is not rebutted or contradicted, it will remain sufficient.

principle A fundamental truth that will tend to apply in new situations in much the same way as it has applied in situations already observed.

principle of least eligibility The principle that prisoners should earn less than free citizens doing the same work and should be less eligible than schoolchildren and welfare clients when competing for the same tax dollars.

prisoners' rights The constitutional rights that survive prisoners' incarceration.

privatization The private management of correctional facilities.

pro bono **assistance** The representation of criminal defendants without a fee.

pro se **filing** A court proceeding in which a prisoner files his or her own papers.

proactive police operations The operations initiated by police.

probable cause A reasonable cause having more evidence for than against it. It is an apparent state of facts that would induce a reasonably intelligent and prudent person to believe, in a criminal case, that the accused person had committed the crime as charged. It is more than suspicion but less than certainty, the quantum of proof required to search or arrest.

probation The release of a convicted defendant by a court under conditions imposed by the court for a specified period during which the imposition of sentence is suspended. Probation is in lieu of incarceration and is a judicial act.

problem solving The process of identifying and removing barriers to the setting and attainment of goals.

procedural due process The process that places limits on criminal procedure.

procedural law The legal machinery for carrying on a suit or action.

procedure A standardized method of performing specified work; the mode of proceeding by which a legal right is enforced, as distinguished from the law, which gives or defines the right; the machinery, as distinguished from its product; a form, manner, and order of conducting prosecutions.

process evaluation The assessment of a plan during the time it is being implemented. The evaluation should be done at least weekly, and some critical parts of the plan should be assessed daily. This allows the planner to stay on top of the plan as it is being put into action.

proof beyond a reasonable doubt The accumulation of enough facts to convict a criminal defendant.

prosecutor One who prosecutes another for a crime in the name of the government.

prosecutor's information A written accusation by a district attorney filed with a New York court that charges one or more defendants with the commission of one or more offenses (none of which is felony) and that serves as a basis for prosecution in the state of New York.

prostitution A sex offense of a commercialized nature.

protective custody unit A unit devoted to the protection of prisoners with special problems.

provocation The act of inciting another to do a particular deed; an action that arouses, moves, calls forth, causes, or occasions.

proximate cause An action that, in a natural and continuous sequence, is unbroken by any efficient intervening cause, produces the injury. Without the action, the result would not have occurred.

public defender An attorney designated by law or appointed by the court to represent indigent defendants in criminal proceedings. A public defender is paid by the state or by private agency, or serves without fee.

public order offense A minor crime of public annoyance.

public works crew A group of prisoners who work in groups performing public services.

quality arrest An arrest resulting in conviction.

quantification The determination or measurement of a quantity or amount.

quantum of proof The amount of evidence that justifies government action.

quasi-judicial proceeding A proceeding that mixes formal rules and discretionary judgments.

quasi-military line A form of bureaucracy with a hierarchical authority structure.

random sample A sample in which any person or item in the population has an equal chance of being chosen on each selection.

rape The unlawful carnal knowledge of a woman by a man forcibly and against her will.

rational decision making The process of making decisions based on defined goals, alternatives, and information.

real evidence The evidence furnished by things themselves on view or inspection, as distinguished from a description of them given by a witness.

reasonable suspicion The quantum of proof required for a stop-and-frisk procedure.

rebuttable presumption A presumption that may be rebutted by evidence; a species of legal presumption that holds good until disproved.

rebuttal The introduction of rebutting evidence; the demonstration that a statement of a witness as to what occurred is not true; the stage of a trial at which such evidence may be introduced. It is also used to describe the presentation of rebutting evidence.

rebutting evidence The evidence given to explain, repel, counteract, or disprove facts given in evidence by the adverse party.

receiving stolen property The act of buying, receiving, and/or possessing stolen property with knowledge that it is stolen or that is available under circumstances requiring inquiry as to its origins.

recidivist A repeat offender.

record A written account of an act, transaction, or instrument; a written memorial of all the acts and proceedings in an action or suit, in a court of record; the official and authentic history of the cause, consisting in entries in each successive step in the proceedings. In common law, a record is a roll or parchment on which the proceedings and transactions of a court are entered.

rehabilitation The prevention of crime by changing the behavior of individual offenders.

relative deprivation The feeling of deprivation by one person when compared to persons who are doing better.

release on (own) recognizance The release of a defendant on his or her promise to appear in court.

relevant Applying to the matter in question. A fact is relevant to another fact when, according to a common course of events, the existence of one taken alone or in connection with the other fact renders the existence of the other certain or more probable.

relevant evidence The evidence that relates to the elements of a crime.

reported capacity The number of prisoners that a jurisdiction decides is the capacity of a facility.

res gestae A Latin phrase meaning "things done," referring to the whole of the transaction under investigation and every part of it. *Res gestae* is considered an exception to the hearsay rule and is extended to include not only declarations by the parties to the suit but also statements made by bystanders and strangers under certain circumstances.

respondent The defendant on appeal; the party who contends against an appeal.

response time The time it takes for the police to respond to citizen calls.

responsibility The responsibility of a subordinate to a superior for authority received by delegation. It is both absolute and tenuous: absolute as long as the subordinate maintains and executes the responsibility and authority appropriately, and tenuous in that it can be taken back at any time by a higher authority in the organization. In any case, no superior can escape ultimate responsibility for any delegation or any activities of subordinates.

restitution The repayment by offenders for the injuries their crimes caused.

retribution A look back in order to punish for the crime committed.

reus A Latin word referring to a person judicially accused of a crime or a person criminally proceeded against.

revocation The retraction of parole.

right of allocution The right of the convicted person to speak in his own defense before judgment is pronounced. *See also* allocution.

right–wrong test An insanity definition focusing on impairment of reason.

robbery The act of stealing or taking anything of value from a person by force or violence or by putting that person in fear.

role The specific relationship one person has to other people or to an organization. Any given person can have many roles, depending on how many relationships he or she has or how many "hats" he or she wears in the organization. Role also has to be seen as a two-way street: Half the role is how people see themselves in a relationship, and the other half comes from how the other people or the organization sees those people in that relationship.

role management The continuous examination and assessment of role(s), either one person's role or the roles of others as they affect that person's role. The purpose is to modify or adjust a role or to help others adjust their roles in order to maintain common interpersonal and organizational objectives.

rule of law The principle that rules, rather than discretion, govern decisions in criminal law and procedure.

runaway A juvenile offense; also an offender who has run away from home without his or her parents' permission.

safety-valve policy The reduction of the minimum sentence of prisoners when a prison exceeds its capacity.

sample A small group that, ideally, is representative of a larger group.

sampling frame The specific part of a population from which a sample is drawn for a survey.

sciential Knowingly; with guilty knowledge.

Scottsboro case The case that established the fundamental fairness doctrine.

search The examination of a person or property to discover evidence, a weapon, or contraband.

search incident to arrest A search without a warrant conducted at the time of arrest.

Section 1983 action A legal action brought under the Ku Klux Klan Act permitting citizens to sue government officials for the violation of civil rights.

securing order An order of a court in New York committing a principal to the custody of a sheriff, fixing bail, or releasing the person on his or her own recognizance.

selective hypothesis fallacy The choice of subjects for research that favors a particular outcome.

selective incapacitation The policy of imprisoning offenders who commit the most crimes.

self-report The type of data based on sampling members of the population who have committed crimes.

sentence The judgment that is formally pronounced by the court or judge on a defendant after his or her conviction in a criminal prosecution and that stipulates the punishment to be inflicted.

sentence bargaining The plea negotiations over the sentence a judge will grant.

sentencing discrimination The determination of sentences by unacceptable criteria, such as race.

sentencing disparity A difference in the sentences received by persons who committed similar offenses under similar circumstances.

sentencing guidelines A range within which judges prescribe specific sentences.

separation of powers The doctrine that permits the three branches of government—legislative, executive, and judiciary—to perform their own functions without interference from the others.

sequester To keep a jury together and in isolation from other persons under charge of the bailiff while a trial is pending, sometimes called separation of the jury; to keep witnesses apart from other witnesses so that they are unable to hear the other testimony.

service of process The service of writs, summonses, rules, and so on signifies delivering them to whom they ought to be delivered or leaving them with the party they should be left with. When they are delivered, they are said to be served.

sex offenses An offense such as rape, prostitution, commercialized vice, or statutory rape or an offense against chastity, common decency, or morals.

shelter A temporary, nonsecure, community-based holding facility.

show cause To order to appear as directed and to present to the court reasons and considerations as to why certain circumstances should be continued, permitted, or prohibited, as the case may be.

simple assault An assault that is not of an aggravated nature. *See also* assault.

simplified traffic information A written accusation by a police officer filed with a local criminal court that charges a person with a traffic violation or misdemeanors relating to traffic, which may serve both to begin a criminal action for such offense and to act as a basis for its prosecution.

skill A person's physical, emotional, or mental capacity to perform a certain function or task. It could range from the physical skill of operating an office machine to the emotional skill of working with people to the mental skill of computing a complex budget.

social control The process by which subgroups and persons are influenced to conduct themselves in conformity to group expectations.

social control perspective The view that obedience to rules depends on institutions to keep the desire to break the rules in check.

social structure of the case The extralegal or sociological influences on legal decisions.

solicitation The request of one person to another to commit a crime.

solvability factor A type of information that leads to the solution of a crime.

special management inmate A prisoner in need of special care.

specialization The attempt to confine the work of each person to a single related set of functions, with sets of similar functions grouped together under one department or unit.

specific intent The intent to do something in addition to the criminal act.

split sentence The type of sentencing in which part of a sentence is served in jail and the remainder is served on probation.

split-sentence probation The type of sentencing in which a prisoner is sentenced to a specified term of incarceration followed by a specified time on probation.

staffing The act of putting people into the proper jobs; the idea of having the right person in the right job at the right time. Staffing includes the selection, placement, development, and appraisal of people for organizational activities.

standing The qualifications needed to bring legal action.

stare decisis A Latin phrase meaning "to abide by, or adhere to, decided cases," used to refer to the doctrine stating that when a court has once laid down a principle, it be applied to all future cases where facts are substantially the same, regardless of whether the person and the property are the same.

state The supreme political community; also, a state of the United States.

statistics Figures that summarize and represent factual data.

status offense A behavior that only juveniles commit.

statutory law A law enacted by federal, state, or local legislatures.

statutory rape Carnal knowledge of a female child below the age fixed by statute. Neither force nor lack of content is a necessary element of this offense.

stop and frisk The less intrusive seizure and search protected by the Fourth Amendment.

straight plea A plea of guilty without plea negotiations.

strain theory A belief that pressures in the social structure cause crime.

street crime A one-on-one crime against a stranger.

strict liability A type of criminal liability without criminal intent.

subculture of competition The concept that success is more important than the means by which it is achieved.

subculture of violence A subculture that condones violence.

subpoena A process issued by a court to cause a witness to appear and give testimony for the party named.

substantial capacity test An insanity definition focusing on impairments of either or both reason and will.

substantive due process The constitutional limit on criminal law.

summons A notification of proceedings against defendants and the requirement of their appearance in court.

superior court A term used generally to denote courts of general trial jurisdiction. It is the name given to felony courts in California and Illinois.

supervision The day-to-day direct management of personnel and activities within a program. Each person and each activity should have an immediate supervisor who is responsible for the proper application of that person's skills and the proper direction of that activity.

Supreme Court The highest court of the United States, created by the Constitution; the name given in most states to the highest court of appeals, the court of last resort.

suspect To have a slight or even vague idea (not necessarily involving knowledge) concerning; a likelihood about someone or something, sometimes used in place of the word *believe*; also, a person who is suspected of having committed an offense or who is believed to have committed an offense.

systems paradigm The decision-making perspective that treats all the criminal justice agencies as an integrated whole.

task The specific item of activity for which each person in an organization is held accountable.

testimony The evidence given by a competent witness, under oath or affirmation, as distinguished from evidence derived from writings and other sources. Testimony is one species of evidence, but the words *testimony* and *evidence* are often used interchangeably.

the great writ A name given to the writ of habeas corpus.

theft A popular name for larceny.

Theory X A management theory that employees can be motivated only by fear (of job loss, for example).

Theory Y A management theory that employees can be motivated by better challenges, personal growth, and improved work performance and productivity.

Theory Z A management theory that employees should be involved, should participate, and should be treated like family.

tort A noncriminal legal wrong; a private or civil wrong or injury; a legal wrong committed upon a person or property independent of contract, which is redressed in a civil court. A personal tort involves or consists of an injury to the person or to the reputation of feelings as distinguished from an injury or damage to real or personal property, called a property tort.

tort reasor One who commits a tort.

training The provision of a variety of ongoing opportunities for staff development, including coaching, workshops, seminars, and classes in higher education.

training school A secure detention facility.

transcript of record The printed record as made up in case for review by a higher court; also, a copy of any kind. In referring to the written documents on appeal, the words *transcript*, *record*, and *record on appeal* are used interchangeably.

transferred intent The concept that the intent to cause one harm results in causing harm to another.

trial jurisdiction The jurisdiction by a criminal court of an offense when an indictment or an information charging an offense may properly be filed with the court and when the court has authority to accept a plea to try or otherwise finally dispose of the accusatory instrument. *See also* original jurisdiction.

typology A classification of phenomena according to differing characteristics.

Uniform Crime Reports A summary of information provided by local police agencies to the Federal Bureau of Investigation.

unity of command The principle that the more complete a reporting relationship a person has to a single superior, the less the problem of conflict in instructions and evaluation and the greater the feeling of personal responsibility for results.

unity of objectives The concept that if persons in each position fulfill clearly defined objectives logically related to each other, the goal of the entire organization will be met.

utilitarian punishment A method of punishment meant to prevent crime in the future.

validity The characteristic that a measuring instrument (such as a survey) has when it actually measures what it purports to measure.

value A belief, attitude, or behavior of a person based on what the person will accept, reject, or feel neutral about.

vandalism The willful or malicious destruction, injury, disfigurement, or defacement of property without consent of the owner or the person having custody or control of it.

variable The element of an equation, experiment, or formula that is under study and subject to change in accordance with changes in the environment; anything that varies.

vehicle search The search of vehicles without a warrant, but not without probable cause.

venire A Latin word for "to come" or "to appear," used to refer to the name given to the writ for summoning a jury; also, the body of a summoned jury.

venireman A member of a jury; a juror summoned by the writ of venire *facias*.

venue A neighborhood, place, or county in which an injury is declared to have been done or a fact declared to have happened. The jurisdiction of the court is the inherent power to decide a case, whereas venue designates the particular county or city in which a court with jurisdiction may hear and determine the case.

verdict (from the Latin *verdictum*, a "true declaration") A formal and unanimous decision or finding made by a jury, impaneled and sworn for trial of a cause, and reported to the court on the matters or questions duly submitted to them upon the trial.

victimless crime A crime without any complaining victims.

violation An incident punishable by a small fine that does not carry with it a criminal record.

violence The use of physical force.

violent predator A career criminal who commits a range of street crimes.

void for vagueness The violation of the standard that a statute must define a crime precisely.

voir dire (literally, "to speak the truth") The preliminary examination of a witness or juror as to his or her competency, interest, and so on.

waive To abandon or throw away; in modern law, to abandon, throw away, renounce, repudiate, or surrender a claim, privilege, or right, or the opportunity to take advantage of some defect, irregularity, or wrong.

warrant A document issued by a magistrate that the Constitution requires for a search or arrest.

warrant of arrest A written order issued and signed by a magistrate, directed to a peace officer or some other person specially named, commanding him or her to arrest the body of a person named in it, who is accused of an offense.

watchman style of policing A policing style focused on order maintenance and discretionary decision making.

work release A program allowing prisoners to leave confinement in order to work.

writ of habeas corpus A writ directed to a person detaining another and commanding him or her to produce the body of the prisoner or person detained.

zero-based budgeting A method of budgeting that starts with no base from the preceding budget period. Most criminal justice vendors are subject to this method.

References

American Sociological Association. 2007. *American Sociological Association Style Guide*. 3rd ed. Washington, D.C.: American Sociological Association.

————. 2010. *Publication Manual of the American Psychological Association*. 6th ed. Washington, D.C.: American Psychological Association.

————. 2010. *American Sociological Association Style Guide*. 4th ed. Washington, D.C.: American Sociological Association.

Becker, Howard S., Blanche Geer, Everett C. Hughes, and Anselm L. Strauss. 1961. *Boys in White: Student Culture in Medical School*. Chicago, IL: University of Chicago Press.

Bouma, Gary D. and G. B. J. Atkinson. 1995. *A Handbook of Social Science Research: A Comprehensive and Practical Guide for Students*. 2nd ed. New York: Oxford University Press.

Chicago Manual of Style. 2003. 15th ed. Chicago, IL: University of Chicago Press.

Chicago Manual of Style. 2010. 16th ed. Chicago, IL: University of Chicago Press.

Davis, Joseph N. 2004. *Painless Police Report Writing*. Upper Saddle River, NJ: Pearson-Prentice Hall.

Doyle, Michael and Robert Meadows. 1997. "A Writing-Intensive Approach to Criminal Justice Education: The California Lutheran University Model." *Justice Professional* 10(1):19–30.

Edwards, Richard H., ed. 1995. *Encyclopedia of Social Work*. New York: National Association of Social Workers.

Kennedy, John F. 1961. "Inaugural Address, January 20, 1961." *John F. Kennedy Presidential Library and Museum*. Retrieved February 10, 2013 (http://www.jfklibrary.org/Asset-Viewer/BqXIEM9F17SVAjA.aspx).

Hartwell, Patrick. 1985. "Grammar, Grammars, and the Teaching of Grammar." *College English* 47:111.

Hunter, David E. and Phillip Whitten, eds. 1976. *Encyclopedia of Anthropology*. New York: Harper and Row.

Isaac, Stephen and William B. Michael. 1981. *Handbook in Research and Evaluation*. 2d ed. San Diego, CA: EdITS Publishers.

Lunsford, Andrea and Robert Connors. 1992. *The St. Martin's Handbook*. 2d ed. (annotated instructor's edition). New York: St. Martin's.

Marta, Timothy P. 2004. "Police Reporting." School of Law Enforcement Supervision, Criminal Justice Institute.

Pearce, Catherine Owens, ed. 1958. *A Scientist of Two Worlds: Louis Agassiz*. Philadelphia, PA: Lippincott.

Perry, Gene. 2013. "Action Items for Oklahoma: Criminal Justice: Increase Safety and Savings with Smart on Crime Reforms." *OKPolicy.org*. Oklahoma Policy Institute, March 21. Retrieved June 12, 2013 (http://okpolicy.org/action-items-for-oklahoma-criminal-justice).

Philliber, Susan G., Mary R. Schwab, and G. Sam Sloss. 1980. *Social Research*. Itasca, IL: F. E. Peacock.

"Police Report Writing." n.d. San Francisco City Government, Office of Budget Analyst, Section 1.3.

Roosevelt, Franklin D. 2013. "Address by Franklin D. Roosevelt, 1933." *Fifty-Seventh Presidental Inaugural, January 21, 2013*. Retrieved February 10, 2013 (http://www.inaugural.senate.gov/swearing-in/address-by-franklin-d-roosevelt-1933).

Ross, Alec and David Plant. 1977. *Writing Police Reports*. Northbrook, IL: MTI Teleprograms, Inc.

U.S. Bureau of the Census. 1988. *County and City Data Book*. Washington, D.C.: Government Printing Office.

Index